CARDINAL CONTARINI AT
REGENSBURG

Cardinal Contarini
at Regensburg

———

PETER MATHESON

CLARENDON PRESS · OXFORD

1972

Oxford University Press, Ely House, London W.1

GLASGOW NEW YORK TORONTO MELBOURNE WELLINGTON
CAPE TOWN IBADAN NAIROBI DAR ES SALAAM LUSAKA ADDIS ABABA
DELHI BOMBAY CALCUTTA MADRAS KARACHI LAHORE DACCA
KUALA LUMPUR SINGAPORE HONG KONG TOKYO

PRINTED IN GREAT BRITAIN
BY WILLIAM CLOWES & SONS, LIMITED
LONDON, BECCLES AND COLCHESTER

FOR GESINE

Preface

THE sixteenth century, like our own, had to learn to cope with conflict on an unparalleled scale, to live with a crisis of authority which left few questions unasked. To recover some sense of the astringency of these questions is the none too modest aim of this book.

Two main debts have to be acknowledged. Firstly to that extraordinary group of late nineteenth-century German historians, Catholic and Protestant, whose monumental diligence and integrity has given us undeserving moderns such a solid foundation to work on; and secondly to the noble and largely unsung army of librarians who go to such lengths to help the unlikeliest of scholars. In particular my thanks are due to the university libraries in Tübingen and Bonn, to the Bayerische Staatsbibliothek in Munich, and to New College Library, Edinburgh.

My first interest in the area of pre-tridentine Catholicism was whetted by Professor Alec. Cheyne, and to him, together with Professors Denys Hay and Gordon Rupp, I am indebted for much encouragement and advice. The Clarendon Press, finally, has done much to ease the painful transition from doctoral thesis to book.

New College
September 1971

CONTENTS

LIST OF ABBREVIATIONS
USED IN THE FOOTNOTES

AC	*Apology* to the Augsburg Confession.
ARG	*Archiv für Reformationsgeschichte.*
CA	*Confessio Augustana.*
CR	*Corpus Reformatorum.*
D/B	Dittrich's biography of Contarini.
D/R	Dittrich, *Regesten und Briefe Contarinis.*
D/*Morone*	Dittrich, *Nuntiaturberichte Morones. 1539, 1540.*
DG	Ranke, *Deutsche Geschichte im Zeitalter der Reformation*
HJ	*Historisches Jahrbuch der Görres-Gesellschaft.*
Jedin, *History*	Jedin, *A History of the Council of Trent.*
KDB	Mader, *Die Kunstdenkmäler von Bayern*, XXII. Stadt Regensburg.
NAV	*Nuovo Archivio Veneto.*
NB	*Nuntiaturberichte aus Deutschland.*
RE	*Realenzyklopädie für protestantische Theologie.*
SVRG	Schriften des Vereins für Reformationsgeschichte.
WA	Weimar edition of Luther's works.
WAB	Weimar edition of Luther's letters.
ZBLG	*Zeitschrift für Bayerische Landesgeschichte.*
ZKG	*Zeitschrift für Kirchengeschichte.*

I

The Ruin of Germany

THE so-called medieval synthesis, with its often bewildering combination of Classical, Christian, and barbarian elements, was already well on the way to collapse when the Reformation took place. Yet Rome had been for many a centre of stability, and for contemporaries the sacking of the city in 1527 by the mutinous troops of the Holy Roman Emperor was a profound shock. It signalized the end of an era as clearly as the sack of Rome in 410 by Alaric. For in the long run Christian Rome had been as unsuccessful as her pagan predecessor in imposing her will on the peoples of the north. Once more, it seemed, the barbarians were pounding on the gates of Rome, but this time it was theological thunder-bolts that they hurled. Germany was in ruin and threatened to bring down all Christian Europe with it.

The astonishing speed with which the Reformation spread seemed to take on apocalyptic dimensions. Within two decades it had surged through Germany and beyond with all the violence of a tidal wave. It had swept far beyond the narrow confines of monastery, university, and ecclesiastical structures. The Germanic peoples, apparently domesticated, apparently resigned to playing handmaid to their Roman mistress, suddenly shook off the shackles of Mediterranean domination.

It was the age of preaching, but also the one in which the written word came into its own. The invention of printing had confronted the world with a new and highly subversive medium by which the traditional centres and custodians of learning could be by-passed. Already it had Europeanized the ideas of Erasmus—to the notable discomfiture of the monastic and scholastic establishments. And now, in the wake of the Reformation, there came a further development, the printed pamphlet and the broadsheet. Infinitely more seditious than the book, this popular literature rolled off the presses, thrusting down into the ranks of the semi-literate, reaching with slogans the minds of the unsophisticated, articulating their hopes and fears in crude but effective form. The Humanist movement had rested on the patronage of a new lay culture, of the teacher, the knight, the merchant. Now a popular culture began to emerge, supplementing the eloquence of the preacher with a flood of catechisms, devotional and controversial tracts, vernacular Bibles, woodcuts, and rough-hewn doggerel. The German language was beginning to discover its power.

Overnight the cultural landscape was transformed. Aristotelian logic and canon law, the authority of Rome and the hallowed traditions of centuries, the intercession of the saints and the mediation of the priest were cast aside. And as the ancient values crumbled, so too did the institutions which had cradled them. After all, as Luther boasted, a child armed with the new teachings knew more than the most venerable authorities of the past.

The new Gospel gave birth to a new Church, an aggressively German Church, centred round family and local community, rejoicing in the support of its princely protectors. The preacher replaced the priest; nuns and monks married; the dead were left unprayed for.

Social patterns were revolutionized as secularization proceeded apace. Chantries, collegiate churches, and friaries had their revenues appropriated. Protestant schools arose to teach the new élite—the learned, or at least literate preacher and his formidable ally, the pious jurist. The virtues of industry and neighbourliness shouldered out those of heroic asceticism. The beggar found himself regarded as a social problem.

Politically, territorialism continued on its rampage with the added consolation of a good conscience. There was Philip of Hesse, for example: sensual, energetic, impatient with fools, crashing through his peasants' fields with his hunting companions, a stalwart defender of the Lutheran gospel, a devout reader of the Bible. Men such as he engineered the alliances which were to sunder Germany into two armed camps, Catholic on the one side, Protestant on the other; men driven by a strange blend of scepticism and bigotry, of political calculation and personal rivalry, of incipient nationalism and the blindest particularism, of the desire for peace and the age-old tradition of resistance to Pope and Emperor.

Politically, socially, culturally, and ecclesiastically the world was being turned upside-down. A style of life, radically different from the Catholic one, was emerging. Its exponents may have been a varied lot: burgesses, pastors, knights, theologians, Humanists, and not least parents. Yet they shared the vision of a worldly piety and a secular ethic. They denied the possibility of an escape from godlessness into a realm of perfect obedience. Man, they believed, must learn to accept himself and his limitations, for he is irrevocably bound to his humanity. He cannot deny his flesh. Indeed, his worldly obedience, for all its shortcomings, has a high seriousness and dignity. Through the offices of his daily life—as father and husband, as peasant or tradesman, as a useful member of the community—he serves Christ. He is, in Luther's startling formulation, a Christ to his neighbour.

Thus the problem of confessionalism which began to exercise Germans from the end of the 1520s did not exhaust itself in the confrontation of two opposing systems of theology. Following the Diets of Speyer in 1529 and Augsburg in 1530 and the inauguration of the Visitations in Electoral Saxony, Protestantism emerged as a political and cultural phenomenon as well as an ecclesiastical one. The totality of social, political, and cultural life came under its disruptive influence, and two different cultures faced one another across the confessional divide.

The alarm and despondency of the German Catholics was therefore well founded. The spread of the Lutheran error seemed to know no limit. From its home base in Wittenberg it had taken root throughout Electoral Saxony. Hesse had fallen to it at an early stage, and in 1539 Ducal Saxony. Brandenburg was on the brink. Indeed the whole of north Germany seemed likely to succumb. In the south many of the imperial cities were, like Augsburg and Nuremberg, openly Lutheran. In 1534 Württemberg followed their example. Even the spiritual Electorates were not immune, and under Hermann von Wied Cologne seemed to be preparing for defection. Even in nominally Catholic territories morale was at a low ebb and loyalty to the Roman See conspicuous by its absence. The complete ruin of Germany, it appeared, was imminent. Already Switzerland, Scandinavia, and England were threatening to follow its example. France, Spain and Italy might yet hold firm, but they were the Latin peoples of the Mediterranean. The peoples of the north, on the other hand, seemed to be almost with one accord deserting the old faith.

Theologically the Catholic controversialists had proved them-selves singularly ill-equipped to meet the Lutheran challenge. The best that can be said about Eck, Cochlaeus, and Nausea is that they were sincere, conscientious, and not without courage. They ensured, as Lortz points out, that the Catholic voice did not go completely unheard. Their message, however, was a dourly traditionalist one, their style painfully pedestrian, their reactions of Pavlovian predictibility. They were a dwindling band, the remnant of a once proud 'establishment', slighted and ignored and mis-understood, moving through a twilight world between reaction and reform, forced into perpetual polemic, battling alternately for their honour or their theology or their Church. Perhaps their most signal service was to alarm the Roman See into a tardy recognition of the realities of the situation.

Nor could the Catholics look for spiritual guidance to their bishops, who were noted neither for their scholarship nor for their pastoral concern. Like Albert of Mainz they tended to be concern-ed primarily with the administration of their secular responsibi-lities. With honourable and dishonourable exceptions they were moderate men who sought to fulfil within reason the little that was expected of them.

It is less easy to characterize the regular and secular clergy. Undeniably they had lost some of their best men to the heretics, and without doubt the moral and intellectual state of many of them left much to be desired. Yet there were reformers among them, too. Luther himself, of course, had moved through a reformist stage before he came to the point of outright rebellion, and he retained the greatest respect for his provincial superior, John Staupitz. Among the parish priests there must have been many, like Pastor Diel in Mainz, who took their pastoral responsi-bilities with the utmost seriousness. George Witzel exemplifies the convert to Lutheran ideas who returned to the old faith, disgusted with what he had experienced: sectarianism, bitter polemic, the breakdown of moral discipline, the loss of the breath and depth of the faith.

Among the laity the natural tendency to cling to the old ways was offset by a deep-seated anti-clericalism. There was, too, a weariness with the burdensome penitential system and a resent-ment that good German money should be drained away across the Alps. The attack on the Hebrew scholarship of Reuchlin had soured many a teacher and lawyer against the scholastic theologians and their monkish confederates, while the criticisms by Erasmus of the contemporary Church had found no small echo among the educated classes.

Luther's protest had fallen on fertile soil. Certainly each grouping in society tended to interpret his message to suit its own interests. The way was paved here by the imperial knights, but it was soon to be followed by princes, peasants, and merchants. The outcome of this interaction was the Reformation, for it was the wide diversity of the interested groups to whom Luther's ideas appealed which transformed a scholar's concern into a national movement. A purely theological Reformation never existed, and by the time of the Diet of Regensburg in 1541 doctrinal and socio-political questions were inextricably bound up with one another. It was because of this urgent relation to the fabric of daily life that the Reformation caught fire in Germany. Yet precisely this was the reason for the grave reservations which a third party, identified with neither Protestant nor Catholic, had about the Reformation.

For those in the Erasmian tradition, the Reformation had been by no means pure gain. On the contrary, by a premature polarization of the situation, it appeared to have destroyed the chances of a moderate reform of the Church. Its extremism drove the cautious into reaction, the enthusiasts into a fanatical radicalism. It had not only broken the ties with Rome; it had set German against German at a time when a sense of national pride and unity seemed at last to be beginning to emerge.

The ecclesiastical consequences of this were grave enough. Still more pressing were the political and social issues. The population was being unsettled by the endless succession of innovation and controversy. Confused by the stream of polemics many began to entertain the wildest ideas. New sects burgeoned, bands of destructive peasants raged through the land, the spectre of Münster haunted men's minds. With the discrediting of the penitential system all moral constraints were being thrown to the winds. Was society breaking apart at the seams? Did the future offer anything except anarchy and bloodshed?

The priority, it seemed, was the restoration of law and order. Without it civilized life would become impossible, travel and commerce would come to a halt, the pursuit of scholarship would cease. An escalation of the existing confessional tensions, on the other hand, could only lead to a savage civil war. Already local skirmishes had taken place: the Knight's War of 1522–3, the tussle over Württemberg, the sporadic hostilities between Philip of Hesse and Henry of Brunswick. A full-scale confrontation between the two hostile blocs could only be a matter of time. Meanwhile France and the Turks were ready to pounce on a divided land. For the sake of both the internal stability and the external security of Germany an accommodation between the two confessions was imperative.

Surely, Erasmus argued, men of goodwill from both sides could meet together and hammer out the difficulties in an amicable and scholarly manner. Points held in common should be stressed, and there should be tolerance for differing views on non-essential matters. The finer points of doctrine could be left to the continuing debate of the theologians. For the ordinary man, however, the important thing was that there should be agreement on the substance of the faith.[1] Given this, the social and political tensions could be eased and a gradual return made to settled conditions. Peace would not prevent the progress of reform; indeed it was the precondition for any genuine and lasting reform.

The first major attempt to apply this policy was made at the Diet of Augsburg in 1530. There was even a suggestion that Erasmus might be invited to attend. Charles V, returning to Germany for the first time since 1521, recognized that the attempt to suppress Lutheranism forcibly along the lines of the Edict of Worms had failed miserably. The Lutheran movement had gathered impetus during the twenties, and at the Diet of Speyer only a year previously the 'Protestants' had emerged as a political force to be reckoned with. The Emperor lacked the money and the resources to crush them by force; nor could he rely on the German Catholic princes to act effectively in his support.

When, therefore, the Protestants refused to give way under pressure at Augsburg and met the Catholic 'refutation' of their 'confession' with derision, the only option open appeared to be a colloquy on the Erasmian pattern. A vigorous attempt was made to resolve the doctrinal differences as the first stage of a peaceful

---

[1] The classical statement of Erasmus's position is found in his *De Amabile Ecclesiae Concordia*, written in 1533 and dedicated to Julius Pflug.

settlement of the religious crisis. After some initial success, however, the theologians failed to agree.

Melanchthon had emerged from the negotiations as a key figure for any future strategy of reconciliation. One of the most notable of Luther's early converts, he combined a close personal friendship with the reformer with a passionate belief in the unity of the Church. Emotionally he recoiled from the bitterness of confessional strife and was genuinely appalled at the prospect of a fratricidal civil war. He had kept in touch with Erasmus even after the latter had openly broken with Luther on the question of free will.

At Augsburg he sought to demonstrate the truly catholic nature of Protestantism. The Augsburg Confession, for which he was largely responsible, was a moderate statement of the Lutheran position. Not for the last time, however, his conciliatory temperament led him to make concessions which were unacceptable to his fellow Lutherans. At one stage he was not only prepared to envisage a return to an episcopal system and to some recognition of the supreme pastoral role of the Papacy, but to reduce the essential Protestant demands to communion in both kinds and the acceptance of a married priesthood. Understandably the other Lutheran theologians hastened to throw in their veto and nudge Melanchthon back towards a more recognisably 'Protestant' position.

After Augsburg Melanchthon's irenical activity encouraged many to believe that the continuance of the schism was not inevitable. Throughout Europe the Humanist circles used their considerable influence in the interests of reconciliation during the 1530s.[2] In France they secured the invitation of Melanchthon and Martin Bucer to a colloquy whose aim was the amicable settlement of the religious differences. Only John Frederick's veto prevented Melanchthon's acceptance.

Another Erasmian group was gathered around the Dresden court of George, Duke of Saxony, himself a strong defender of the old faith. It was on the initiative of one of its most prominent members, Julius Pflug, that a colloquy was summoned to Leipzig. Together with the ducal chancellor Carlowitz and representatives of the Archbishop of Mainz, Pflug met Melanchthon on 29 and 30 April 1534. Agreement was reached on the doctrine of justification, but the colloquy foundered on the question of the Mass.

[2] Cf. R. Stupperich, *Der Humanismus und die Wiedervereinigung der Konfessionen.* Leipzig: 1936.

Carlowitz himself was the initiator of a second colloquy at Leipzig which began, without the knowledge of his prince, on 2 January 1539. Hesse and Electoral Saxony were represented by the theologians Bucer and Melanchthon and the jurists Feige and Brück, Ducal Saxony (unofficially) by Carlowitz, Fachs, and later Witzel.

Carlowitz's programme was anti-papal, anti-imperial, and anti-clerical. The territorial authorities should have the right to determine their own doctrine and practice, following the pattern of the early Church. This attempt to by-pass the confessional strife by a return to the common ground of the Apostolic Age failed when the Protestants demonstrated that the diversity of practice within the early Church prevented it from being an adequate criterion. The thought that this diversity itself could be a criterion occurred, of course, to no one.

A measure of agreement was, however, reached. On the question as to the role played by faith and good works in justification, a formula was worked out by Bucer and Witzel. This described good works as the inevitable and commendable fruits of faith, but as having no merit in themselves. Only as the gifts of Christ did they have merit. This formulation was regarded by Carlowitz as proof that as far as doctrine was concerned there was no real dispute between Catholic and Protestant. The delegation from Hesse also found it acceptable, but the Wittenbergers felt it was a dangerous compromising of the truth. At the assembly of the princes at Gelnhausen only the irenic Elector of Brandenburg was ready to give it his backing.

Joachim of Brandenburg had been taking advice from the moderates in both camps, from Melanchthon and Pflug and, above all, from Witzel, who helped to draft the reformed Church Order for Brandenburg. This latter had combined what were, in effect, Lutheran teachings with the ecclesiastical structures of the old Church. Luther felt able to give it his partial approval.

It is no surprise, therefore, that it was a suggestion of Joachim in May 1538 to Ferdinand of Austria, the Emperor's brother and vicegerent in Germany, which persuaded Charles V to abandon, at least for the moment, the hope of a General Council of the Church which he had pursued since the failure of the colloquy at Augsburg in 1530. The Elector of Brandenburg argued that instead of a Council, which the Protestants would not attend and which could only lead to war, a peaceful conference should be convoked within Germany by the Emperor. At the cost of certain concessions to the Protestants, Germany could be reunited and the much needed subsidy against the Turks secured.

Ever since the death of Clement VII in 1534 it had been becoming increasingly clear to Charles V that the important question was not whether a Council should be held, but what sort of Council it was going to be. By 1538 he knew that there was no prospect whatsoever of a Council which would concentrate on the reform of the Church and the restoration of its unity. On the contrary, all the signs pointed to a Council pre-eminently concerned with restoring doctrinal unanimity and papal authority. In principle these aims might be worthy enough. In practice they would still further weaken imperial authority in Germany by heightening the religious crisis and the confessional differences.

Charles was forced to the conclusion that if he were to restore his political authority in Germany he would first have to take independent measures to heal the religious schism. At the same time he must seek to minimize the theological consequences of such a policy by referring any decisions which a German colloquy might arrive at to the ultimate decision of the promised Council. In theory he remained true to the principles of the Roman Church. In practice he found himself side-stepping them.

His ultimate aim remained the anachronistic dream of the restoration of Christendom, of one Church and one Empire, working hand in hand for the good of man and the glory of God. Yet the logic of the political situation forced him to negotiate with the heretics and rebuff the Papacy. To buy time he had to put his convictions in pawn, for the moment at least. The Diet at Frankfurt in 1539 marks the first step along this new path.

2

A Respite from the Gallows

THE alarm and dismay of Rome at the new course of events were unmistakable. At the Diet of Frankfurt the imperial representative, the Archbishop of Lund, had allowed a 'Respite', or truce, to be passed on 19 April 1539 which provided for a gathering of laymen and theologians in Nuremberg to settle the religious question. The Pope and his legate were not so much as mentioned.

Hitherto the imperial power had acted at least as a moral and psychological brake to the progress of the Protestants, who were now at the height of their fortunes and threatening to carry all before them. Now even this was threatening to give way. While scarcely 'determined to prevent the unification of the Germans',[1] the Papacy, with its back to the wall, feared that the proposed conference would sell out the Catholic cause to the Protestants.

The classical statement of the case against the holding of such colloquies had been made by the Sorbonne in 1534. Here it was argued that discussion with heretics is only possible after they have acknowledged their error. From the very beginning it must be made clear that the proper criteria of judgement are the decisions of the Councils and the decrees of the Popes, Apostolic tradition and Catholic practice. Otherwise only one criterion will be admitted—the authority of the Scriptures—and the Protestants will wilfully distort these to suit their case. Hence discussions with them are to no avail and function only as a sounding-board for Lutheran propaganda.[2]

At Rome this remained the dominant view, and it was by no means only the fanatical rigorists and curialists who were alarmed

---

[1] 'Ihr Ziel stand fest: die Einigung der Deutschen zu verhindern.' Stupperich, op. cit., p. 61.

[2] Le Plat, *Monumentorum ad historiam Concilii Tridentini . . . collectio*, ii. 770 ff.

by the events at Frankfurt. Contarini agreed with Cardinal Pole that unless measures were speedily taken against such private gatherings a still worse schism would arise.[3] Giovanni Morone, the papal nuncio to Ferdinand, joined all the other papal representatives in Germany in a fierce denunciation of the 'reckless and inept' policy to which the Archbishop of Lund had given his approval.[4]

The Emperor, riding out the storm of indignation, neither rejected nor confirmed the Recess of the Diet, and the colloquy planned for Nuremberg did not, in fact, take place. The relief of the Papacy was, however, to be of brief duration. Towards the end of 1539 the high hopes which the well-informed Aleander, the papal legate to Ferdinand, had put in the imminent visit of Charles V to Germany turned to concern that the Emperor would take up a neutral, mediating position between Catholic and Protestant. In view of the doubtful loyalty of the German episcopate, this could well, wrote Morone, lead to the unification of Germany on the basis of independence from Rome.[5]

The Curia acted speedily. The whole weight of its diplomacy was thrown into the scales against the threatened compromise with the Protestants. Its formula was simple: concerted Catholic action against the Turks and the Protestants, including England. To this end the Emperor and the French King, Francis I, must resolve their political differences, and a properly convoked General Council would settle the religious problems.[6] Nothing was more dangerous than a conciliatory approach to people of such insolence as the Lutherans.[7]

Such admonitions, however, fell on deaf ears. Cardinal Farnese, sent as a special legate to promote peace between France and the Empire, found the Emperor 'lukewarm' in his attitude to the Lutherans. Morone feared the worst from the vacillating attitude of the Catholics as a whole and even found it necessary to warn the Archbishop of Mainz, whom he characterized as 'superficial, timid, and ambitious', against a draft basis of unity, 'full of poison

---

[3] Pole/Contarini 8 June 1539, *Epistolarum Reginaldi Poli . . . collectio*, ed. Angelo M. Quirini, ii. 157–9; Contarini/Pole 22 June 1539, ibid., p. 159.

[4] Morone/Farnese 19 Aug. 1539, D/*Morone*, pp. 12–14.

[5] Morone/Farnese 13 Dec. 1539, *NB* I. v. 24–5.

[6] Cf. the Instruction to Farnese 28 Nov. 1539, ibid., pp. 40–2.

[7] Thus Morone in a conversation with Ferdinand. Farnese/Paul III, 5 Mar. 1540, ibid., pp. 105–9.

in many points', compiled by Melanchthon and Bucer.[8] Eck lamented that the Lutherans were much more active on behalf of their heresy than the Catholics for the true faith.[9]

The Emperor's reported lack of firmness in dealing with the Protestants was the natural outcome of the waning hopes of a peace with France. Milan remained the chief stone of offence. Neither the friendly reception of the Emperor as he passed through France to the Netherlands at the end of 1539 nor the various marriage alliances proposed in the months following could disguise the basic incompatibility of Charles's dynastic and imperial ambitions with Francis I's hopes for the future of France.

When Charles was joined in Ghent by Ferdinand, who was already deeply involved in the negotiations with the Protestants and desperately concerned that effective measures be taken against the Turks, the balance swung decisively against a *rapprochement* with France. By the beginning of February 1540 Farnese was reporting to Rome that the prospects of peace were uncertain, and as the weeks went by his initial optimism turned to doubt and then irritation at the procrastinating tactics of the Emperor. By the beginning of April it was abundantly clear that all hopes of peace were dead.[10]

This, in turn, knocked on the head the Roman hopes of a united Catholic crusade against the heretics, and there could be no doubt that the break with France would incur the grave displeasure of the Papacy. On the other hand the insistence with which the papal representatives had harped on the theme of peace when, to Charles's mind, the French conditions were unacceptable, had reinforced his suspicions about the Francophile tendency of papal policy. Both France and Rome had supported the chimerical idea of a campaign against England. A number of dynastic, Italian disputes between the Emperor and the Pope helped to exacerbate relations further.

Farnese painted the situation in the grimmest colours. The Emperor might have to choose between a Lutheran Germany and his allegiance to the Roman See. If he submitted to the Protestant

---

[8] Morone/Sforza 6 Mar. 1540, ibid., pp. 110–11; D/*Morone*, pp. 88–92.

[9] '. . . vigilantiores sunt in perfidia quam nostri pro fide.' Eck/Fabri 9 Feb. 1540, *ZKG* xix. (1899), p. 240.

[10] Farnese/Paul III, 1 Apr. 1540, *NB* I. v. 144–5.

threats this could well lead to the apostasy of all Germany.[11] Morone, surely one of the ablest diplomats ever to serve the Curia, was equally pessimistic. He rejected a military solution as impractical and morally questionable. The sole effective remedy, despite the enormous difficulties it posed, would be a Council, preceded by reform and backed by a really determined Papacy.[12]

Charles, however, expected from Paul III neither reform, nor determination, nor a Council. On 11 April Morone received from Ferdinand the bald intimation that within six months a gathering of Catholic princes would be held, probably at Speyer, to discuss the religious question. Morone's guarded approval soon vanished when it transpired that Protestants, too, were to be invited. Religious considerations would, he feared, be subordinated to political, questions of principle to a policy of 'peace at all costs'. The Papacy could expect little support from the German Catholics.[13]

Farnese submitted a formal protest. The Protestants are 'slippery eels' who do not even abide by their own Augsburg Confession. Negotiations with them would undermine Catholic doctrine, and be the first stage in the speedy dissolution of the whole structure of the Church, for they would only make concessions in exchange for the defection of Germany from the Roman obedience.[14] The only solution to the religious question would be a General Council which would either effect the submission of the Protestants, or, by branding them before the world as heretics, authorize their overlords to reduce them 'ad saniorem mentem'.[15]

We have reached a critical point. The centre of interest is moving from the diplomatic scene to the theological, from negotiations with France to dealings with the Protestants, from the question of Milan to the question of Germany, from a reasonably harmonious co-operation between Emperor and Pope to a bitter, long-drawn-out struggle between them. The recognition begins to dawn that the gain of the one side must be at the expense of the

---

[11] It could well come to pass that 'la parte catholica deventi anche lei subito lutherana et già molti se ne lassano intendere, tal che la feda si può tener per perduta in quella provincia'. ibid., pp. 135–7.

[12] Ibid., p. 153   [13] Ibid., p. 170.

[14] A recurrent nightmare of the papal representatives in Germany. Morone also feared a concentration of the Lutheran attack on this point. Farnese believed that to gain their way on this question ' . . . qual solo è il scopo della loro malignità . . .', the Protestants would agree with the Catholics on the other doctrinal issues. Farnese/Paul III, 17 Apr. 1540, ibid., pp. 175–82.

[15] Le Plat, ii. 634–40.

other, that either the unity of Germany or Papal authority in Germany must be sacrificed.[16] For if the right of autonomous judgement is granted to a German colloquy, then Rome and the Papacy can be side-stepped at will. If authority to determine possible concessions lies in Speyer and not in Rome, then why even bother to have recourse to Rome or to Council at all? Questions of ultimate priorities lie behind all the particular controversies about Council and colloquies, peace and war which were fought out in the months immediately preceding the Diet of Regensburg.

The question of priorities was also a question of time. The Emperor, harried by Turk and France alike, pressed for immediate decisions. He had nothing to gain, and everything to lose, from protracted triangular negotiations between himself, the Papacy, and the Germans. Hence his drive to settle the issue himself, in Germany, and without further delay. As he pointed out to Farnese, a Council would neither provide the money needed for the Turkish campaign, nor would it, unless it were held in Germany, be attended by any German delegates. The colloquy at Speyer must go ahead.[17]

Since it was now evident that, with or without papal approval, the policy of mediation would be carried through, the Curia could only try to stall. The divided counsels within the Curia, the involvement of Paul in other personal matters, and his chronic indecisiveness all militated against the formulation of any positive alternative policy. Neither reform, nor the preparations for a Council, nor the consolidation of the Catholic forces in Germany were pursued with the necessary urgency. Even the dispatches from Germany were dealt with in an inconceivably lethargic and offhanded manner.[18]

The papal representatives at the imperial court were finding their position increasingly intolerable. Ill-informed as to the real wishes of Rome, and excluded from the counsels of the Emperor, they were none the less being pushed into taking weighty decisions on their own initiative. Already Farnese had overstepped his

---

[16] Farnese commented that if the unity of Germany were achieved as the result of Speyer this would be fateful for both the Apostolic See and for France. *NB* I. v. 180.

[17] Le Plat, ii. 640.

[18] e.g. Morone's complaint about 'questa ignorantia mia delle cose di Roma' and his entreaty to Farnese, by now back in Rome: 'Per tanto supplico V.S.R. si degni far scriver, perche dubitando, non si habbia cura de le cose di qua, mi casca l'animo di servir' (7 July 1540). Hugo Lämmer, *Monumenta Vaticana* (Friburgi Brisgoviae: 1861), p. 288.

instructions by offering the Emperor the immediate convocation of a General Council as an alternative to Speyer.[19] Morone was anxious to avoid taking similar responsibilities upon himself at the coming colloquy. Hence they urged that someone of the stature of Pole or Contarini should be dispatched to Speyer, since only a papal representative of the highest standing, one intimately acquainted with the papal intentions, would be able to weld together the Catholic party, resist effectively the neutralist tendencies of the Emperor,[20] and take whatever decisions the urgency of the hour might demand.[21]

Charles himself was not averse to the despatch of a legate, but warned that 'care would have to be taken that someone did not come who would worsen the situation. A hard-liner like Aleander, for example, would not be welcome.[22] Contarini, on the other hand, would be more than acceptable.[23] Morone, no mean judge of men, also felt that Contarini had all the qualifications—authority, scholarship, and simplicity of life—which would be required.[24] From the beginning, then, respect for Contarini tended to transcend the usual divisions.

But while Germany smouldered, Rome dithered. At first it decided simply to commission the nuncio Morone to attend the colloquy. This would reduce the danger of the authority of the Apostolic See being compromised if affairs went badly. He was to avoid becoming involved in any disputation, and leave the city immediately if the Papacy were slighted in any way.

A legate might be sent at a later stage, but even then there could be no question of his being granted plenary powers to settle the religious crisis in Germany. Aleander, who drafted Morone's instructions, waxed indignant at the very idea. 'The heart of the

---

[19] *NB* I. v. 186–9.

[20] One current rumour passed on by the Bishop of Trent was that the Lutherans were offering to make the Emperor the spiritual as well as the temporal ruler of Germany, on the English analogy. Farnese/Paul III, 21 Apr. 1540, ibid., p. 187.

[21] Among the dispatches urging the sending of a legate are: Morone/Paul III, 17 Apr. 1540, ibid., p. 182; Farnese/Paul III, 30 Apr. 1540, ibid., p. 226.

[22] Ibid., p. 201.

[23] '. . . et parlando de alchuni, vedo che gli piaceria assai fusse il Revmo Contarini . . .' Poggio/Paul III, 24 Apr. 1540, ibid., pp. 197–8.

[24] D/*Morone*, p. 116–18. The respect appears to have been mutual. As early as 1537 Contarini wrote of Morone: 'Ego equidem summopere amo eum hominem et virtutes eius non vulgares suspicio.' D/R, p. 279.

matter is this. The Pope and the Holy College, nay the heavens above, the earth beneath, and the very stones of the earth, cry out against matters of such import being entrusted to four or five people or even to a whole province . . .'[25]

Then for a time it seemed as though Contarini would, after all, be sent to the colloquy, now transferred to Hagenau due to an outbreak of the plague in Speyer. There was, however, strong opposition to his nomination in the Consistory, probably from the French party in the Curia.[26] Contarini was expected to leave Rome on 9 June for Belluno, his diocese in the north of Italy, to await there a favourable turn of events to justify his departure. In the meantime Cervini, the newly appointed legate to Charles V, would have general oversight and authority in Germany.[27]

The papal decision was enthusiastically welcomed by the reforming party in Italy, by the papal representatives in Germany, and by the imperial court. The rejoicing proved premature. On 9 June Contarini's departure was postponed indefinitely, and in fact he never left for Hagenau.

The official explanation for the change in policy—that the new treaty between Venice and Turkey would make Contarini, a patriotic and aristocratic Venetian, *persona non grata* with the Emperor—is at best only part of the truth.[28] For even after Charles V had made it clear that this was not the case, still other, and even less convincing reasons were found for the delay.

The lonely ruler of the Vatican, sending out his nuncios and legates to probe the situation on the far side of the Alps, like Noah his dove from the ark, must have decided that the floods had not yet receded sufficiently for him or his representative to venture out. He would bide his time, postpone a final decision, and in the interim collect more information.

Morone was worried. There was work, he felt, for ten papal representatives at Hagenau. Perhaps his main concern was to avoid a fatal embittering of the relations between the Habsburgs and the Papacy. Already it was being said that the latter was

---

[25] Lämmer, p. 267.

[26] He was nominated legate to Germany on 21 May. The hawkish Aleander claimed the credit for overcoming the opposition to Contarini. Aleander/Maffei, 21 May 1540, *NB* I. v. pp. 258–9.

[27] Ibid., pp. 252–3, 269.

[28] Farnese/Cervini, 26 June 1540, ibid., p. 317.

opposed to the concord of Germany.[29] The failure to send a legate might well be taken as proof of this.

The key question, of course, was that of the intentions of the Emperor. His request that the legate come armed with plenary authority indicated the trend of his thinking. The decisions should be taken in Germany, not Rome. This request Morone rejected out-of-hand. Even if an angel were sent he did not believe the Apostolic See would give him such a mandate. Every part of the coming negotiations must be referred back to the Pope.[30]

The Habsburgs were liberal with their professions of loyalty to Rome, and Morone was convinced of the good intentions of Ferdinand, who was to represent the Emperor at Hagenau. But the irresolution of the Catholic Estates gave grave cause for concern. Bernardo Santi, the Bishop of Aquila, whose chief source of information was the imperial barber, did, it is true, have high hopes for the outcome of the colloquy.[31] His judgement, however, was always erratic in the extreme.

There was, indeed, scant room for optimism. The Protestants were in militant mood. They had been by no means wholly satisfied with the outcome of the Frankfurt Diet. Yet by conceding them an open discussion of matters of the faith with the Catholics, free of papal or episcopal surveillance, the Emperor had taken an unprecedented step. As Bucer wrote to Philip of Hesse, the leader of the Schmalkaldic League, in May 1539, it was an opportunity they dared not miss. A colloquy like this was what the Protestants had been demanding from the very beginning.[32] Philip agreed and tried to persuade the Elector John Frederick of Saxony to join him in promoting the colloquy. His theologians, he wrote, were ready to allow the Catholics their Mass and their ceremonies provided the pure Word was preached.[33] John Frederick's theologians, on the other hand, insisted that in religious questions there could be no middle way. The choice must be made between pure doctrine and error. They could not depart from the truth as declared in the Gospel and expounded in the Augsburg Confession. To mask disagreement with ambiguous phrases was futile. The sole purpose

---

[29] Morone/Contarini, 15 June 1540, Quirini, iii. 262–6.

[30] Morone/Farnese, 3 June 1540, D/*Morone*, p. 137.

[31] *NB* I. v. 281.

[32] Max Lenz (ed.), *Briefwechsel Landgraf Philipps* (Leipzig; 1880–91), i. 68–70.

[33] Ibid., p. 84 n. 2.

of a colloquy would be to test the willingness of the other party to admit the truth of the Lutheran doctrines.[34]

In the meantime another plan for a very different type of colloquy had appeared on the horizon. On 7 November 1539 the Catholic Archbishop of Trier, Johann von Metzenhausen, wrote to Philip of Hesse. He had heard that the Pope and the Emperor had agreed to launch an attack on certain German princes under the pretext of religion. To prevent a bloody civil war, the princes of the Empire should forge a defensive alliance against the Emperor. Its basis would be a religious settlement to be worked out by the princes before the arrival of the Emperor in Germany. 'If agreement can be reached on the religious question, well and good; if not, such matters as remain in dispute can be set aside until the next convenient occasion.'[35]

This proposal to by-pass the Pope, thwart the Emperor, and arrange an amicable settlement of the religious crisis was taken up eagerly by Philip. As he pointed out to Bucer, the 'Respite of Frankfurt' had expired, and the militant Catholics—the Dukes of Bavaria, the Archbishop of Mainz, and the Duke of Brunswick—were arming. It seemed the part of wisdom to accept this offer and thus split the Catholic camp. The bishops appeared to be ready to make far-reaching concessions on priestly celibacy, communion in both kinds, and on the transfer of their spiritual power to coadjutors.[36]

The new project also harmonized admirably with Bucer's conviction that to protect her liberties and further the true faith Germany must unite against the Emperor and the Pope. This political unity must rest on a common determination to carry through a thorough-going reformation of Church and nation. '. . . We cannot hope for the lasting peace, happiness, or welfare of the German people except on the basis of a reformation of the churches and a religious settlement. God will not allow it. It is against all God's ways and against nature.'[37]

[34] Stupperich, *Humanismus*, pp. 63–4.
[35] Lenz, i. 431.
[36] Philip/Bucer, 11 Feb. 1539, ibid., p. 115.
[37] Bucer/Philip, 14 Jan. 1540, ibid., p. 126; a conviction he expressed again and again: 'Der eusser frid, die religion onvertragen, ist bei mir ein vergeblich onmöglich und den kirchen Christi ein hoch schedlich ding.' Ibid., p. 151. The whole aim of any colloquy would be to convince friendly or wavering powers such as the Palatinate, Cologne, Augsburg, Trier, that the real concern of the Protestants was a true reform of the Church. Ibid., p. 217.

A common front must be built up to constrain the Emperor to abide by the Frankfurt decision that a colloquy should be held. The reason why Pope and priests are agitating so violently against Frankfurt is that they know 'that they cannot stand up to honest discussion'. The Palatinate and Brandenburg, however, are in favour of a colloquy and the spiritual princes of Cologne and Trier could be won over, perhaps even Mainz and Bavaria. At such a colloquy the 'sword of the divine word could be used aright', and the Protestants, like the ancient Israelites, while grasping a weapon in the one hand, would be able to build up the walls of Jerusalem with the other.[38]

Throughout the winter 1539/40 ambassadors scurried from one German court to the other in an attempt to bring this plan to fruition. Nothing particularly outrageous was seen in this attempt to unite Protestant princes and cities with Catholic territories such as Bavaria or even with the spiritual princes of the Rhine. That it failed was due more to the hesitations of Ulrich of Württemberg, Henry of Saxony, and the south German cities, to the rivalries between Jülich and Hesse, the Palatinate and Saxony, and perhaps above all to the natural fears of the ecclesiastical princes on the Rhine as the Emperor's army approached, than to any considerations of principle. It would have been a politically motivated attempt to secure religious unity or at least tolerance in order to conduct a successful defence of the 'German liberties'. Germany, whether Catholic or Protestant, would have been united against the Emperor, not united under him.

This was a programme which never ceased to exercise its fascination on Hesse, who was at the centre of all these intrigues, and on his religious adviser, Martin Bucer. Bucer, who will play a key role at the Diet of Regensburg, is not an easy figure to classify. Recent research has taught us to take him much more seriously as an independent thinker than has been done in the past. It will not do to dismiss him as a mere activist, whirled along in an ecstasy of agitation. Certainly, however, he is the most militantly German of the reformers—far more nationalistic, for example, than Luther himself. For him the cause of God's Kingdom and the interests of the German *vatterland* are most intimately related to one another. Both are threatened by the same unholy alliance of Pope and

[38] Ibid., p. 126.

Emperor. Both can be protected and championed by the Protestant prince.

Hence Bucer tends to see the extension of the Kingdom of God in very earthy or earthly terms. Even at the risk of war the Christian ruler must do everything in his power to further its extension. Thus the Protestant political alliance is no mere secular matter. Its members are members 'in Christ'. To depart from the alliance would be to 'tear oneself away from Christ the Lord'.[39]

This is the language of full-blooded enthusiasm. The concerns of political Protestantism are identified with those of the Kingdom. The Schmalkaldic League becomes the eschatological community. The veil between temporal and eternal has been virtually lifted.

Like all enthusiasts Bucer tends to be rather less than particular about the means by which his vision will be achieved. Although, for example, fully aware of the self-interested motives of the Bavarians in their opposition to the Emperor, he is able to persuade himself that these somewhat dubious allies may be God's instruments against the undue tyranny of others.[40] Again, for the sake of the Kingdom he is ready to embark on an elaborate deception of Granvelle as to the real aims of the Protestants.[41] In the figures of Bucer and his princely patron, Philip of Hesse, curial diplomacy has certainly found its equal.

When, therefore, the Hagenau conference opened in June 1540 the chances for an imperial peace offensive did not seem very great. The anti-imperial conspiracy had only just collapsed, the Papacy was hostile, the Catholics irresolute, the Protestants cool. John Frederick of Saxony and Philip of Hesse absented themselves from the proceedings.

The imperial 'Proposition', or basis for negotiation, which Ferdinand presented to the Catholic Estates on 12 June was phrased in irenical terms. The Papacy was not so much as mentioned. It spoke in general terms of 'Christian unity and agreement', 'tolerable and Christian means', a return to 'Christian unity and a due obedience', and drew a distinction between those matters essential to the substance of the Christian faith and the so-called 'positive' articles, relating to disciplinary questions.[42]

The papal representatives were appalled. Morone talked darkly of

---

[39] ' . . . sich von Christo dem herren abreissen . . .' Ibid., p. 192.
[40] Ibid., p. 136.   [41] Ibid., p. 153.   [42] Le Plat, ii. 650–4.

the imminent ruin of Catholicism.[43] Cervini suspected that for the sake of peace and quiet Charles was prepared to come to terms with the Protestants 'regardless of the interests of religion or anything else' and said as much to the Emperor in what must have been a lively audience. Charles, for his part, denounced the attitude of the Papacy as completely negative. It must surely realize that a military solution was unthinkable in the present circumstances. But what did it do? One of its legates sat tight in Italy, another refused to leave Brussels (Cervini), while Morone, the sole papal representative at Hagenau, did his best to torpedo the conference. He could assure the Pope that nothing detrimental to the interests of the faith would occur. Tolerance was requested for the Protestants as far as the 'positive' articles were concerned until the Council, but there seemed good reason to hope that many of them would then return to the Apostolic obedience.[44]

Although the Hagenau conference in fact achieved little Charles was determined to persist in his new policy. A second conference was planned for Worms in the autumn, with an imperial Diet at Regensburg to follow it. Increasingly Morone and Cervini came to feel that Rome's attitude was untenable. The discouraging news from Hagenau had confirmed Paul in his previous irresolution and there were no signs of Contarini leaving Rome for Worms, though his attendance at the Regensburg Diet had been agreed to.[45]

Rome was, in fact, boycotting the imperial plans. It was refusing to give the least shadow of its sanction to a settlement that might well favour the Lutherans. But was this policy realistic? Morone was only too aware of the dangers which Worms might pose. But one could not defend the papal authority in Germany by alienating the mainstay of its support there—the Habsburgs. By refusing to send a legate to Worms, the Curia would only drive the Habsburgs into the hands of the neutralists, and lead all Germany—indeed all Christendom—to believe that the Papacy cared neither for religion nor for Germany. To prevent Contarini coming would be to do Charles the greatest possible favour, for he would then proceed to an accommodation with the Lutherans and claim that it

[43] Morone/Farnese, 15 June 1540, NB I. v. 431.
[44] Cf. the despatches of Poggio and Cervini on 25 June and 2 July, ibid., pp. 306, 315, 321–5, 327, and Cervini's on 3 July, ibid., p. 328.
[45] Farnese/Cervini, 9 June 1540, ibid., p. 281; Aleander/Morone, 23 July 1540, ibid., p. 453; Farnese/Cervini, 29 Aug. 1540, ibid., pp. 383–5.

was all the fault of the Pope. The dangers had to be met and averted on the spot by a papal legate accompanied by a group of first-class scholars.[46]

In the end a compromise solution was decided on in Rome. At the beginning of September 1540 Contarini had again been ready to leave, but at the last moment his departure, which had been supported by Ghinucci and Aleander, was cancelled. Thomas Campeggio, Bishop of Feltre, the guileless brother of the late Cardinal Lorenzo Campeggio, was despatched instead.[47] Paul, however, made no secret of his distaste for the proposed Worms colloquy.[48]

When, however, negotiations finally got under way at Worms on 25 November, the first victory went to the papal party. The Hagenau Recess had foreseen a disputation between eleven representatives of each of the confessions. Of the eleven 'Catholic' representatives no less than three—Brandenburg, Cleves, and the Palatinate—were openly Protestant in their theology, while the loyalty of Cologne, Trier, and Strasbourg to the Apostolic See was doubtful.[49] Campeggio even believed that the three spiritual Electors, together with the Elector Palatine and the Bishops of Bamberg and Würzburg, had a secret alliance with the Lutherans.[50] It was at any rate evident that in every decision that was taken the loyal papalist group would be outnumbered and outvoted. Morone and Campeggio, who were jointly responsible for representing the papal case, concluded that at all costs voting must be prevented.

And prevented it was. By an adroit alliance with the anti-imperial forces among the Catholics—led by the Duke of Bavaria, the Duke of Brunswick, and the Archbishop of Mainz—whose opposition to a peaceful religious settlement was as much political

---

[46] Cervini/Farnese, 5–6 Sept. and 12 Sept. 1540, ibid., pp. 388–92, 398–9; D/*Morone*, p. 202.

[47] According to Farnese, Charles V himself, through his ambassador Aquilar, made it known that he would prefer a simple prelate to be sent to Worms, reserving the dispatch of a cardinal to the coming imperial Diet at Regensburg. *NB* I. v. 472–6; *NB* I. vi. 152–5, 160–2.

[48] Ibid., pp. 5–13.

[49] Campeggio/Farnese, 15 Dec. 1540, ibid., pp. 68–79; the disunity of the 'Catholics' went so far that on 23 December Campeggio had to report to Rome that they had submitted *four* different statements to the Protestants on the questions of original sin, justification, faith and works. Ibid., pp. 82–90; cf. Morone's judgement on 12 January: '. . . la Teologia ora è fatta ministra delle passioni degli uomini.' Morandi, I. ii. 101–2.

[50] *NB* I. vi. 16.

as religious, Morone managed to force Granvelle, who was representing the Emperor, to abandon the proposed mode of procedure. The Emperor, though furious at what he regarded as an attempt to sabotage the colloquy, dared not precipitate a complete break with the Papacy.[51] Granvelle had to capitulate. It was decided that only one spokesman from each side would be allowed—Eck and Melanchthon respectively—and thus the divisions within the 'Catholic' party were rendered harmless.[52]

It soon transpired that the public disputations on the basis of the Augsburg Confession were unlikely to lead to any agreement. The Protestants had the strictest injunctions not to depart from the letter of the Confession. They made not the slightest positive response to the genuinely ecumenical attitude of Campeggio. The only reaction of Calvin, for example, to an irenical speech by the latter on 8 December, was to gloat over Campeggio's discomfiture when in their reply to him the Estates did not even mention the Pope's name.[53]

Eck, for his part, needed no injunctions to keep him on the path of orthodoxy. He had had his fill of disputations and reported gloomily to Contarini on the failure to achieve anything at Hagenau and the excellent prospect of another such failure at Worms.[54]

Thus on the open field the party of conciliation had been out-manœuvred. Granvelle, however, an infinitely resourceful politician, had another card up his sleeve. While allowing the public debate to continue—and in fact agreement was reached on the doctrine of original sin—he shifted the centre of gravity from the public to the secret plane. There, he hoped, away from the glare of publicity and the scrutiny of all-too-interested parties, a compromise could be hammered out. His grand design was to present the rigorists on both sides with a theological *fait-accompli*—a draft plan of concord agreeable to all parties, which would then be ratified at the Diet of Regensburg. Accordingly he summoned Bucer and the Hessian preacher Capito on 14 December and

[51] Morone/Farnese, 15 Dec. 1540, ibid., p. 63; 15 Dec. 1540, L. von Ranke, *Deutsche Geschichte im Zeitalter der Reformation*, vi. 173. Cf. Poggio/Farnese, 22 Dec. 1540, *NB* I. vi. 174–6.

[52] Ibid., p. 104.

[53] Calvin/Farel, mid-December 1540, Herminjard, *Correspondance des Réformateurs*, vi. 410–11.

[54] Le Plat, ii. 674–5.

eventually gained their agreement to the proposal of a secret colloquy.[55]

This dramatic step had been preceded by a diplomatic coup of the first importance. As a result of his bigamous marriage Philip of Hesse had fallen into disfavour with his Protestant allies. He could not even count on their support if Charles V used the pretext of his bigamy to put him under the ban of the Empire.[56] Hesse professed himself bitterly disappointed at this uncomradely reaction. His previous profligacy, he complained, had never aroused so much indignation as this new attempt to regulate his relationships.[57] As early as July 1540 we find him complaining to Bucer that if he found no understanding from the Protestants he would seek the support of the Emperor and the Pope.[58] By Christmas this angry threat has become reality. Since he lacks the confidence of his allies, he writes to Bucer, he is compelled to give up the military leadership of the Protestant forces and to accept the olive-branch so timeously offered by the Emperor.[59]

It is scarcely necessary to underline the importance of this step for Granvelle's plans. The Protestant alliance lost its most forceful leader. Philip could now be induced to support the imperial plans for the settlement of the religious discord in Germany as the price for immunity from the imperial ban. The danger that Jülich, with French help and Protestant backing, would sever the lifelines of the Habsburg territories and lead the way to a complete Protestantization of the Rhine territories would be averted. In every respect the militancy of Protestantism would be tamed, and the chances for a moderate settlement of the religious issues enhanced.

When at the beginning of November Bucer heard that Philip had commenced negotiations with the Emperor, the news came as a shattering blow. He saw it as a lack of faith in God, who 'has bestowed upon us Germans his Kingdom and continually given it glorious expansion'. He had no confidence in the wiles of Granvelle, and trembled in every limb when he thought of the endless treachery of the Burgundian court. In the name of the 'suffering

---

[55] Bucer/Philip of Hesse, 20 Dec. 1540 Lenz, i. 274–9; cf. R. Stupperich, 'Der Ursprung des "Regensburger Buches" von 1541 und seine Rechtfertigungslehre', *ARG* xxxvi (1939), 88–116.

[56] Lenz, i. 251.

[57] 'Wir finden, das uns in diesem handel viel vervolgung begegnet, der uns doch im hurenleben keine begegnet.' Ibid., p. 181.

[58] Ibid., p. 184.   [59] Philip/Bucer, 25 Dec. 1540, ibid., p. 283.

and passion and glorious incarnation of our dear Lord Jesus' he warns Hesse of the price he will have to pay for help from an Emperor who persecutes the Christians in the Netherlands and is more concerned with Italy and Spain than for Germany.[60] The peace the Emperor is offering is no true religious peace, but only a 'poor, wretched, uncertain respite from the gallows'.[61]

Philip, however, was not to be moved. He argued that he would best be able to further the interests of the Protestants if he were on good terms with the Emperor.[62] Probably, however, he did not see in the arrangement anything more than the winning of a breathing space, until the Emperor left Germany again. Lenz's suggestion that he was intoxicated by the flattery of Granvelle seems scarcely likely. The truth is probably that Hesse was for the moment weary of his militancy. Since the beginning of 1540 he had been complaining that of all the Protestant Estates only he and the Elector of Saxony were ready to take action and bear responsibility. 'For in all truth we are right eager to do what we can for a proper reform of the Church and the upholding of the freedom of the German nation. But in all truth it is little help we have had either from the princes or the towns; everyone is out for himself.'[63] The Protestants seemed hopelessly divided. The country was weary of war and schism. In view of all this, would it not be folly to reject the very reasonable terms which the Emperor was offering the adherents of the new religion?

Hesse, of course, had no intention of betraying the Protestant gospel, but as we have already seen he allowed himself and his theologians a more flexible interpretation of it than John Frederick of Saxony. Hence he instructed Bucer to participate in the secret colloquy proposed by Granvelle, but not to make too many concessions, abiding 'as far as possible' by the standpoint of Luther.[64] The dialogue between Catholic and Protestant could begin.

[60] Bucer/Philip, 3 Nov. 1540, ibid., pp. 221–5.
[61] '. . . ein so arme, elende, ongewisse galgenfrist . . .' 26 Nov. 1540, ibid., p. 243.
[62] Ibid., p. 267.   [63] Ibid., p. 150.   [64] Ibid., pp. 279–85.

3

God Grant it is Well Done

WE shall present ourselves as those to whom God has given his pure Gospel and convince the others of the way to the true reformation of the Church they have devastated.'[1] Martin Bucer had never been opposed to the idea of a colloquy, indeed for him it was an aggressive weapon to be used for the extension of the Kingdom. This enabled him to adjust himself to the radical change of course which Philip had now embarked upon. Now he sought to exploit the possibilities of a peaceful expansion of the Kingdom, this time under the aegis of the Emperor.

Now as before the chief enemy remained the Pope, and the very fact that the latter was so violently opposed to the colloquies was an eloquent argument in their favour. At a colloquy Christ himself is present through his Word. 'For where he is confessed and his teaching explained and defended, there he himself is present . . .' The power of the Lord will work through his holy Word and at least some of the lost sheep will be brought back to the fold.[2]

Bucer argued for flexibility on non-essential matters but could not countenance any compromising of the evangelical truth. He would 'rather suffer anything than commit himself to an agreement in which we began to approach the errors of our opponents'. But a colloquy could provide a 'grand beginning to a true reformation of the Churches'. Even though it did not meet all the demands of the Protestants it would be acceptable if it made their present position more tolerable, did not close any doors to further progress, and on the basic issues accepted the Protestant premisses.[3]

The colloquy is here assigned a key role in the Protestant strategy of mission. Bucer never doubted that in the long run Protestantism would triumph; it was simply a matter of time. The

[1] Lenz, i. 97.   [2] Ibid.   [3] Ibid.

future of Germany would be a Protestant one. Already the Estates were in general anti-papal, and all the time the seed of the Word was being scattered further. His tolerance does not indicate a willingness to accept something equivalent to a plurality of theological standpoints, but rests on the conviction that time was on his side.

Bucer's hopes for a colloquy were thus radically different from those of Granvelle, who followed the Erasmian concept of a colloquy as being primarily a means to reconcile divergent views, not as a missionary platform. This may warn us against characterizing Bucer too glibly as a 'Humanist'. The same is true of Contarini and Melanchthon. Certainly there were men on both sides of the confessional divide who shared with Erasmus his abhorrence of war, his concern for the unity of the Church, his conviction of the necessity for moral reform. Certainly, too, it was these men who spearheaded the movement for reconciliation of the religious schism. They remain, however, a highly differentiated grouping. The blanket term 'Erasmian' or 'Humanist' should be used with caution in relation to them.

Thus Bucer viewed Granvelle's initial advances with some scepticism.[4] Granvelle, of course, had assigned to the secret colloquy an eminently political role. Since no progress had been made at Worms, pressure had to be brought to bear on the moderates in both camps. The agreement which was expected to issue from the secret colloquy was designed to do just this. With the leverage which could now be applied on Hesse (and through him on Bucer) it looked as though a case of bigamy might have consequences as important for the German religious situation as a divorce for the English.

What both the Emperor and Hesse needed was a theological legitimation for the cessation of hostilities, a religious undergirding for a new political settlement. The 'Old Faith' no longer provided the framework of the 'given', the common ground and shared convictions within which all—Protestants and Catholics alike—could peaceably coexist. A new set of conventions had to be established which would enshrine or at least tolerate both the virtues of the Reformation and the permanent values of the 'Old Faith'. The Emperor, it appeared, was aware of the need for reform and concessions. The spiritual princes might be ready to

4 'Es wird aber wasser sein.' 14 Dec. 1540, ibid., p. 269.

renounce the spiritual side of their functions in favour of coadjutors and thus pave the way to reform. The Protestants
agreed that not all was well in their own house, and that there were
men of good will in the other. Could not something be done to
avoid what seemed to be the only alternative to a peaceful settlement of the religious issue—civil war?

A theological concord was thus widely regarded, whether rightly
or wrongly, as the necessary precondition for progress in any other
field. Whether the campaign was against the Emperor or the Turk
or the most Christian King of France, it was assumed that only a
Germany united in religion could fight it. Nor could the war
against ignorance, immorality, and disorder be fought without a
prior unity of belief. The religious settlement would be used, that
is, as a means to social and political ends. Or, to put it in another
way, at this stage political action still sought theological sanction
and assumed that the latter could be formulated in propositional
terms.

Bucer was, however, deeply suspicious that the proposed
colloquy would subordinate religious interests to secular considerations. He had no real confidence in Granvelle, doubting his
concern for religion.[5] Nor had the atmosphere at Worms thus far
been exactly cordial. Yet Granvelle's agent, Gerhard Veltwyck,[6]
impressed Bucer with his learning and he became convinced that
the other proposed discussion partner, Johann Gropper, the
Cologne churchman and theologian,[7] was genuinely concerned
with reforming the Church. It was from this rather extraordinary
partnership between Gropper and Bucer that the Regensburg
Book was to emerge, and with it the hope of preventing the
collapse of Christendom pulling down with it the unity of the
Christian Church.

Veltwyck and Gropper urged Capito and Bucer to engage with
them in a confidential discussion of the theological questions at
debate between Catholic and Protestant. It was emphasized that
the discussions would not be binding on either side, that they
would not be in any way prejudicial to the public colloquy or the
Protestant Estates, and that everything would be kept absolutely
secret. After consulting with Feige and Jacob Sturm of Strasbourg

Bucer finally overcame his hesitations and he and Capito agreed to take part in the discussions.[8]

To cover himself against possible reactions from Saxony and from Strasbourg Bucer requested and gained a warrant to engage in these discussions from Hesse,[9] and a written promise of secrecy under the imperial seal from Granvelle. He remained suspicious. Why did Granvelle himself refuse to be drawn into any statement of his point of view on the theological issues? If so great a desire for concord and peace existed why was this not more evident in the main colloquy? Was not the suggestion that at first only Hesse be consulted and kept informed on the course of the discussions a dangerous move to detach him still further from the other Protestant allies? On the other hand Granvelle had sworn that his intentions were of the purest, and that he desired nothing but peace, reformation of the churches, and good relations with Hesse.

Bucer's aim in engaging in this secret colloquy was to prove the apostolicity of Protestantism. He would expound its central tenets in such a way that 'any Christian who wanted to make up his mind on these matters would be convinced that we believe and teach nothing other than the ancient and true apostolic Church has believed and taught from the beginning'.

A key point was the role envisaged for the Emperor should progress be made. Bucer believed that the greatest hindrance to any hope of agreement was the Pope's irrevocable opposition to any true reform, and that therefore the Emperor should take the initiative into his own hands and thus rally all Germany behind him.[10] Feige, who believed that there was a strong group around the Emperor which genuinely wanted a fair peace with the Protestants, struck a similar note in a discussion with Granvelle. The latter replied that although the Emperor still adhered to the old religion, he was by no means the blind tool of the Pope. He recognized that the abuses had to be reformed, and did not intend to further the interests of either of the two parties but rather to promote what was consonant with the divine truth and the Holy

[8] Lenz, i. 274–9.

[9] Philip/Bucer, 25 Dec. 1540, ibid., p. 280. Cf. Feige/Philip, 20 Dec. 1540, ibid., p. 517.

[10] 20 Dec. 1540, ibid., p. 275; Bucer believed that the whole aim of the Pope was to defeat any attempts at reformation. Bucer/Joachim II, 10 Jan. 1541, ibid., p. 529.

Scriptures. This insinuation that the Emperor stood above the confessional differences is no less interesting than the protestation that if a good beginning were made at Worms the Emperor would not be too concerned about the papal attitude. 'For his Majesty is the greatest prince in Christendom and will do what he considers necessary regardless of what anyone may think.' Granvelle's *cri de cœur* at the end of the conversation: 'But let me get on with it. You always want me to compromise myself completely. But if that happens I will be unable to achieve anything', illustrates how difficult it was, even for this adroit statesman, to manœuvre successfully between the two confessions.[11]

In the meantime the discussions proceeded quite well, on the basis of the draft articles drawn up by Gropper. But Bucer reported that he was 'just about off his head with these people', as their motives were anything but unambiguous. At one moment it seemed that they genuinely sought a true reformation, but on reflection there was always the fear that they were merely seeking to exploit the hopes of the Protestants in order to gain assistance against the Turks or for other worldly ends.[12]

Hesse's relations with Württemberg and the Elector of Saxony, whom he accused of sodomy, continued to deteriorate and he found himself forced to consort ever more closely with the imperial party. He energetically refused, however, to allow himself to be manœuvred into an approval of the articles agreed upon at the secret colloquy without the consent of the other Protestant princes, although he believed they would serve as a basis for agreement.[13]

Bucer was aware that the articles on which the four collocutors had agreed at Worms might well be regarded as too conciliatory. His and Capito's criticism, he recognized, had not gone far enough, but he hoped that they would serve as a basis for discussion which after amendments by both sides would be acceptable to any Christian. The theological analysis of the articles we must

---

[11] Feige/Philip, 30 Dec. 1540, ibid., p. 523–5.

[12] 25 Dec. 1540, ibid., p. 286–7, speaking of the Emperor's recognition of the need for reform some three weeks later Bucer commented, 'Ob aber diss geschehe auss gottesforcht oder auss not obligender hendel, als vom Turcken, Franckreich und andere, will ich nit richten, sonder, das sich zum reich Christi fürderlich erzeiget, ein gnädigs erregen göttlicher gnaden erkennen.' Bucer/ Joachim II, 10 Jan. 1541, ibid., p. 531.

[13] Philip/Bucer, 3 and 7 Jan. 1541, ibid., pp. 304 and 309.

leave to a later chapter. Here it must suffice to point out that Bucer was agreeably surprised by the degree of unity that had been achieved, and believed—at first sight an unusually superficial judgement—that the crux of the difficulty would lie in the questions of prayers for the dead, the adoration of the saints, and such like. On the central issues, he believed, complete concord could be achieved at once. On other issues differences would remain, but these could be allowed to rest for a while until the passage of time had calmed down the more fiery spirits and allowed the seed of the good doctrine to have its effect.

The important thing was to encourage the men of goodwill on both sides, for Satan has blinded even godfearing men from seeing that 'on many issues they are really much closer to being at one in the truth than they themselves realize or can express to one another verbally'. The differences between the two confessions, he believed, were more apparent than real. The Protestant faith, for example, is calumniated and misunderstood as a rejection of all morality and discipline, and not altogether surprisingly in view of the Protestants' failings in this regard and their tendency at first to make extreme statements, although Melanchthon has moderated this to some extent. The result has been that both sides have become increasingly alienated from one another and that anyone who attempts to mediate is immediately suspected of being about to fall away to the opposing party.

In view of all these difficulties the language of the articles agreed on at Worms had been kept deliberately restrained and moderate so that above all the crucial article on Justification could be acceptable to the moderate Catholics and free them from their unjustified suspicions and prejudices about the Protestants; and this applied still more to the secondary articles. The important point, however, is that while the language is different from that to which the Protestants have been accustomed nothing is said which is contrary to the truth.[14] 'God grant it is well done.'

[14] 'Weil nun die sach zwischen uns und dem gegenteil steht, wie erzelet, ist vilberurter schrifft in worten dermassen temperiret und gemessiget worden, das den guthertzigen auf jenem teil im artikel der justification, an dem alles gelegen, und andern haubtartikeln desto weniger anstoss entgegen geworfen würde, und deshalb alles, so vil möglich, dahin gerichtet, das man vor eingebildter und unrechter meinung und verdacht gegen uns fuglich begegnet wurde. Und derhalben . . . hatt man auch die nebenartikel so weitlaufig hinbeigesetzt, in denen doch on weiderhandlung und correction die vergleichung der religion nit möchte troffen werden.' Bucer/Joachim II, 10 Jan. 1541, ibid., p. 534. Bucer is

Bucer, in the language of contemporary sociology, is a representative of 'marginal man'. He can stand on the frontier between different cultural options and recognize their relative merits. He has an unusual awareness of the limitations of language, of the relativity of any linguistic or logical model.

In Gropper and Veltwyck he had found men whom he could respect and trust. They were, in a word, fellow Christians. Between him and them there was a basic unity which outweighed divergent views on particular points. The latter derived mainly from misunderstandings and semantic problems which time and patience could be trusted to remove, given an atmosphere of mutual confidence.

The question is, of course, whether this approach must not lead to a trivialization of the real issues. Could the cultural revolution brought about by the new gospel be digested by Catholic tradition? Or were the discontinuities too radical and the Roman system too inflexible for a new synthesis to emerge?

All in all it was a strange constellation of circumstances that had made possible the birth of the Regensburg Book. The loose morality of Philip of Hesse, the 'grand design' of Granvelle, the humanistic circles among theologians, politicians, and jurists, and the failure of the Protestant and Catholic 'defensive' alliances to override particular interests and thus dominate the political situation had all played their part. A strange complex of hopes, expectations, anxieties, and fears occupied the minds of the chief participants in the time before the Diet.

Above all we should keep in mind the secrecy in which the whole affair was clothed, a secrecy which was quite remarkably well kept. Apart from Hesse only Brandenburg was informed about the Book prior to the Diet.[15] This was the essential condition for its success. It had to appear out of the blue, dropped as it were from the heavens by a disinterested but learned deity. It also, however, points unmistakably to the difficulty of the whole undertaking. Saxony, home and centre of the Reformation, of Luther, and of Wittenberg, had played no role in its production. The Elector was to stay away from the Diet, and the great Luther himself was to

---

aware, then, of the limitations of the articles. 'Nun wir haben hie die sachen gemilteret, so fil wir konden: Gott gebe, das gut ist.' 20 Feb. 1541, Lenz ii, Nr. 118, p. 18.

[15] Bucer/Joachim II, 10 Jan. 1541, Lenz, i. 529–38.

write off the colloquy as a well-meant attempt at the impossible. But of what sort of a concord would the Book form the basis, if Saxony, Wittenberg and Luther were not participant thereof? The difficulties, one sees, had only just begun.

The secret colloquy at Worms had come to an end on 31 December. Meanwhile, as we have seen, the public disputations between Eck and Melanchthon had been continuing. The papal representatives, however, were aware that something was going on behind the scenes. Morone, in a New Year's Day letter to Contarini, complained bitterly that he was being prevented from having any influence on the course of events. Only a legate, he believed, could uphold the authority of the Apostolic See, for the nuncios themselves had neither the authority nor the ability to cope with the situation.[16]

He had, all the same, good reason to be content with his achievements at Worms. Together with Campeggio, he had secured the virtual rescinding of the Recess of Hagenau, thus preventing any decisions from being reached under conditions unusually unfavourable to the Apostolic See. The political and numerical predominance of the Protestant or non-papal forces had not been allowed to be brought to bear. Time had been gained, a breathing space found, the steam-roller impact of the imperial concord policy broken. 'God be thanked that we have emerged from the snares of this colloquy', he sighed with some justification, as it finally came to an end on 18 January.[17]

The Protestants were rather depressed at the outcome. Not that they had ever nursed exaggerated hopes of it.[18] But at first their bearing had been described by Campeggio as 'very arrogant and confident'; their aim, he felt, was not to negotiate a settlement but to gain adherents.[19] Their divisions, he remarks interestingly,

[16] Morone/Contarini, 10 Jan. 1541, NB I. vi. 116 '... in somma noi altri Nuntii non avemo nè sufficienza, nè grazia, nè autorità'.

[17] Morone/Farnese, 18 Jan. 1541, Lämmer, p. 337.

[18] If both sides were to seek after God, wrote Bucer to Philip of Hesse from Worms, agreement would soon be arrived at. But the Emperor seeks only to extend his power; he regards 'die theure gabe Gottes, die deutsche freiheit gewisslich für ein onleidliche ongehorsame ...'; and there is no hope of those like Eck who desire no true reformation. 'So kann man auch kein freundtlich und christlich gesprech haben dann allein mit freunden und christen.' The main hope was to prepare the way for the Diet by unmasking the unreasonableness of the others. Bucer/Philip, 3 Nov. 1540, Lenz, i. 221–4.

[19] They were 'molto superbi et elati'. Campeggio/Farnese, 6 Nov. 1540, NB I. vi. 19.

could well be exploited by the Emperor, for they feared the effects of the imperial ban on their commerce, without which they could not live.[20] The Bishop of Aquila likewise described their self-confidence and their feverish activity.[21] They regarded this new colloquy as confirmation that they ranked as the equals of the Catholics, that the issues were now being discussed on their terms, and that they outdid the Catholics in eloquence and scholarship.[22] Hence Campeggio had little confidence in Granvelle's view that the Protestant councillors and theologians could be won over 'by force of money' if not by force of arms, and suggested the postponement of this question to the Diet at Regensburg.[23]

Morone, to whom the concept 'Germany' was now almost synonymous with that of 'ruin', also found the Protestants confident, most of the Catholics on the other hand 'timid, almost desperate'.[24] The very peacefulness of the Protestants' demeanour might deceive the Emperor, Campeggio feared, into granting them freedom of belief and worship, which would entail a progressive loss of papal and episcopal authority.[25] Already the Protestants were said to be making their presence at the coming Diet of Regensburg conditional on the annulling of the judgements of the Imperial Court against them, and on their being granted the right of preaching during the Diet in the city.[26]

Yet the Protestants had signally failed to exploit the dissensions within the Catholic camp, they had allowed the Recess of Hagenau to be pushed aside, they had been in every respect outmanœuvred by the papal diplomats. We may not care to pay too much attention to the observation of Campeggio that on the way to the first confrontation between Eck and Melanchthon the Catholics were in a cheerful, the Protestants in a depressed mood.[27] If, however, the Protestants were not in fact depressed, then perhaps they should have been. They had let not a few opportunities slip through their fingers.

On the other hand, the victory for the Catholics at Worms was

---

[20] Campeggio/Farnese, 11 Nov. 1540, ibid., p. 24.
[21] '. . . semper disputant, semper scribunt, multa confingunt . . .' Sanzio/Cervini, 16 Nov. 1540, ibid., p. 31.
[22] Sanzio/Farnese, 25 Nov. 1540, ibid., p. 33.
[23] Campeggio/Farnese, 26 Nov. 1540, ibid., p. 44.
[24] 'Timidi et quasi disperati', Morone/Farnese, 15 Dec. 1540, *DG* vi. 174.
[25] Campeggio/Farnese, 23 Dec. 1540, *NB* I. vi. 88.
[26] Campeggio/Farnese, 15 Jan. 1541, ibid., pp. 124–6.   [27] Ibid.

perhaps more apparent than real. It had, like everything, its price. The Regensburg Book was part of that price. A further embittering of papal-imperial relations was another. The papal representatives had served their master on the far side of the Alps well. It was, however, a master on the far side of the Alps whom they had served. The Protestants, on the contrary, were Germans, conscious of their nationality, in their way even aggressively patriotic. Throughout the colloquy their studied moderation had hammered away at one point with which they hoped to impress the Emperor: if the policy of concord was in danger then the blame could not be laid at the door of the Protestants. The conclusion to be drawn was clear. Whether or not the Emperor would draw the consequences from it would be seen at the forthcoming Diet at Regensburg.

4

To Be of Some Service

THE appointment of Contarini to the German Legation in May 1540 had, as we have seen, given rise to enthusiasm on all sides, and in particular among the papal representatives and the imperial party in Germany, and among the reforming circles in Italy. The Emperor was speaking for many when he expressed his confidence that Contarini was eminently well suited for the task ahead of him, and added that personally 'I regard him as a good friend'.[1] Correspondingly great was the disappointment when his departure was put off from month to month. Once again, it seemed, Germany was to be fobbed off with empty promises.

On 8 January 1541, however, the Pope finally decided to send him to Regensburg, and on the 28th of the same month he set out from Rome.[2] The die was cast.

It had not been without hesitation, not without the direst forebodings, that Paul III had eventually decided that the dispatch of the legate would be the lesser of the evils he had to face. Pulled on the one side by the enthusiasm of Contarini,[3] and pushed on the other by the pressure from Germany, he had given way in the end with good grace. Cardinal Farnese, defending the papal decision in a dispatch to Dandino, the nuncio at the French Court, spoke of a 'unanimous' request for the appointment of Contarini,[4] and certainly as it became clear at the beginning of 1541 that this time the legate was really on his way, the news was received with almost

---

[1] *NB* I. v. 298.

[2] Farnese/Poggi, 8 Jan 1541, *NB* I. vi. 182–4; on 10 Jan. he was commissioned. 'Fuit Consistorium *S.D.N.* creavit in *S.R.E.* Legatum de latere Rmum Gasparem Presbyterum Cardinalem Contarenum in partibus Germaniae et ad ea potissimum loca, ad quae eum declinare contigerit cum facultatibus prout in literis.' D/*R*, p. 140.

[3] Contarini refers to the many conversations he had held with the Pope about the coming colloquy. Contarini/Farnese, 12 Dec. 1541, ibid., p. 146.

[4] Farnese/Dandino, 17 Jan. 1541, *NB* I. vi. 137 n. 2.

universal satisfaction. As on Contarini's elevation to the cardinalate it appeared to many that new perspectives were opening up.
At last something was going to be done. And Contarini seemed the
right man to do it.

The name Contarini, then, struck a responsive chord in the
most diverse circles—Humanist, ecclesiastical and political. Even
the Protestants held him in high respect.[5] Which all seemed to
augur well for the success of his undertaking. Even at this stage,
however, a word of warning is in place.

First, a legate's powers were severely limited. Even with the
most liberal of instructions Contarini's freedom to develop
initiatives of his own would have been circumscribed. As Poggio,
nuncio to the Imperial Court, emphasized to Granvelle, at best he
would only be authorized to participate in the negotiations, to
assist the participants by his counsel, and to report on the events to
Rome.[6] From the outset, that is, there was no prospect of Contarini
playing anything more than a marginal role at Regensburg. The
chief actors, those who actually determined the course of events,
were those who could make real decisions—their own decisions.
Contarini could encourage and he could obstruct, and, in the event,
he did both. But the important decisions he could not make. His
instructions excluded that from the beginning. Hence his coming
could not have been expected to effect in itself any radical alteration
in the situation.

Secondly, as is natural with a man of such outstanding gifts, a
certain mythology had begun to spring up about Contarini, and
even the standard biography by Dittrich is not free from hagio-
graphical tendencies. The source of the trouble seems to be a
rather uncritical acceptance of the baroque eloquence of Contarini's
own contemporaries, who never tired of describing Contarini as an
ornament of his age, a paragon of learning, one renowned far and
wide for his piety, integrity, and sanctity. Flaminio, for example,
on Contarini's elevation to the cardinalate, speaks of the choice of

---

[5] Campeggio/Farnese, 23 Dec. 1540. Campeggio reported a statement by
Granvelle according to which Contarini, Sadoleto, Pole, and Fregoso (the
Bishop of Salerno) were the men in whom the Protestants had most confidence.
D/R, 137–8; cf. the later characterization of Contarini by Sarpi as 'huomo
stimato di eccellente bontà et dottrina', Pietro Soave Polano (Paolo Sarpi),
Historia del Concilio Tridentino (2nd edn. Geneva: 1629), iii, 51, p. 97.

[6] Poggio/Farnese, 5 Feb. 1541, *HJ* iv. 661.

this 'perfect man', with which a new epoch was opening.[7] His biographer Beccadelli can find nothing but virtues in him, though he recognizes that to those who do not know Contarini personally this may seem mere adulation.[8] Dittrich, throughout his biography, never tires of drawing the reader's attention to the outstanding merits of his hero, whether as student, diplomat, patriot, reformer, theologian, or peace-maker.[9] The fact that the purpose of the book, as the Preface explains, is the 'paying of a debt of honour, which the Catholic Church and scholarship owe to one of their most zealous and energetic champions in a difficult time',[10] helps to make this understandable. Jedin pictures Contarini as one almost too good for this world, so convinced of the merits of charity and humility and goodwill that he believed they alone would suffice to settle the religious turmoil that beset Church and State.[11] In fact something between a saint and a fool.

We must grant the myth its half-truths. Contarini, however, was no saint and certainly no fool. He was a man who knew the meaning—and the necessity—of compromise, a man of the world as well as a man of the Church, an experienced diplomat, trained to observe the world as it was, to exploit human weakness, to flatter and cajole, to express the non-existent confidence or goodwill of

[7] God had chosen him, wrote Flaminio, 'per istrumento di qualche effetto novo, e segnalato, o che tutti i buoni aspettavano da lui tutte quelle eccellenti effetti, et operationi virtuose, che si denno aspettare da un' uomo perfetto'. Lodovico Beccadelli, *Monumenti di Varia Letteratura*, ed. G. Morandi (Bologna: 1797–1804), I. ii. 24. In similar vein Gregorio Cortese hoped it might herald a renewal of the Church. D/B, p. 329.

[8] Morandi, I. ii. 9; cf. Pallavicini's judgement that his clarity was complemented by profundity, his subtlety by eloquence, his reverence by sincerity. Sforza Pallavicino, *Vera Concilii Tridentini Historia*, trans. P. J. B. Giattino (Antwerpae: 1673), I. iv. 13.

[9] Dittrich sees in him 'das Idealbild eines Studenten'. ('Ein Bedürfnis nach sinnlichen Freuden oder gar geschlechtlichen Genüssen empfand er nicht . . . Die Erhabenhei der Wissenschaft erfüllte und befriedigte ganz seine Seele.') D/B, p. 17; he then becomes 'der gewandte Diplomat', and finally the accomplished Cardinal, ibid., pp. 127, 321 ff.

[10] '. . . eine Ehrenschuld abtragen, welche die katholische Kirche und Wissenschaft einem ihrer eifrigsten und tüchtigsten Vorkämpfer in schwerer Zeit schuldig ist.' Ibid., p. iii.

[11] 'In Regensburg musste Contarini die schmerzliche Erfahrung machen, dass der gute Wille und die heisse Liebe zu den Seelen, die er beide mitbrachte, nicht mehr genügten, um die verlorene kirchliche Einheit wieder herzustellen.' Hubert Jedin, *Kardinal Contarini als Kontroverstheologe* (Münster: 1949), p. 17. Similarly Dittrich: Contarini was 'stets geneigt, all Menschen nach seinem guten Willen und nach seinen idealen Bestrebungen zu beurteilen'. D/B, p. 563.

his superior. In the course of his diplomatic career he had not been above exploiting, or attempting to exploit, the Christian convictions of the Emperor to the advantage of the Republic of Venice, nor even of obstructing, or attempting to obstruct, peace in Europe if this were to be dangerous to the interests of this same Republic.[12] To the end of his life he remained an intensely conservative man, an aristocrat of Venice and of the Church, conscious of the weight of the centuries behind him, moving with ease through the familiar pomp of Court and Curia.

He was also, of course, to use an unfashionable word, a quite unusually good man. His whole life was spent in the service of others—of the citizens of Venice and of the members of the Church. He had an exalted view of public duty: humanist as he was, he refused, despite the constant interruption to his studies, to allow access to himself to be barred against those who sought his offices as Cardinal on their behalf. 'I do not think that the good Lord has called me to this high office for my own gratification but in order that I may be of service to others. Hence I am not here to pursue my own desires but to be at the disposal of those who need me.'[13] He used to say that he had great fellow-feeling for the Pope, for the higher the office the greater the toil.[14] He himself worked

---

[12] On his adept handling of Gattinara cf. Contarini/Council of Ten, 16 Aug. 1524, Brown, iii. 376. 'It is requisite first of all to sustain the fancies of the Chancellor, and then adroitly to dispel them, because he is a man of very small brains, and when he once takes an impression, he then becomes obstinate.' Or of Clement VII: 'Io mi sforzo quanto posso di adolcire et mitigare l'animo di S. Sant., con la quale bisogna usare diverse insinuationi, ne bisogna passare certi termini a chi cerchi di non irritarlo, ma mitigarlo.' Contarini/Senate, 14 June 1528, D/R, p. 31. Similarly ibid., Nr. 91, p. 31; Brown, iv, Nr. 324, p. 161. For illustrations of the sophistry he could practise on occasions cf. his defence of Venice's failure to carry out its obligations under the Treaty of London (Contarini/Council of Ten, 18 Sept. 1521, Brown, iii. 179), of its seizure of the papal towns Cervia and Ravenna (D/B, pp. 129 ff.), of its offensive measures against Faenza on the (false) report of Clement VII's death (he claimed that the latter were due to a concern to protect the cities from the Emperor! D/B, p. 158). As to his obstruction of peace, in 1524 he advocated a more vigorous pursuit of the war between France and the Emperor. Venice had just decided to join the imperial side, and feared that if Charles were not occupied with France he would turn his attention and his armies towards Italy. Contarini/Council of Ten, 16 Aug. 1524, Brown, iii. 376; D/B, pp. 81 ff. Three years previously Contarini—again pursuing Venetian interests—had urged precisely the opposite course: a suspension of hostilities. (Brown, iii. 157). There was, of course, nothing extraordinary about such conduct, but that is precisely the point we wish to make.

[13] Morandi, I. ii. 46; if Casa is to be believed it was out of a sense of public duty that he accepted the cardinalate in 1535. D/B, pp. 320-1.

[14] Morandi, I. ii. 47.

hard and long and executed his duties as ambassador, reformer, and legate with scrupulous care. He was not petty; he was free from ambition.[15] In true Erasmian manner he abhorred the fanatic. On the other hand, as we see particularly from his reforming activity, he was a man of strong convictions and did not shrink from speaking his mind frankly whenever the occasion—and his conscience—seemed to demand it.[16]

The civic and scholarly virtues displayed by Contarini are those of Italian Humanism at its best. They are also virtues calculated to appeal to the adherents of the new Lutheran ethic, with its stress on vocation, the calling to service in the world. There is nothing spectacular and few traces of the ascetic in Contarini's spirituality; indeed compared with some of the exotic saints with which Italy abounded at this time his character seems positively pedestrian.

Yet there *is* something of the saint or the prophet or the charismatic about Contarini. About his outrageous optimism. About the influence he exercised on men whose opinions appeared to be diametrically opposed to his own. About, in this particular case, his ability to see in Regensburg not a danger, or a shoal to be successfully negotiated, or a futile exercise in rhetoric, but an opportunity to be grasped with both hands, an opportunity for which God should be thanked. 'I thank God', he wrote to Farnese from Bologna as he made his way towards Germany, '. . . for the *colloquium*, and for the good beginning that has already been made, and I hope in God that irrelevant considerations will not intrude themselves, and that, as I have many times said to his Holiness, there will not be such a great disagreement in the essentials as many believe . . .'[17] Was this a foolish dream of understanding?

The evidence would appear to speak against such a view. On his

[15] There seems no doubt that he was personally a man of great humility. Beccadelli described him as 'tanto modesto, et cosi privo d'ambitione, quanto si conviene alla bonta ch'e conosciuta, et predicata di lui'. Ibid., p. 22.

[16] 'Die Offenheit und der Freimut, jene Charaktereigenschaften, die ihn bei Carl V so beliebt gemacht hatten, behielt Contarini auch als Cardinal bei . . . Es war etwas nahezu unerhörtes, dass ein Cardinal im Consistorium selbst dem Papst opponirte und sich dessen Lieblingsplänen widersetzte. Contarini tat das mehr als einmal.' D/B, p. 327. Beccadelli, e.g. records the occasion when Contarini championed the rights of the Varani family against the papal annexationist policy in the name of justice and the honour of the Apostolic See. Morandi, I. ii. 44–5.

[17] Contarini/Farnese, 12 Feb. 1541, D/R, p. 146.

original appointment as legate in May 1540 he had certainly had no illusions about the difficulty of the task before him.[18] If there was a sober realism about his approach, then this was largely due to the fact that he was one of the best-informed men in Rome on the German situation. He had been in Worms in 1521 as Venetian ambassador to the Emperor when Luther had made his famous stand. Remaining at the Imperial Court until 1525 he had had ample opportunity to acquaint himself with the growing seriousness of the situation. Again, as the Republic's representative at the Curia from 1528 to 1530, he had noted the helplessness of the Papacy in face of the problem.[19] And finally after his elevation to the cardinalate, his interest as the leader of the reform party had been primarily given to the preparation for the Council, whose main purpose would be to find a remedy for the German schism.

For two decades, then, he had been in the closest touch with events in Germany, and in the latter months of 1540, with his dispatch as legate expected any moment, he had been in constant communication with the papal representatives in Germany and had full access to all their dispatches to Rome.[20] When, therefore, he set out for Regensburg he knew very well that the scale of probabilities was heavily weighted against success. He told Ruggieri, the Ferrarese ambassador to the Papal Court, that he foresaw an arduous and difficult task ahead of him, especially in view of the

[18] It was far beyond his powers, mental and physical, he wrote to Cervini, yet out of obedience to the Pope and the desire to do what he can for the blessed Church of Christ he gladly accepts the burden. 26 May 1540, Morandi, I. ii. 84–5; he writes to Sadoleto similarly on the same day. Ibid., p. 81.

[19] His earlier dispatches, it is true, have almost nothing to say about Lutheranism, and the wider implications of the Reformation are obviously beyond the compass of his thought at this stage. In five years of dispatches from 1521 to 1525 there are as many references to Lutheranism. By the late 1520s the situation has changed completely. Commenting on Clement's unwillingness to call the Council demanded by Charles V, he wrote at the end of 1528 to the Senate that he considered the Church of Rome to be in great trouble, and did not know to what end the Almighty would lead it. 11 Dec. 1528, Brown, iv, Nr. 378, p. 179. Clement 'dimostra di essere desiderosa di vedere gli abusi di Santa Chiesa regolati ma nientedimeno egli non manda ad esecuzione alcun simile pensiero, ne si risolve in far provisione alcuna'. *Relazione degli ambasciatori veneti al Senato*, ed. Eugenio Albéri, II. iii. 265. His dispatches are full of references to the spread of Lutheranism in Germany and Savoy, e.g. 7 Apr. 1529, D/R, p. 50; 10 July 1529, Brown, iv. Nr. 486, p. 221. Cf. D/B, pp. 146–51.

[20] Morandi actually assumed that many of Morone's dispatches had been sent to Contarini in the first instance, and not to Farnese! (e.g. that of 12 Jan. 1541, with its detailed analysis of the German situation.) Morandi, I. ii. 100–5.

entanglement of matters of state with those of religion.[21] There is scant evidence of undue optimism here and indeed Contarini seems to have inclined temperamentally to the opposite pole, to melancholy and depression.[22]

Perhaps the best illustration of his attitude is an exchange of letters with Eck. At the end of August 1540 Eck had written Contarini speaking out strongly against the whole idea of entering into discussions with the Protestants. 'There should not be any disputations with the heretics. Those who break their pledged word to the Emperor by continuing to expand their following and by seizing more and more Church lands cannot be dealt with in this way.'[23]

Contarini replied that he had been badly shaken to hear how little hope Eck held out of a reconciliation of the schism. Whatever human reason may say to the contrary, we must hope against hope. Where there is trust in the providence of God and the mercy of Christ there can be no room for despair. Rather let us pray, pray to the author of all peace to establish the unity of His Church, by sending down His Holy Spirit to be with us to the end of time. As to us, let us overcome evil with good so that our adversaries will be ashamed—or at least ought to be—of holding themselves apart from their loving brethren. The rest we can leave to God.[24]

Over against such prophecies of doom Contarini had a curious freedom. In his view, nothing could be taken for granted, for good or ill, for the future is not at our disposal. He recognized that the Diet might well pass resolutions inimical to the Faith and to the Apostolic See, and that the Emperor might well close the Diet and grant the Protestants similar concessions to those they had secured at Frankfurt.[25] But one must take the risk. Man's duty in this situation is an ultimate optimism.

[21] Farnese/Poggio, 8 Jan. 1541, *NB* I. vi. 183 *Anm.* I; Nino Servini wrote to Cardinal Gonzaga on 22 January that from what he heard from his secretary Contarini '. . . ha poca speranza di posser fare cosa buona, scrivendogli il m. *ro* del sacro palazzo, che si vede pochissimo verso, essendo quei diavoli disuniti più che mai fra di loro, et è il manco quello che si harebbe da trattare della fede, l'autorità del papa, ma fra di loro è una rabbia crudelissima . . . et cosi hanno poco animo di fare cosa buona . . .' *NAV* n.s. xxv (1907), 18.

[22] e.g. his complaint to Pole in 1536 is being 'Saepe maesto'. Pole/Contarini, 24 June 1536, Quirini, I. 459.

[23] Eck/Contarini, 26 Aug. 1540, *ZKG* xix. 259–61.

[24] Contarini/Eck, 6 Jan. 1541, D/*R*, pp. 314–15.

[25] Memoriale Rmi Domini Card. Contareni, antequam discederet Germaniam versus, datum Rmo Card. S. Crucis. D/*R*, p. 140.

His attitude to the colloquy is thus remarkably similar to Bucer's. It is based on a firm conviction of the rightness and the eventual triumph of his cause, and evinces the same concern to do his duty by his Christian brother.[26] It is scarcely an accident that both these champions of dialogue possessed this inner security. Conversely one has grounds for suspicion that the violent opposition of Eck and indeed Luther to the colloquy is not unrelated to their own personal anxieties and insecurities.

It was, of course, precisely this maturity of outlook which had prompted Charles V to recommend the appointment of Contarini. Without doubt, Charles's previous knowledge of Contarini as Venetian ambassador to the Imperial Court from 1521 to 1525, and the further encounter with him at Bologna in 1529 had a large influence on his choice.[27] Despite the fact that throughout this period Venice, in its concern to defend Italian independence, had pursued a pro-French policy, Contarini himself had won the favour of the Emperor. He had proved himself not only a good diplomat,[28] but a cultured and personable man of the world. He often engaged in friendly conversation with the Emperor about non-political matters,[29] having among other things, so Beccadelli tells us, a common interest with Charles in cosmography, a subject of particular interest at a time when the riches of the New World were beginning to come to the notice of Europe.[30]

---

[26] 'S'io posso in questa Legatione farci servitio, quella mi commandi con quella sicurta che recerca l'amor nostro fraterno.' Contarini/Sadoleto, 13 Jan. 1541, Morandi, I. ii. 95.

[27] Cf. D/B, pp. 26–124, and Brown, iii. 114–470, on which Dittrich's account is almost exclusively based.

[28] But cf. Brown, iii. 338 n. 2. He certainly had good judgement, was a fine orator, and enjoyed general popularity. On occasions he tended to credulity, as his conviction that the French King would not desert his Italian allies—expressed to Giberti just prior to the peace of Cambrai—shows. D/R, Nr. 157, p. 51.

[29] Brown, iii. Nr. 564, p. 280. On Contarini's scientific interests cf. D/B, pp. 265–79.

[30] Morandi, I. ii. 33. For a Venetian report of the Bologna negotiations cf. *Relazioni degli Ambasciatori al Senato*, ed. Eugenio Alberi, Ser. 2, vol. iii, pp. 142–253, esp. the report on Contarini's reception by Charles V. Contarini was received not as a representative of the Republic, '. . . ma come a messer Gasparo Contarini, con cui aveva avuta grande dimestichezza quando fu a lui oratore in Spagna: e qui di nuova lo recevette con tanta benignità di paroli e dimostrazione di gesti della persona, che tutti li circonstanti ne presero maraviglia . . .' Ibid., p. 162. Cf. also Contarini's own report to Venice. Ibid., pp. 257–74.

The importance of this previous acquaintance should not be pressed too far. Throughout his period in Rome as Venetian ambassador there (May 1528 to December 1529) Contarini had been a zealous advocate of the anti-imperial policy of Venice,[31] and the Emperor cannot have been ignorant of this. Indeed it is important to realize that Contarini remained until his cardinalate very much the Venetian patriot. It is the freedoms of Italy, not the future of Christendom, which are in the forefront of his mind, although precisely the interests of Venice had led him to see the desirability of a lasting and equitable peace between France and the Empire and a concentration of warlike energies on the Turkish threat.

More important for the Emperor's choice would be Contarini's scholarly reputation. Though of a breadth that today would draw the accusation of dilettantism, his learning, in philosophy and theology particularly, commanded the admiration of all his contemporaries. Beccadelli relates that a professional philosopher of Bologna, Messer Lodovico Bocca di ferro, said that of the many scholars he knew there was none with more learning and better judgement than Contarini. The latter, although for years away from his studies, could answer without hesitation the problems he had brought before him. 'I felt as if I were conversing with an angel rather than with a man.'[32] He is referring here primarily to Contarini's mastery of Aristotle.

As regards theology he had a thorough knowledge of the *Summa* of Aquinas, and of the Fathers was well read in Augustine, Basil, Chrysostom, Nazianzus, and others. In the long summer days his favourite recreation was reading in the Classics, in Latin and Greek history, in Homer, Horace, Virgil, and Cicero.[33] His learning would thus adorn the deliberations at the colloquy, and if his approval were gained for any agreement, it would be exceedingly difficult for Rome later to reject it.

Again, not only as a humanist but as a member of the 'evan-

[31] On hearing, e.g. of the papal treaty with the Emperor in 1529 Contarini did not conceal his dismay and told Clement VII that the Spaniards 'sempre vano cosi cauti ne' le conventione che fano et in li altri progressi sui, et sempre tengono un capo in mano, per potersi schermir et assassinar il compagno'. D/R, Nr. 190, p. 59. Sim. D/R, Nr. 178, p. 56. At this stage the Emperor is for Contarini the arch-enemy.

[32] Morandi, I. ii. 42; Pietro Pomponazzi dedicated one of his writings to him as a token of his respect. D/B, p. 219.

[33] Morandi, I. ii. 42–3.

gelical' group in Italy he would act as a magnet for the Erasmian forces in Germany—on both sides of the religious divide. The imperial party was only too well aware how ill the Catholic apologetic had thus far been conducted in Germany. As Brieger points out, the Catholic cause would now be championed not by Morone, who in Granvelle's opinion had held up the conversations at Worms for months, but by someone who might be expected to promote the work of reconciliation.[34] Contarini was a man of very different stamp from the German controversial theologians. His writings were free from all personal bitterness and polemic.[35] He, if anyone, would be able to win over at least the reasonable elements in the Protestant camp to the Catholic side.

His reforming activities in the much-abused Curia, his concern for the pastoral office of the clergy, the fact that since his elevation to the cardinalate in 1535 he had been generally recognized as the leader of the 'Catholic Reformation' in Italy,[36] together with his own unchallenged personal integrity, would commend him further to the Protestants, and also to the Catholic Estates, who had now for two decades been calling for a redress of their gravamina, for an end to the abuses and absurdities which were threatening the credibility of the old faith.

Finally, by the beginning of the 1540s he had become a 'good European'. His experience in Rome had broadened his horizons and extended his loyalties. He had learned to see the problems of Europe as a whole, and while too much of a layman to think like an Italian prince of the Church, he was now also too much of a Churchman to think as a Venetian patrician. The variety of his experience as humanist, diplomat, and cardinal had given him a rare openness and breadth of vision. He was, above all, aware of the urgent need

---

[34] Theodor Brieger, *Gasparo Contarini und das Regensburger Concordienwerk des Jahres 1541*, p. 5.

[35] In the concluding words to his *Confutatio articulorum Lutheranorum* Contarini wrote: 'Non est opus concilio, non disputationibus et syllogismis, non locis ex sacra scriptura excerptis ad sedandos hos Lutheranorum motus; opus est tantum bona voluntate, charitate erga Deum et proximum, animi humilitate opus est . . .' *Gasparo Contarini, Gegenreformatorische Schriften, (1530 c.–1542)*, ed. F. Hünermann, p. 22. In his personal life, too, he was as conciliatory as possible. 'Non era nelle dispute contentioso, ma mite et benigno, et s'havesse senso, buono, a quello s'appigliava, et quello metteva innanzi, et così non lassava, che altri rimanesse confuso.' Beccadelli in Morandi, I. ii. 41–2.

[36] D/B, pp. 317–422. Almost all the leading reformers—Pole, Sadoleto, Cortese, Badia, Giberti, Caraffa, Fregoso, to name only a few—were personal friends of Contarini.

for action to meet the chaos in Germany, the schism in the Church, the Turkish menace in the East. He believed, like the Emperor, in Christendom, and shared with him the dream of a restoration of the lost harmonies.

That all his concerns, as theologian, as reformer, and as one passionately concerned for the peace of Europe, culminated in his ecumenical concern, his yearning for the recovery of the shattered unity of the Church seemed to fit him ideally for the task which the Emperor, through his chancellor Granvelle, had prepared for him.

As Brieger points out, the presence of Contarini transformed the whole situation. In place of the hope for reconciliation between the new and the old Church in Germany it seemed now that a reunion of Wittenberg and Rome was in the offing, and it was the positive attitude of Contarini to the policy of conciliation that was the basis of this momentous possibility.[37]

First of all as a non-conformist himself he believed he understood the language of rebels. He deplored much on the Catholic side that the Protestants also deplored. The wild polemic of some of the Catholic controversialists offended not only his cultured taste but seemed to him often, in its enthusiasm to castigate everything Protestant, quite uncatholic in, for example, its depreciation of faith and grace.[38] Institutional Catholicism was never attractive to him. One recollects his famous words to Paul III when the latter hinted that his opposition to the nomination of some new cardinals lay in a fear that the influence of the present members would thus be diminished: 'For my part, I must confess that I do not consider the red hat to be my greatest honour.'[39]

His faith had been nurtured in the critical atmosphere of Venice,[40] among his own circle of friends and pilgrims in the

[37] Brieger, *Contarini*, pp. 9–10.

[38] In two letters in the summer of 1537 he expresses his fear that such writers, in their zeal to oppose Luther, in fact oppose Augustine, Ambrose, Bernard, Jerome, and Thomas, and verge towards the Pelagian heresy. D/R, pp. 270, 288–90.

[39] 'Per mio conto, a dir el vero, io non reputo che il Cappello sia il mio maggior honore.' Morandi, I. ii. 47.

[40] Dittrich describes Padua's university as one which had long been suspect of heresy (D/B, p. 220). It is certainly interesting to remark what very sympathetic treatment the Lutherans often received at the hands of the Venetian observer. Carlo Contarini, e.g. even grants the peasants a certain justification for their revolt in 1525 and displays some *schadenfreude* at the discomfiture of the Bishop of Ulm (Brown, iii. Nr. 976, p. 423). Other observers: ibid., Nr. 990, p. 427, and Nr. 1007, pp. 433 ff; Nr. 1086 contains this very sympathetic statement:

spiritual life, in his own passionate struggle to reach certainty of salvation.[41] His diplomatic career had stripped him of any illusions as regards the Papacy in its worldly aspect,[42] and he had proved himself in the 1530s to be an outspoken opponent of an exaggerated Curialism.[43] His activity as a cardinal had been one long struggle against the reactionary forces of the Curia.[44] His knowledge of the history of the Church led him to be critical of many traditional practices, and to recognize that there was guilt on the Catholic side.[45] And yet despite all his criticism he had fought his way through to what he believed to be a both reasonable and biblical position within the Catholic Church.

It would not, therefore, be the Catholicism of the canonist[46] or

---

'Luther's whole faith, in short, consists in loving God above all things, and one's neighbour as one's self; and he maintained that so many external ceremonies are unnecessary, because Christ by his passion made atonement for everything . . .' Ibid., p. 468. Finally one should mention a letter from Zuan Francisco Contarini (Carlo's brother): 'Tell the most noble Messer Martin Sanuto that here one cannot even speak of Luther, still less have his works, as this Prince (Archduke Ferdinand) makes the Bishop of Vienna search for Lutherans, and if found woe betide them; so he must excuse me in this matter.' Vienna, 9 Oct. 1524, ibid., Nr. 83, pp. 385 ff.

[41] Hubert Jedin, *Contarini und Camaldoli* (Edizione di Storia e Letteratura; Estratte dall' Archivio Italiane per la Storia della Pietà, vol. ii, 1953); also Jedin's article, 'Das Turmerlebnis des jungen Contarini', *HJ* lxx. 115 ff.

[42] In 1521 he criticized the belligerence of the Pope when the latter, with his eyes on Parma and Piacenza (promised him by the Emperor), opposed any reconciliation with France. Brown, iii. Nr. 289, p. 157. 'Should a conflict ensue', he wrote, 'it must cause great detriment to Christendom, and those who thwarted the adjustment [at Calais] . . . for the purpose of augmenting their positions in Italy, will have to give account to the Almighty.' Ibid., Nr. 345, p. 182. Four years later, hearing of the treaty the Pope had signed with England and the Emperor because of his fear of the latter, he exclaimed, 'Dio voglia, che questa timidità sua non sii causa de la ruina d'Italia.' D/R, Nr. 57, p. 23. In a treaty with the Emperor Contarini did not hesitate to inform the Senate that '. . . la natura del Pontefice e supra modum timida e vile . . .' D/R, Nr. 191, p. 60. He strongly criticized the Pope's pursuit of his own private interests, and defended the refusal of Venice to return Ravenna and Cervia to the Papacy, '. . . perche Ravenna et Cervia sono il pretexto del desiderio infinito, che ha de Fiorenza et alle cose de Ferrara, le qual li tochano al commodo privato et al disegno che ha fatto de la exaltation de casa sua'. D/R, 28 Dec. 1528, Nr. 121, p. 39.

[43] e.g. his writing *De Potestate Pontificis in Compositionibus*, D/B, pp. 384–9.

[44] Ibid., pp. 317–422.

[45] He recommended, for example, the publication of the reforming 'consilium de ecclesia emendanda' as a papal bull in 1537, although this would have amounted to nothing less than a public confession of guilt. D/B, pp. 368 ff.

[46] He never interested himself in the study of law '. . . et la teneva per vana', according to Beccadelli, who also mentions his impatience with cavilling of any

the school theologian which he would be offering the Protestants, but a Catholicism which he believed to be the fulfilment
of the deepest concerns of the Protestants.[47] Is it even possible
that he saw them, or at least some of them, as possible future
allies in his own fight against reaction within the Curia and elsewhere?

Secondly, as himself a fervid advocate of reform, he had much in
common with a Melanchthon or a Bucer. None of the reformers
was more concerned to restore the pastoral work of the clergy to its
central place than he. Nor did they outdo him in his zeal to provide
instruction in the faith, from the parish level to the universities, or
indeed in his love for learning as such. The very list of the friends
whom he had hoped to take with him to Regensburg is significant
in this respect—Sadoleto, Marcantonio Flaminio, Cortese.[48] He
could already point with justification to the progress that had
attended his efforts and those of the reforming party thus far—the
raising of the moral and intellectual standard of the cardinalate, the
beginnings of the reform of the Curia, and the campaign against
absentee bishops.[49] The Church was already being renewed and
cleansed from within! When they realized this, how would the

---

kind, following the dictum of his teacher Pietro of Mantua 'nil subtilius falsitate',
Morandi, I. ii. 40–1. We have already noticed his opposition to the exaggerated
papalism of the canon lawyers. Dittrich comments, 'Nach seiner Überzeugung
war Grund und Quelle der verkehrten Praxis [of compositions] an der Curie die
Lehre gewisser extremer Canonisten, dass der Papst Herr der kirchlichen
Gnadenschätze, sowie der ihm von Christus übertragenen jurisdictionellen
Befugnisse sei und folglich darüber auch unumschränkt disponiren, dieselben
also auch verkaufen könne, ohne sich der Simonie schildig zu machen.' D/B.
p. 384.

[47] Cf. his writing, De Poenitentia. D/R, pp. 353–61, esp. 354–5.

[48] D/R, pp. 126, 134, 135.

[49] Cf. Jedin, History, i. 378, 410 ff. There is no doubt that Contarini was,
inter alia, instrumental in persuading his friends to take an active part in the
reform programme, e.g. Pole, D/B, p. 360, Anm. I. Admittedly Dittrich over-
states the position when, discussing the papal plans for the reform of the Church,
he adds 'hiebei stand ihm stets mahnend und rathend Contarini zur Seite, dem
er sein Vertrauen zuwandte und mit dem er häufig gerade über die Angelegenheit
der Reformen conferirte'. Ibid., p. 350. It is true that Contarini had the ear of
the Pope. Yet this is equally true of the leaders of the more conservative party.
Paul listened to Contarini and encouraged his reforming endeavours, but
refused to identify himself too closely with the party of reform. Dittrich himself
notes that, in view of the disagreement between the two groups, Paul 'could not
immediately come to a decision' in favour of the progressive party: D/B, p. 389.
In reality Contarini's alternate moods of hope and despair reflect very pointedly
the fact that he did not possess the full confidence of the Pope, who sought to
pursue a middle course between the two alternatives. Cf. D/B, pp. 390, 402 ff.

Protestants continue to justify their rending of the seamless robe by this ungodly and fearful schism?

Thirdly—and perhaps this is the crucial point—he believed that he not only understood but shared the *basic conviction* of the Protestants—that of the all-importance of justification by faith. In his theological writing the relation of faith and works was the central concern, and he held that the Lutheran concern for justification by faith was in fact the essence of Catholic faith also.[50] Protestantism, in other words, is essentially Catholic! Only in the false consequences which it draws from its basic doctrines must it be corrected. But if this is so, then the Protestant schism was caused by a misunderstanding of Catholicism. To do away with this misunderstanding, which was preventing the Protestants from appreciating the 'real' Catholicism, was his great hope.

If we are to learn from Christ mildness and humility of heart then the waging of bitter polemic against our opponents is impossible, he wrote at the end of 1538 to Cochlaeus, congratulating him on the mild tone of his refutation of an attack by Johannes Sturm on the 'consilium de ecclesia emendanda'.[51] The difficulty is that however piously and irreprehensibly we write these days the Lutherans take grave offence.[52]

Without doubt Contarini would see in Regensburg this long-sought opportunity. He was, by inclination and temperament, the born teacher. He never lost his temper, Beccadelli tells us. Although

---

[50] 'Il fundamento dello aedificio de Luterani e verissimo, ne per alcun modo devemo dirli contra, ma accetarlo come vero et catholico, immo come fundamento della religione christiana.' D/R, p. 358.

[51] Contarini/Cochlaeus, 8 Nov. 1538, D/R, pp. 296–7. Similarly he urged Pole to excise the hefty polemic from his *Pro ecclesiasticae unitatis defensione*, directed to Henry VIII. D/B, p. 430.

[52] 'Dabit fortasse deus optimus maximus nobis occasionem, qua poterimus simul esse, simul agere de his controversiis ac eis ostendere, quam falsa plerumque nobis attribuant, quam negligenter legerint excellentissimos viros, quos damnant, quod in nonnullis immutarint vocabula, idem tamen dicant, quod scholastici omnes. Ea vero quae falsa praedicant ac in coetus suos receperunt, ostendamus, quantum pugnet cum ratione, cum patribus nostris et cum doctrina sacrae paginae, non verbis amarulentis, non conviciis, sed animo benevolentissimo, amicis verbis, omnique corporis gestu miti ac mansueto, qui christianum hominem deceat.' Cochlaeus has given of his knowledge, experience, and piety for the sake of healing the schism, '. . . ut nostra tempestate videamus ecclesiam Dei unam esse vinculo caritatis et pacis, ac ecclesia germanica, nobilissima et potentissima christianae reipublicae pars, tandem quiescat ac sibi parcat provideatque, ne seditionibus his durantibus suis ipsa se viribus conficiat'. Contarini/Cochlaeus, 8 Nov. 1538, D/R, pp. 296–7.

he had a passionate temperament, the extreme limit of his anger is said to have been that he called a servant a goose![53] He never sought to display his knowledge, but enjoyed teaching, saying that, 'to him who has it is given, and he who is miserly with the grace given him will lose it'. He was able to use language that would be understandable to the learner, a skill that might not be without its importance for the confrontation with the Protestants.[54]

Yet, as we shall see, his instruction drastically curtailed his freedom of action in respect to the Protestants. It is significant in this respect that another of his questions found no echo in the instruction. He had asked whether, if the colloquy should come to a decision which left the decision on certain peripheral questions ('articoli indifferenti') open, resort could be had to a gathering of theologians under the authority of the Papacy, if it should prove that a General Council was not in prospect.[55] Even this modest attempt to increase somewhat his freedom of manœuvre was evidently found unacceptable by the Curia.

The Curia could constrain him to abandon his 'dangerous' tactics. His exalted hopes, however, he clung to. The result was that the latter were left stranded high and dry, that there crept in a glaring contradiction between his audacious expectations and the totally incongruous methods with which he hoped to realize them. It is with this contradiction—rather than with any supposed illegitimacy or impossibility of the hopes as such—that the historian has to deal. Contarini was perhaps clear enough about what he wanted to achieve. On the question of how it was to be achieved he was intolerably and inexcusably vague.

Without doubt he expected that he would be able to bring to bear his influence on the Emperor so that political considerations the 'rispetti estrinsechi', could be excluded, and a truly Catholic concord attained. Here however he not only fell victim to the typical illusion of the Renaissance diplomat—that history is made by the delivery of speeches—but he overestimated both the power of the Emperor and the community of interest between imperial and papal policy. His dream of the revival of Christendom was an essentially medieval ideal with but scant relevance to the actual situation—to the rise of particularism that was challenging the imperial authority in the interest of the territories, to the collapse of the imperial legal and administrative framework, to the alliance

[53] Morandi, I. ii. 48.   [54] Ibid., p. 42.   [55] Quirini, iii. 224–5.

of France and Turkey, to the underlying economic realities, to the new secular spirit that resisted the claims of any overarching spiritual hierarchy.

Nor does he appear to have given any consideration to the anomaly of his position as papal legate, to the fact that his authority would be recognized by only one of the two parties at Regensburg. John Frederick, for example, had instructed his representatives to reject any attempt by the legate to exercise the authority of the Pope as the head of the Church.[56] True, the unpopularity of the Papacy in Germany meant that he would seem to some extent the representative of an alien power to both parties, but this was a thought that can hardly have afforded him much comfort.

How was he to walk the tightrope between betraying the papal interests—which he was there to represent—and between rebuffing the Protestants, whose recovery for the 'Church' was the whole point of the exercise? It was not enough to reply here that if the unity of the Church were to come to pass it would not be the outcome of any human effort, but of the working of the Holy Spirit in men's hearts, the answer to prayer,[57] unexceptionable though the sentiment may be; pious verbiage is here making a confusion of thought. If the brand of Catholicism which Contarini was eager to champion to the Protestants was not in fact quite as near to Protestantism as he believed it was, was it not equally distant from the variety of Catholicism which was predominant in the Curia and which was, in chaste and exalted form, to find expression in the decrees of the Council of Trent?

Contarini's significance has nothing to do with demonstrating the illusoriness of the hope of reunion. It lies rather in the confusion of thinking from which he could not free himself. It lies in his failure to think through the consequences of his own critique of Catholicism. He stood between two fronts, drawn inwardly now by the one, now by the other. His goal was the evangelizing of the Catholic as much as the catholicizing of the Evangelical. He had made his decision to stay within the Catholic camp, to work from within it for its inner renewal. But was he clear in his own mind as to the frontiers beyond which a loyalty to the tradition and the institutions would become a betrayal of his goal? Had he decided whether his task was to reconcile Catholics and Protestants on a basis of 'evangelical Catholicism', or whether it was to win back

[56] CR iv. 125-6.   [57] D/R, p. 314.

the Protestants to the existing Catholic Church? This one is inclined to doubt. The result was confusion of thought. The result was that he allowed events to dictate to him, took the easier line of resistance—he was, after all, no youthful radical—and hence retreated under pressure behind the orthodox formulae and the hierarchical structures.

It is not being argued here that Contarini was 'really' a Protestant. Nor even that he was not 'unexceptionably Catholic'.[58] Simply that these terms in themselves do not help us much here, and that a too hasty readiness to use such labels obscures rather than illumines the issues before us. We shall be able to return to this subject after a closer examination of Contarini's actions and attitudes at Regensburg.

[58] 'Einwandfrei katholisch.' Jedin, *Contarini als Kontroverstheologe*, p. 16.

5

The Authority of this Holy See

THE Protestants had broken with Rome. The Catholic Reformers followed another option: that of a critical solidarity with the Old Church. According to circumstances the emphasis could lie either on the criticism or on the solidarity, but it was in the tension between these poles that they found themselves. It was a sophisticated position. Later, when the Inquisition got under way, it was also to become a dangerous one. Its adherents required both patience and determination to see beyond the immediate frustrations and day-to-day compromises to the vision of a renewed and reunited Church. There were moral as well as tactical problems. When does the pursuit of radical change from within an institution phase into subversion of the institution itself! What if acceptance of new ideas means the betrayal of old friends? Where is the point of no return from which one cannot return to the fold?

We have noted the expectations with which Contarini approached Regensburg. How compatible were they with those of the Papacy? Could the legate be sure of backing in Rome for the decisions he took in Regensburg? Could Rome be confident that whatever decisions he did take would promote her best interests?

There does indeed seem to be a startling contrast between Contarini's cautious optimism about Regensburg and the attitude of the Curia, frozen into a defensive posture, dreading every new development in Germany. Retreating as far as it could behind the barriers of orthodoxy and traditionalism, the Curia expressed its anxiety for the future in an uncritical adulation of the past. Contarini had left with great zeal and high hopes of finding a way to reunite the Church, wrote Ruggieri, 'but it seems to others that although he shows high courage he has taken upon himself a troublesome assignment'. For him to emerge from it honourably would be a superhuman achievement. None of the other cardinals, he added, envied Contarini in the least.[1] The general view was that the Lutherans would be unyielding on all the main questions, not out of any religious concern, but simply from the desire to continue in their previous licentious way of life.[2]

Contarini, then, was under the suspicion of pursuing a policy of appeasement from the outset. Driven by circumstance into sending a legate to Regensburg, into giving its unwilling benediction to what it could only regard as an exceedingly dangerous departure from Catholic practice, Rome's chief concern was to avoid being committed to a doctrinal compromise at Regensburg. The whole project was approached in Rome, as in Wittenberg, with the utmost caution and suspicion. The only outcome that was hoped from it was failure, which would at least demonstrate once and for all the futility of such colloquies.

The dispatch of Contarini was really nothing more than a gesture, a tactical manœuvre, dictated by the need to retain the goodwill of the Emperor. It would demonstrate that the Pope had done everything possible to contain the Protestant threat. It had been alleged that if the colloquy failed this would be due to the lack of papal support. The sending of the legate would 'remove the pretext for this calumny', wrote Farnese to Dandino,[3] perhaps a little too hopefully.

The lack of enthusiasm in Rome for the colloquy, quite apart from considerations of principle, was, after all, understandable enough. If no legate were sent, the Papacy would be accused of a total lack of concern for Germany. If, on the other hand, one were sent, his fate would almost certainly be similar to that of the papal representatives at Worms—he would, that is, be accused of obstructing the progress of the work of reconciliation. A further danger was that what was done at Regensburg might be regarded as binding on the Papacy. To cover itself against at least this contingency the Pope was careful to stress that the responsibility for the outcome rested on the Emperor's shoulders.[4] This would not only make the latter more circumspect in his actions. If the worst came to the worst, the whole project could be disowned.

Rome's pessimism was fed by the reports from its representatives in Germany. Morone himself was pessimistic about the outcome. Smarting from his experiences in Worms he was deeply worried

---

[1] NB I. vi. 189, Anm. 1.   [2] Ibid., p. 196, Anm. 1.
[3] Ibid., p. 137, Anm. 2.   [4] Ibid., pp. 161–2.

that the religious issue would be made subservient to purely political considerations. He had seen the Catholic theologians at Worms bowing to the will of their respective princes. 'Theology is made subservient here to human passions.' Although, apart from Cleves, the Palatinate, and Brandenburg, the Catholics were agreed on the basic doctrines, their attitude to what they termed the 'indifferent articles' varied according to what was politically most advantageous to them. Only Mainz and the Bavarians held the Papacy in any affection. By comparison the Protestants presented a relatively united front, based on adherence to the Augsburg Confession and Apology and on opposition to the Pope. The most moderate among them were the south German cities— Ulm, Augsburg, Nuremberg—together with the Margrave George of Brandenburg.[5]

Further evidence of the predominance of political considerations he found in the imperial plans. Granvelle, he believed, was trying to create divisions within the Catholic ranks in order to facilitate accord with the Lutherans, and imperial policy seemed to be ready to enter into 'any agreement, even a bad one' in order to secure the subsidy against the Turks. The negotiations therefore could not but be detrimental to the interests of the Apostolic See and the Catholic faith.[6]

He had hoped at Worms that the Emperor and Ferdinand would at least have their eyes opened to the real intentions of the Protestants. But this, it was now clear, had not happened; already too much consideration was being given to the Protestants.[7] Morone's expectations therefore were of the gloomiest. His pessimism was shared by Vergerio, Bishop of Capod' Istria, who, looking back at Worms, felt it resembled a National Council more than anything else,[8] and by the Scot Wauchop, who was convinced on the basis of Worms that such colloquies were not a way to concord, but on the contrary, only spurred the heretics on to greater fury, and served as a sounding-board for Protestant propaganda.[9]

Campeggio tended towards a hesitant approval of the project. The Emperor, he believed, was the sole hope in the situation. He

[5] Ibid., pp. 122 ff.
[6] Morone/Farnese, 1 Mar. 1541, Lämmer, pp. 363–6.
[7] Morone/Farnese, 25 Feb. 1541, D/R, p. 149.
[8] Vergerio/Aleander, 23 Feb. 1541, Lämmer, p. 357.
[9] Wauchop/Farnese, 19 Feb. 1541, ibid., pp. 356–7.

might fail to act effectively, and he might make impermissible concessions to the Lutherans.[10] On the whole, however, Campeggio was guardedly optimistic about the possibilities of a reconciliation, especially in view of the decision to send Contarini.[11] It appeared from what Granvelle said that Brandenburg and Hesse would be amenable, that all the princes would come to Regensburg in an obedient spirit, that the threatened National Council could be avoided, and that a gradual improvement of the situation would set in. Granvelle, he was convinced, would do the best he could. Certain concessions would, however, have to be made to the Protestants, if concord were to be achieved. The Emperor seemed to be preparing to make substantial concessions on the questions of the Church lands, of the cases before the Imperial Court, of clerical marriage, and of the common cup. Agreement would, he thought, be reached on as many issues as possible and the disputed points would be referred to the next General Council.[12]

Poggio, the nuncio at the Imperial Court, also refused to give up all hope of a successful issue to the Diet, although he did not deceive himself as to the difficulties that would have to be surmounted.[13] The Bishop of Aquila was, as might be expected, quite confident of success, if only the Papacy would give its full support. The Emperor seemed to have won the goodwill of the princes, and even the Protestants appeared determined to settle the religious crisis.[14]

The judgement of Morone, however, was the one which carried weight in Rome. The result was that the legation was now primarily orientated towards the Emperor. It was the Emperor, not the Protestants, from whom Rome had most to fear, and therefore Contarini's main function would be to put a brake on the overconciliatory tendencies of the imperial party. Contarini, believing in the possibility of a genuine reconciliation with the Protestants, had seen his legation as being primarily directed towards them.

---

[10] The Emperor's primary aim, he felt, was a peaceful settlement of the problem, and ' . . . se non potrà quello vorà, vorà quello potrà et darà il carico ad altri che non habino accettati li ricordi soi et satisfatto alle richieste soe'. Campeggio/Farnese, 28 Nov. 1540, *NB* I. vi. 54.

[11] Campeggio/Farnese, 23 Jan. 1541, ibid., pp. 133–4.

[12] Cf. the dispatches of 20 Jan. 1541, 23 Feb. 1541, ibid., pp. 128–9, 146; and 18 Feb. 1541, Lämmer, pp. 351–2.

[13] 'Non vi è gia persona che non cognoschi la difficultà della causa quasi desperata, pure in questa desperatione, si spera come dico.' Ibid., p. 354.

[14] *D/R*, p. 138; *NB* I. vi. 131; *HJ* iv. 668–70; Lämmer, p. 363.

Because, on the other hand, the Curia was sure that there was no hope of any reasonable accommodation with the Protestants, it laid the main stress on the need to persuade the Emperor against accepting, in desperation at the breakdown of the colloquy, an injudicious peace.

The instruction for Contarini was drafted by Ghinucci, the Cardinal Santa Croce and Aleander, and revised by Farnese and the Pope himself.[15] Aleander's suggestion to Farnese that it would be advisable for the latter to instruct Contarini to study the articles with great care, and to govern his actions accordingly—and should there be anything in it of which he did not approve to write for fresh instructions[16]—is a veiled indication of the differing conceptions of the purpose of the mission held by Contarini and by Aleander and his colleagues. It is clear that it was expected that the legate would find his instruction distasteful. It reached him in Trent, when he was on the point of leaving. His acknowledgement is brief, and confirms his resolution to defend the interests of the Holy See.[17]

In the latter part of the instruction reference is made to Contarini's request for permission to make personal contacts with the Protestants. One would give much to know exactly what was said in the conversations that he had with Farnese and the Pope, and probably also with the three Cardinals who drafted his instructions, prior to his departure from Rome. That his optimistic and irenical outlook did not find uncritical acceptance is confirmed by the grudging manner in which his request is granted. He is to remember how easily such goodwill visits to the Protestants could be falsely interpreted—as a sign of weakness and indecision on his part, or on the other hand, as an attempt to suborn the Protestants. Hence, while showing friendliness to the Protestant scholars in so far as this can be done without harm, he should be careful to show the prudence and dignity worthy of a legate of the Pope and of the Apostolic See.[18] It is the voice of caution that speaks here and

[15] Aleander/Farnese, 15 Feb. 1541, *NB* I. vii. 3; Contarini had worked closely together with both Ghinucci and Aleander in the work of reform in Rome, and in the preparation for a Council. D/B, pp. 345, 376 ff.

[16] Aleander/Farnese, 15 Feb. 1541, *NB* I. vii. Nr. 1, pp. 4–5.

[17] Contarini/Farnese, 24 Feb. 1541, D/R, p. 148.

[18] 'Instruction Rmo Dno Card. Contareno in Germaniam Legato die XXVIII mensis Januarii MDXLI.' Text in Morandi, I. ii. 112–22; and Quirini, iii. 286–99.

the points it makes are not without their force. But the audacious undertaking that Contarini had in mind—the presentation of a totally new image of Catholicism—could never hope to succeed if such pedestrian considerations were to dominate. The Curia's fear was that in attempting to win all, Contarini would only harm the Catholic cause still further. The result was that no real dialogue between him and the Protestants—lay or clerical—took place at Regensburg.

The conflict of interests is clear. To Contarini the first priority at Regensburg was the achievement of reunion on the religious level, while for the Papacy the first priority was the defence of papal authority. True, the instruction explicitly states that the purpose of his mission was the pursuit of a true and holy concord in the name of the Pope. Immediately following this profession, however, are the reasons why it had been decided not to endow Contarini with a 'full mandate to come to terms with the Protestants'. These reasons give us pause for thought.

Firstly, it is argued, since it is not known what the Protestants' intentions are as regards the basic tenets of the faith, including the Primacy, the Sacraments, and other articles, it seemed wiser not to grant this power. This argument might carry some conviction if it were not immediately followed by another to the effect that since from an examination of the Protestants' articles one *can* almost divine what they will ask, it would be scandalous to make any decision without the consent of the other nations of Christendom. In both cases the conclusion is the same: not even the Pope himself could act on his own responsibility in such questions, far less a mere legate! But the grounds for the conclusion are diametrically opposed. In one case it is because one knows, in another because one does not know what the Protestants are likely to ask. The nature of the arguments, we conclude, is immaterial. Any argument will serve its turn if it supports the conclusion that nothing can be decided at Regensburg, everything must be referred to Rome.

The danger of a concord being undertaken without due regard to papal interests is very much in the forefront throughout, though it is piously noted that the Pope can hardly believe this is possible. There can be no question of tolerating an agreement of this sort, for it would be a direct attack on 'our honour and the authority of this Holy See, on which the well-being of the universal Church is entirely dependent'. Contarini is to do his utmost to dissuade the

Emperor from such a course, and in particular to stress that a General Council is the sole fitting antidote to schism and heresy.

Should the Emperor persevere, despite all his efforts, he must declare that he cannot be a witness to such an agreement, and in the name of the Pope forbid it, and if even this is to no avail he is to declare it null and void and withdraw. A similar course of action is to be pursued if the Protestants are granted toleration pending a General Council, or if convocation of the latter in Germany is demanded. Any suggestion of a National Council is also to be rejected.

That the Papacy saw the primary function of Contarini to be the defence of her own interests and authority is not so very surprising. He was, after all, her ambassador. The defence of papal interests, moreover, was not a mere struggle of one power complex against another. For the Papacy, and to a large extent for Contarini himself,[19] the interests of the Papacy were those of Christendom. A large part of the instruction was devoted to the need to promote peace between Charles V and France. Was not this for the good of Christendom—a united front against the Turkish threat? He was to seek the reconciliation of the Protestants and what was more essential for Germany—the greatest bastion of Christendom—than this? True, this must be effected by 'appropriate means', either through a General Council convened by the Pope or after mature consideration by the Pope himself, but was this in fact a restriction? For any other attempted mediation, on a national level, or without the sanction of the head of the universal Church, would only provoke schism, not heal it. For the same reason it had been impossible to promise ratification of decisions arrived at during the Diet. A blank cheque to this effect would have been out of the question.

Peace on the political level could not be bought by concessions on the spiritual. Peace, to be genuine, presupposed the restitution of the true faith and of the rule of justice, that is, the restoration of the lands and properties seized in defiance of all law by the Lutherans from the Church, their rightful owner. There could, therefore, be but one way to peace and the unity of the Church—a

---

[19] Contarini certainly never had the slightest intention of going behind the back of the Pope. Cf. Beccadelli's comment that 'nè mai si fermò conclusione, o sillaba in quel Colloquio, che non s'avesse la risposta da Roma del consenso del Papa'. Morandi, I. ii. 34–5.

Diet in Germany to settle the temporal matters, and a properly convoked Council for the spiritual.

It need not be doubted that the Pope was concerned with the political stability of Europe. Nor is there any question but that he felt himself committed, as the successor of Peter and vicegerent of Christ, to the defence of the true faith, handed down from the beginning to the present generation, in whose name he now had to hand it over unimpaired to the generations to come. He recognized also the need for reform, especially of and in the Curia itself. And yet the immediacy and the primacy of his concern lay with the maintenance of the authority of the Holy See. Hence when Farnese exclaimed bitterly in a dispatch to Poggio that the Pope was as concerned as anyone for the end of the schism in Germany, and that there was no need for the Emperor to goad him on to this,[20] he was fully justified. And yet, of course, it all revolved round the question of how reunion was conceived. Farnese could declare that it was because of his concern for Germany that the Pope was opposed to the colloquies,[21] and this might well be true. But for the Pope the good of Germany was equated with the maintenance of the authority of the Papacy and the continuance of the traditional faith. Hence a political realism which was prepared to make compromises concerning the latter for the sake of temporary political advantages could be regarded not only as a threat to Rome, but also as contrary to the real interests of Germany itself.

What, then, did the Pope expect of Contarini? An improvement in the relations between Papacy and Empire could not be expected. At best Contarini's personal popularity might serve to prevent a further deterioration of relations, while his scholarship and conciliatory disposition would present the Roman case in the best possible light both to the Emperor and the Estates.[22] In the case of a crisis he could be relied upon to act not only as a loyal son of the Church, but also as a skilled and knowledgeable representative of papal interests. The authority of his rank and person would help to prevent anything 'detrimental to religion' from taking place.[23]

[20] Farnese/Poggio, 29 Feb. 1541, HJ iv. 667.
[21] Farnese/Poggio, 2 Nov. 1540, NB I. vi. 161.
[22] As we have seen it was a widespread view among the adherents of the imperial party that the Pope was not interested in concord. Cf. Campeggio's warning on this point. Campeggio/Farnese, 18 Jan. 1541, Morandi, I. ii. 109.
[23] Farnese/Dandino, 6 Feb. 1541, NB I. vi. 137, Anm. 2.

Any dealings he might have with the Protestants would be of peripheral interest—possibly one or two individuals would be won over. His main task would be to stiffen the back of the Catholic party, with the help of Eck, Morone, and Conrad Braun, the rigorist lay representative of the Archbishop of Mainz at Worms, who had won Morone's praise there as the saviour of the Catholics,[24] and to watch out vigilantly for any course of action that would be prejudicial to the honour of the Apostolic See or the Catholic faith.

Thus the stage was set for high tragedy before Contarini had as much as set foot in Regensburg. His commission put him on a collision course not only with the German Protestants, but with the Emperor and the German Catholics as well. Its terms made no concessions to the new spirit of German pride and self-respect. As the key document for an ecumenical initiative it makes ominously little sense.

[24] Aleander/Farnese, 15 Feb. 1541, *NB* I. vii. 4–5.

6

A Futile Waste of Time

O N Epiphany, 6 January 1541, the day originally set for the opening of the Diet, the 1,500 citizens who were to comprise the civic guard for the great occasion were mustered in the freezing cold. Not for another three months was the Diet to begin, but when it did the good burghers were to find work enough to hand. Every night a hundred armed men patrolled the city, and even this was to prove barely sufficient. For on the tail of the theologians and courtiers and princes there swarmed into Regensburg a more dubious, if colourful company: the camp-followers and profiteers, the players, pedlars, and stall-holders, the whores, beggars, and honest-to-goodness thieves. Despite the exertions of the watch, murder and manslaughter was a daily occurrence. Not a few found a watery end in the Danube; others drank themselves to death with brandy. The city was invaded by merchants hawking all manner of costly goods. Every day a great market was held with every variety of food on display, and twenty field kitchens were set up on Unserer Frauen Platz to feed the hungry masses.[1]

Yet despite the alarms and excursions Regensburg took it all with a certain nonchalance. The city was no stranger to imperial Diets. No less than ten were held there in the sixteenth century alone. It was a proud city, with a long and not inglorious history.

Lying on the northernmost point reached by the Danube, at its junction with the tributaries Laaber, Naab, and Regen, the strategic and commercial importance of the settlement had been recognized by the Romans. The Carolingians had built themselves palaces within its walls. Boniface gave it its first bishop. The Bavarian dukes set up their court there.

---

[1] Hermann Nestler, 'Vermittlungspolitik und Kirchenspaltung auf dem Regensburger Reichstag von 1541', *ZBLG* vi. 389–414. Nestler's article is based largely on the account of the contemporary chronicler Widmann.

It was in the high Middle Ages, however, that Regensburg reached its peak. For a time it was, perhaps, the most populous city in Germany. Its traders fanned out through the length and breadth of Europe, to Champagne in the west and Russia in the east. They were the first Germans to set up centres in Venice for the trade with Byzantium. On the firm basis of commercial prosperity the importance of the city grew. The crusades of 1147 and 1187 set out from Regensburg. Pious foundations flourished, above all the wealthy abbey of St. Emmeram. The burghers wrested for themselves independence from bishop, duke, and emperor to become in 1251 a free, imperial city. Its symbol became the stone bridge over the Danube, 310 metres long and boasting sixteen arches, one of the wonders of the Middle Ages.

By the time of the Reformation the withdrawal of Bavarian patronage and the decline of its commercial importance had long since stripped it of its earlier prominence. Yet its history as a political and ecclesiastical centre provided it with an abundance of hostelries and other facilities which made it an ideal 'conference centre'.

Regensburg, indeed, with its chaos of conflicting jurisdictions, with Anabaptism making inroads upon its handworkers and Lutheranism upon its burghers, was in 1541 a microcosm of the problems all Germany had to face. Its council was pro-Lutheran and had been in correspondence with Wittenberg as far back as 1519. Thus the stage for the proposed reconciliation between Catholic and Protestant was itself a divided city, teetering on the brink of becoming Protestant. Both confessions were to use the occasion of the Diet in an attempt to strengthen their position in Regensburg itself.[2]

On 11 March Contarini arrived in Regensburg. His journey from Rome had taken him through Florence, Bologna, Mantua, Verona, and Trent. Everywhere he had been afforded the friendliest of receptions. In Trent he had at last received his instruction from Rome. Then he had made his way through Germany by way of Brixen, Innsbruck, Rosenheim, and Landshut, learning on the way that the Emperor had already arrived at Regensburg but as yet none of the princes.[3]

---

[2] On the history of Regensburg cf. Felix Mader, *Stadt Regensburg* (Die Kunstdenkmäler von Bayern: Regierungsbezirk Oberpfalz XXII) i. 1–15.

[3] For description of the journey cf. D/R, pp. 145 ff. On the non-arrival of the

We have spoken above of the high hopes which were coupled with the arrival of Contarini and his mission to the Diet. In the light of this the enthusiastic welcome he was accorded in Regensburg is understandable. Crowds lined the streets and, according to his fellow-countryman Francesco Contarini, the Venetian ambassador to the Emperor, cries of 'Benedictus qui venit in nomine Domini' were heard as he made his ceremonial entry to the city on 12 March.[4] Only the palm branches were missing, it seemed, to complete the Messianic atmosphere. Contarini himself remarked on the unexpected cordiality of his reception.[5]

The audience with the Emperor on the following day was marked by an equally friendly tone.[6] Contarini expressed the papal pleasure at the Emperor's convocation of the Diet to settle the religious discord and restore Germany to the 'unity of the Church of Christ'.[7] In response to this imperial decision and the request of the Emperor, the Pope, deeply moved by the pastoral responsibility for the souls committed to him and by the need to unite Christendom against the Turk, had dispatched Contarini to Regensburg as his legate to the Diet.

Despite his inadequacy for such an undertaking, Contarini continued, he had been chosen because His Holiness knew how long he had yearned for an end to the disunity of the Church. A further ground had been the good personal relationships that existed between him and the Emperor. Despite the great difficulties of the task he placed his trust in the wisdom of the Emperor and the goodness of God, and promised his full support to the

---

princes cf. Contarini/Farnese, 1 Mar. 1541, D/R, p. 150; Morone/Contarini, 7 Mar. 1541, ibid., p. 152.

[4] Francesco Contarini/Venice, 13 Mar. 1541, D/R, p. 154, '. . . par che ogn'uno habbi un contento estremo della venuta sua'.

[5] 'A me parve veder assai populo et più reverenza di quella che mi credea ritrovare, benchè la Città sia Catholicà.' ZKG iii. 151. Sim. Contarini/Pole, 14 Mar. 1541, Quirini, iii. 16.

[6] Contarini took care to stress the extent of this goodwill to his superiors in Rome. A special dispatch was devoted to the correction of a previous statement that he had been met at the city gates by the Bishop of Brixen due to the indisposition of the resident bishop. It had been to do him the greater honour that Ferdinand's representative in the Tyrol, the Bishop of Brixen, had been assigned the duty of welcoming him! ZKG iii. 151 n. 1. He remarks similarly that prior to his audience with the Emperor the latter came to meet him as far as the steps 'et li humanissamente mi raccolse'. Ibid., p. 152.

[7] '. . . alla unità della chiesa di Christo.' Not, as Dittrich translates, 'to the one church of Christ' ('zu der einen Kirche Christi'), D/B, p. 575.

former's endeavours, provided, of course, nothing was done contrary to the essential points of the faith, among which he mentioned in particular the status of the Apostolic See.

The Emperor replied courteously, expressing the hope that the Pope would be zealous in promoting the cause of peace as he (the Emperor) had been in promoting that of the Church, and exhorted the papal representatives to concerted action, having no doubt in mind the experience of Worms, where Campeggio and Morone had been frequently at odds.

Morone, the nuncio newly appointed to replace Poggio, unexpectedly recalled by Rome, now presented his credentials. His appointment could hardly have been expected, after Worms, to be welcomed by the Emperor. Its purpose, after all, was almost certainly to provide a more reliable foil to the conciliatory legate than the more irenic Poggio. The departure of the latter was regretted by the Emperor and, indeed, by the whole court,[8] and Contarini himself would have gladly retained him in Regensburg had he not been hamstrung by his instruction which prevented him from taking any independent decision of this kind.[9] Morone, for his part, was reluctant in the extreme to take up the new post, although Contarini had the highest opinion of him.[10] For the moment, however, his fears that his relationship to the Emperor would be an extremely difficult one were dispelled by the gracious welcoming words of the latter, and the audience ended on this cordial note.[11]

The city, meanwhile, was full of rumours. Would the Electors and princes actually arrive, and if so, when?[12] Was it true that

[8] 'La partita del Nuntio Poggio, come è stata inopinata, così dispiace a tutta la corte et non si potrebbe dir, quanto la sentono . . .' *ZKG* iii. 612. He would have been the right person to have established 'un armonia et concerto buono tra la Ces. Maestà et soi Ministri et il Rmo Legato et me', wrote Morone on 23 March. *D/R*, p. 159. On the same day Poggio left Regensburg, 'con tanto bon nome da questa Corte, che non e homo che non li dogli la partita sua fino al core'. Francesco Contarini/Venice, ibid., p. 160.

[9] 'Ambedui (i.e. Morone and Poggio) certamente sono qui in questa Dieta necessarissimi et, se non fusse, che debbo et voglio deferir il tutto alla sapientia di sua Bne., . . . io havrei usato presuntione di retener Mons. Poggio et darne adviso a sua Stà. et aspettar la risposta . . ' *ZKG* iii. 155.

[10] 'Persona tanto prudente, ben qualificata et buon servitore di N.S. . . .' Ibid., p. 156. Throughout the Diet Morone and Contarini worked together with the utmost harmony.

[11] 'Sua Mtà . . . accettò allegramente et con optime parole il R. Vesco di Modena . . .' Ibid., p. 155.

[12] Speculation centred above all on the possibility of the attendance of the

Granvelle had won over some of the leading Protestants? Was Rome really in earnest, and if so why had she sent an ambassador without any authority to conclude any agreement? Would the offensive of the Turks now milling round Buda and Pest in Hungary reach critical proportions?[13] Above all, what were the prospects for a successful outcome to the reunion negotiations?

The new legation had begun under reasonably favourable auspices. The fair words on both sides could, however, be no more than a very precarious bridge of confidence between Empire and Papacy. Behind them lay the sceptical undertones of Contarini's instruction with which only Morone had been acquainted, but as to whose tendency the Imperial Court would have had few illusions. Only a few days previously Farnese had forwarded to Contarini a memorandum 'di bonissimo loco' which he commended to the legate's attention. This insinuated that the Emperor had come to believe that he must either forfeit the allegiance of Germany or abandon the Apostolic See, and that he had accordingly come to the Diet with the fixed intention to settle affairs in Germany whatever the cost might be to religion.[14] Under such circumstances, warned Farnese, the utmost caution was called for. Above all, Contarini should avoid making any rash promises to the Lutherans as had been the case at Worms.[15] For the danger existed that the presence of the legate could be interpreted later as a legitimation for the concessions that the Emperor would make under the plea of necessity.[16] Morone, the professional sceptic, was satisfied, however, on at least one count. Whatever happened, Contarini, with his upright, free, and open way of thinking, would never be partner to any questionable settlement, and if the schemings of the ministers threatened to move in this direction the favour which he had already won on all sides would stand him in good stead, and his influence would be instrumental in convincing

---

Elector of Saxony, without whose presence Morone considered no reunion negotiations could be entered upon—'senza il quale non si potrebbe far trattato alcuno di concordia'. Ibid., p. 612.

[13] Morone/Farnese, 10 Mar. 1541, ibid., pp. 610–11.

[14] '. . . con intention di serrar' l'occhio ad ogni cosa per quietare et accordare la Germania', pursuing solely his own interests 'senza mirare ad altro, et che lui proprio si vede condotto a termine, che gli bisogna o perdere la Germania, o la sede apostolica'. NB I. vii. 15 n. 2.

[15] Perhaps a reference to Campeggio's speech of 8 December?

[16] Farnese/Contarini, 11 Mar. 1541, D/R, p. 153.

the Emperor and many of the other Catholics to oppose such a fatal course.[17]

Contarini had arrived in Regensburg almost a month before the Diet was to get under way. He showed no trace of annoyance at this long wait and used the time to inform himself about the German situation. At first the sole significant personalities present in Regensburg, apart from some of the bishops, were the Emperor himself, the Dukes of Bavaria, and the Duke of Brunswick, and it was with the controversy that had sprung up between the Emperor and the Dukes—that is, a dissension within the Catholic ranks—that Contarini's first diplomatic engagement was concerned.

The Emperor was determined that this time a peaceful settlement must be arrived at. For the sake of Germany, for the sake of the defence of Christendom against the Turks, for the sake of the unity of religion and the consolidation of the Habsburg Empire, and, by no means least, of solidarity against France.

The Bavarians, with their ally Brunswick, were equally determined to do their all to prevent such a settlement. Primarily from political motives. A scheme so favourable to the interests of the Habsburgs, the traditional rivals of the Wittelsbachs, must necessarily be viewed with scepticism if not dismay. Any consolidation of the Habsburg power must *per se* be detrimental to Bavarian interests. This political opposition found its theological rationalization in the dour reactionism of which Johann Eck was the unparalleled master, although it would be a mistake to attribute the Bavarian anti-Protestantism to purely political motives.

This clash of interests found its immediate expression in a battle for the favour of the papal legate. Granvelle, Morone thought, was quite sincere in his belief that a concord could be gained without prejudice to the interests of the Holy See, and he had done his best to assure the Chancellor that he, too, like his predecessor Poggio, desired nothing more than the peace of Germany, provided, as always, the interests of the faith and the Papacy were not put in jeopardy. Granvelle certainly spared no efforts to convince the papal representatives that there was ground for optimism about the success of the colloquy and to assure them 'how zealously his imperial Majesty and himself were concerned

[17] Morone/Farnese, 12 Mar. 1541, *ZKG* iii. 612.

for the well-being of Christianity and the protection of the Apostolic See'.[18]

He continued also to urge that Rome dispatch the money needed to win over the Protestants. There is for us perhaps no more baffling and intriguing feature at this stage of the events at Regensburg than the apparently genuine conviction of Granvelle that many of the Protestant theologians were hesitating in their allegiance, and might well be brought over to the Catholic cause by the distribution of a judicious quantity of hard cash. Bucer had already been won over by him at Worms, he assured Morone, and there was hope that Melanchthon would also be gained. Of the south German cities Strasbourg, Nuremberg, Augsburg, and Ulm would be recovered for the Apostolic See. The whole Protestant front, he implied, was crumbling.[19]

This indeed was the vivid, if somewhat apocalyptic and eccentric picture of the state of events which he gave to Contarini on his first visit to the legate after the formal courtesy call. Everything was tending towards ruin. Protestantism, having spread throughout Germany, was now infiltrating into Italy, France, and other countries, and the Catholics instead of reacting effectively in the face of this crisis were almost all purely self-interested.

But if, on the one side, the danger was great, there were also real signs of hope if the situation were firmly tackled. The Lutherans were divided among themselves, and their followers were becoming increasingly discontented. They saw the consequences of the unbridled way of life which came in the wake of the new teaching. In the cities, moreover, the despotic methods by which Protestantism was enforced had aroused the resentment of the burghers. By now, too, the doctors and theologians were in constant fear, afraid both of the consequences of continuing in their misguided ways and of the revenge of their misled laity should they confess their errors. For them the coming of Contarini would be a welcome escape since a submission to him would not involve the loss of face which a confession of defeat to the German Catholic theologians would have meant.

The whole amounted to a total misreading of the religious situation. How far Granvelle was aware of this, and consciously

[18] Morone/Farnese, 17 Mar. 1541, ibid., p. 614.
[19] Contarini/Farnese, 18 Mar. 1541, ibid., p. 159; Morone/Farnese, 21 Mar. 1541, *HJ* iv. 439.

raised the hopes of the papal representatives in order to make them more amenable to the proposed settlement, is not clear. The possibility, at any rate, that he was partially convinced by his own rhetoric cannot be left out of account. It is at least clear that for him the primary need was the restoration of order. This was the *summum bonum* to which all his energies were directed. And for the sake of this a certain flexibility on both sides would have to be exercised on issues such as that of the Church properties and the theological questions which were not of central importance.

Were the differences, after all, continued Granvelle, really so great? The Protestants recognized the real presence of Christ in the sacraments. Could not the question of transubstantiation be left to the coming General Council to decide? As to the papal primacy there would be no difficulty. The Protestants had said they would return to the episcopal obedience and the bishops to the pontifical, and even the question of the Church properties, with the exceptional case of Württemberg excluded, could be equably adjusted, although it would, of course, have to be a stage-by-stage procedure. The majority of the incomes had been applied in any case to 'pious' purposes. So there seemed no ground for fear about the success of the concord. Contarini could rest assured that he would be consulted at every stage of the proceedings and that nothing would be done without his approval. He himself would be ready to report to the legate in person 'come a presidente'.[20] If in a rational and friendly way goodwill could be built up there would be no undue difficulties either with the *modus procedendi*.

There was, in any case, as Granvelle a few days later emphasized, no alternative. The Protestants were every bit as much Germans as the Catholics and equally bellicose. The Emperor lacked the resources in men and material to crush them militarily, and even if he had them it would be a highly hazardous undertaking with the Turks and the French lurking as possible allies to the Protestants on the sidelines. This was, finally, no way to win the souls of the Protestants. There was, indeed, only one way left, a peaceful solution. A failure at Regensburg would be the ruin of the German nation.[21]

It was a very different tune which was played by the Bavarian Dukes and by their allies the Duke of Brunswick and the Arch-

[20] *ZKG* iii. 159–61, 626.
[21] Morone/Farnese, 3 Apr. 1541, ibid., p. 621.

bishop of Mainz. The latter had arrived on 31 March. The stance
they adopted was that of loyal Catholics, appalled by the steady
spread of Lutheran doctrines and practices throughout the land.
For this, they were convinced, the past leniency of the Emperor
was responsible, and it was time that a lesson was drawn from this
sorry history. The only remedy was to take a firm stand. It was a
futile waste of time[22] to continue the colloquy begun at Worms
and Hagenau, and a solution by means of a General Council was
only a theoretical possibility. The time had come for action and not
for words. The Emperor should in all form declare his will to
enforce the Augsburg Recess, and the Catholic ranks would then
close behind him. For their part they were ready to sacrifice their
goods, their sons, even their own lives for the true faith and the
Apostolic See.[23]

The Emperor, on the other hand, was even proposing to make a
Lutheran prince, Count Frederick of the Palatinate, one of the
Presidents of the Colloquy. If the Emperor persisted in this
intention they would up horse and leave the Diet forthwith.[24] If
at all possible, it was clear, they were determined to prevent the
colloquy from even getting off the ground. The so-called '*modus
procedendi*' which they proposed for the colloquy made this
abundantly clear. It simply called for the enforcement of the
Recess of Augsburg. Such a basis for negotiations would, of
course, never be accepted by the Protestants and was not meant to
be.

The Duke of Brunswick and the Archbishop of Mainz spoke in
much the same terms,[25] the former lacing his professions of
loyalty to the Apostolic See with vituperations against his old
enemy Hesse who had arrived in the city on 27 March,[26] while the
archbishop launched into a quite ungoverned attack on the
Emperor. Mainz had no hope at all of a successful outcome of
the colloquy. 'Verily, verily, it will be a time, not of peace, but

[22] 'tempo gittato via . . .!' Contarini/Farnese, 30 Mar. 1541, *ZKG* iii. 165.
[23] Lämmer, p. 364.
[24] '. . . se costui sia posto in quel luoco, essi montaranno a cavallo et si
partiranno.' *ZKG* iii. 158. Frederick certainly had Protestant sympathies. Cf. his
reaction to the legate's request that the negotiations be referred to him as papal
representative as well as to the Diet. Ibid., p. 625.
[25] Contarini/Farnese, 26 Mar. 1541, D/*R*, p. 318.
[26] Granvelle informed Morone, 'che il Duca di Brunsvich si governa male
contro il Lantgravio et non cessa etiam in questo loco di irritarlo con detti et
scritti!' *ZKG* iii. 620.

of greater discord.'[27] Like the Bavarians he delivered himself of the opinion that Granvelle was receiving Lutheran bribes, but he went on to predict that if the Emperor went through with the colloquy he would lose his reputation, be hoodwinked by Hesse—who really had not the least intention of converting—and, should no settlement be made, probably lose the imperial Crown altogether.[28]

A further voice in the chorus of despond was the French one. The two French ambassadors at Regensburg, one assigned to the Catholics, the other to the Protestants, counselled their respective partners to stand fast by their positions and oppose the work of concord. Dandino, the papal nuncio to the French Court, informed Contarini at the end of March that Francis already had the assurance of several German princes that they would oppose the imperial plans, for they feared that when a settlement had been achieved the Emperor would then turn his power against them. The French Court regarded the proceedings at Regensburg, he continued, with anything but enthusiasm.[29] The real ground for the dismay was transparent enough. A strengthening of the imperial position would be automatically detrimental to France. A united Germany would be a formidable opponent indeed. Francis recognized the danger, and acted accordingly. He warned Contarini to beware the dangers of an unworthy concord, to which the legate could only reply that he would rather surrender his life than assent to anything contrary to the weal of the Church.[30]

Such professions, of course, altered nothing. Throughout the Diet Francis sought to spread scepticism about its outcome, not only among the Protestants and Catholics at Regensburg but in Rome itself. All the more understandable the bitterness of the Emperor at the large number of French cardinals created by Paul. There were as many of them at the French Court, he declared, as ordinary clergy at the imperial.[31]

Nothing could be more fatal to Charles's plans than an ascen-

---

[27] 'Erit, erit dies non pacis, sed majoris discordiae.' Ibid., p. 167. Cf. Cruciger's comment on Mainz, *CR* iv. 147.

[28] Morone/Farnese, 6 Apr. 1541, *ZKG* iii. 625–6.

[29] Morandi, I. ii. 128.

[30] '. . . che io non sono mai per consentir a cosa, la quale non mi pare honesta et al servitio di Dio et di sua santa chiesa. Et prima che far altramente vi lassarei la vita.' Contarini/Dandino, 1 Apr. 1541, *D/R*, p. 318.

[31] *ZKG* iii. 163.

dancy of French influence in the Curia. Nothing could be calculated to further France's interests better than a discrediting of the
conciliation work being undertaken at Regensburg, and if necessary of the legate whose task it was to represent the papal interests
there.

Again the conflict of interests is clear enough. Contarini's
daunting task was to find a way through the maze of intrigues and
pressures that surrounded him without losing the confidence of
either of the wings of the Catholic party. On the one hand he dare
not forfeit the sympathy of the Emperor. To retain this was the
whole point of his mission. On the other hand, he could not
simply rebuff the Bavarians and their allies, the stoutest supporters
of the Curia in Germany.

On the whole he managed to hold himself apart from the controversy, while seeking by his mediatory activity to gain the good
will of both sides. On behalf of the Bavarians, for example, he
raised with Granvelle the question of the status of Count Frederick
in the colloquy, and was able to assure them as a result that the
latter's function would be purely that of reporter to the Emperor
and Diet on the work of the collocutors, and that it would have no
theological or political significance. On the other hand, he and
Morone promised Granvelle to do their best to influence the
Bavarians to a more moderate course.[32]

Contarini, while assuring Rome and his other correspondents
that he would do all he could to further the concord, also took a
very sober view of the situation. There was no one, or hardly anyone at Regensburg, he wrote to Farnese, who served God with a
pure heart.[33] He carefully avoided a head-on confrontation with
either party however. When the Bavarians, on ostensibly dogmatic

---

[32] Ibid., pp. 161, 620.

[33] Contarini/Farnese, 30 Mar. 1541, ibid., p. 166. His estimation of the
motives of the Bavarians was at all events harsh enough: 'Questi Duchi die [sic]
Bavera, vedendo, che il lantgravio sia fatto grande et così il Duca di Saxonia et
expilano molte città, essendo capi di Lutherani, cosi vorriano essi farsi grandi
con l'arme, essendo capi Catholici, et, non havendo un quatrino, pensano di far
la guerra con li denari di N.Sre et delli Clerici di Germania . . . Dio per sua bontà
li ponga la mano, che certo qui in Germania io vedo poco di bono ne mi maraveg-
lio, che li populi siano in questa confusione, essendo nelli capi seculari et
ecclesiastici et nelli Religiosi quelle conditioni, ch'io vedo, nec alia.' Ibid.;
Contarini/Pole, 22 Mar. 1541: 'Vos, ut reor, iam fruimini veris amoenitate
et nos adhuc versamur in algoribus; vos invicem servatis animi pietatem,
apud nos friget pietas et religio.' D/R, p. 159.

grounds, argued against the colloquy, he countered by pointing to the purely pragmatic arguments which made an outright rejection of the colloquy by Catholics seem an unwise move. If, he argued, the Bavarians were right about the motives of the Protestants—which he was well ready to believe—then the colloquy was bound to fail anyway. Would it not in this case be better to lay the blame squarely on their shoulders? Let it be the obstinacy of the Protestants that evoked the wrath of the Emperor and the general opprobrium!

At all costs, as he tried to convince the Duke of Brunswick, the impression must be avoided that on the Catholic side anything had been left undone which might promote concord. But this concern to preserve the good image of the Church must be balanced by a determination to avoid even the slightest deviation from the truth.[34]

On the particular question of the *modus procedendi* he spared no praise for the concern which the Bavarians had shown for the faith or for their loyalty to the Holy See, but quietly declined to take the initiative himself in requesting the Emperor to make the enforcement of the Augsburg Recess the precondition for the coming negotiations. He even departed from his usual practice and brought forward the moral consideration that a Christian should exercise clemency towards the Lutherans and not embitter them.[35]

The main thrust of his concern, however, was to demonstrate to the Dukes and their councillors that he understood, appreciated, and even, to a large extent, shared their position. He never tired of protesting, as to the Archbishop of Mainz, that for him there could be no question of compromise on the essential matters of the faith, and that any proposed change in the liturgical and disciplinary sphere would require the most careful scrutiny. Otherwise it would simply spark off worse schism and disorder than before. He had, he pointed out, been given no commission from the Pope to grant any concessions to the Protestants. Support for the colloquy in no way precluded concern for orthodoxy.

Contarini had no more illusions as to the political motivation for the 'orthodoxy' of the Bavarians than Morone, and his own sympathies lay far more with the Emperor than with such 'hot-

---

34 D/R, p. 318.
35 Morandi, I. ii. 200.

heads'.[36] He had to cover himself, however, against the possibility that the Emperor would embark on a dubious course, in which case the backing of the rigorists would stand him in good stead.

In the case of Granvelle, by contrast, Contarini saw no particular need to extol the merits of a pragmatic approach. He sought, rather, to impress upon the politician the weighty nature of the theological questions at issue. Speaking of the real differences between the Catholics and the Protestants he made use of the distinction—so suspect to Morone at Worms—between the essential and the non-essential articles of the faith. Even the latter embodied the tradition of the universal Church and this led us to believe, as Augustine said, that they rested on the institution of the Apostles. But as regards an article such as that of transubstantiation, an 'articolo essentialissimo et certissimo', there could be no question of compromise. Even a Council—to which Granvelle had suggested the article be referred—could not alter the situation here. Admittedly the Protestants had begun by recognizing at least the real presence of Christ in the sacrament, but from the *Apology* it appeared that their views had since changed. Here Contarini stood quite firm. On the more controversial question of whether the primacy of the Papacy should be recognized as *de iure divino* he was prepared, however, to keep a discreet silence.[37]

The Bavarian attempts to torpedo the colloquy from the outset failed, not least due to the diplomatic skill of Granvelle. The legate, however, had managed to retain the confidence of both of the contending parties. This neutralized to a considerable degree the danger to the Catholic and papal cause which the radical clash of interests between the conciliatory and the rigorist wings would otherwise have portended. That, however, the task of steering between the two groups would require the utmost diplomatic finesse was only too abundantly clear.

It was not made any easier by a further factor which complicated and clouded the relations between Rome and the Emperor—the so-called Colonna affair. This issue arose in the very first audience which the Emperor granted the legate. It is a sobering reminder of

---

[36] 'Ma certamente il negociar con questi cervelli è dificillimo et ben ho bisogno dell'adjuto di Dio, nel quale spero, che non mi mancarà', with reference to the Bavarians. Contarini/Farnese, 16 Mar. 1541, *ZKG* iii. 158.

[37] *ZKG* iii. 159–61. His handling of Granvelle in this discussion gained the full approbation of the Pope. Farnese/Contarini, 16 Apr. 1541, D/*R*, Nr. 676, p. 169.

the scale of values of the time that in the early period of the Diet Farnese's despatches to Contarini, as Dittrich points out, contained more about this minor political disturbance than about the entire religious negotiations.[38]

Ascanio Colonna, one of the Emperor's most loyal supporters in Italy, had already rebelled in 1539 when throughout the papal states the salt tax was raised. In 1541 he proceeded to armed reprisals when the papal officials made to enforce the new tax and when he was summoned to Rome to answer for his conduct, he refused to appear. All attempts at conciliation by the imperial ambassador in Rome, the Marchesa d'Aquilar, were abortive and a papal army under Pier Luigi set out to enforce obedience on the rebellious vassal. The Pope was now demanding not only restitution and compensation for the damages inflicted by Colonna but also satisfaction for the outrage against his sovereignty. Colonna, he insisted, must hand over the fortresses Rocca di Papa, Nettuno, and Palliano. Paul, it would seem, saw in the revolt a welcome opportunity for territorial expansion.[39]

It was widely suspected in the French Court and at the Curia that Charles was behind the whole affair, and intended to use it to bring pressure upon the Pope to accept his projected settlement of the religious question in Germany.[40] Whatever the truth here may be, the exacerbation of the relations with the Emperor was acute, and Contarini was entrusted with the delicate task of securing from Charles a denunciation of Colonna's actions. The Emperor did indeed dissociate himself from this open flouting of the papal sovereignty, but begged that Paul, for his part, would temper his justice with clemency.[41] It was, in itself, but a minor incident. It illustrated, however, not only the incompatibility of the interests of Pope and Emperor in Italy, but also the lack of any real basis of confidence between the two pillars of Catholic Christendom.

A more severe testing of this confidence and of Contarini's diplomatic ability was now, however, in the offing. Hitherto any radical disagreement had been avoided by a careful skirting on both sides of the most controversial issues—above all of the exact relationship of the authority of the Papacy to the decisions to be

---

[38] D/B, p. 593.

[39] D/B, pp. 592 ff. For Morone's statement of the papal case, and the Emperor's reply, cf. Morone/Farnese, 28 Apr. 1541, *HJ* iv. 447 ff.

[40] Morandi, I. ii. 128 ff.   [41] *ZKG* iii. 152–5, 625.

arrived at in Regensburg. All had been shrouded in a haze of good-will and vague promises.

Now, however, precisely this issue came to the fore. On the evening of 4 April the Bishop of Arras, representing Granvelle, his father, who was in bed with catarrh, submitted to Contarini and Morone the draft for the imperial Proposition which would be read at the opening of the Diet before the assembled Estates—or at least such of them as had by then arrived.[42]

It was this draft which precipitated the first real brush of the legate with the Emperor. In the opening passages of the Proposition the legate was, admittedly, mentioned—in highly flattering terms to Contarini personally. Of the part, however, that the legate would play in the colloquy itself there was no mention whatsoever. This Contarini interpreted as an outrageous slight to the Holy See. It was simply stated that the results of the colloquy would be communicated to the Emperor and the Estates. The legate and indeed the Papacy itself, might as well not have existed. A further but subsidiary failing in Contarini's eyes was the lack of any adequate mention of the Augsburg Recess. To this latter he immediately drew the bishop's attention, calling the Recess 'un grandissimo fondamento nostro', and the bishop promised satisfaction on this count. His complaint was, in fact, referred by Granvelle to Count Frederick and the imperial Council and he was assured that in the German copy ample mention was made of the Recess.[43]

On the crucial point—the mention of the legate—Contarini emphasized that here a quite fundamental issue was at stake. It must be made clear that the decision on matters of religion pertained neither to laymen, nor to the Estates, but to His Holiness and his representatives.[44] He had, after all, come to the Diet at the express wish of the Emperor, and the omission seemed to him an indignity alike for the Pope and the Emperor, who being personally present, should have taken care to mention the papal legate. At Hagenau and in the summons to the Diet this had been done. The

[42] Ibid., pp. 620, 169.

[43] Contarini/Farnese, 5 Apr. 1541, ibid., pp. 169–70. German text of the Proposition in CR iv. 151–4. Only the briefest reference is made to the Augsburg Recess.

[44] '. . . il giudicio delle cose della Religione non apertiene a laici nè allo stato dell' Imperio, ma a N.Sre et alli soi representanti . . .' Contarini/Farnese, 5 Apr. 1541, ZKG iii. 170.

desire not to exasperate the Protestants was no adequate ground. A courteous and friendly approach to the latter should not degenerate into pusillanimity. This would be unworthy of the Emperor and would only encourage the Protestants to further insolence. Friendliness must be complemented by a due gravity and dignity.

When the bishop returned with a negative reply from the Council to the effect that to avoid provoking the Protestants—who held that the Pope could not act as an impartial arbiter since he had already condemned them—no further mention of the legate would be possible, Contarini heatedly retorted that this amounted to a breach of the solemn assurance that no prejudice would be done to the authority of His Holiness and of the Apostolic See. It was not a matter of his own personal honour. They could call him an ant for all he cared! But he knew very well that the Pope would not rest content with an answer such as this.[45]

The no doubt somewhat shaken bishop then retreated and reported this latest exchange to his father. Time pressed. Contarini decided with Morone to tackle the Emperor himself on the subject before Mass, for immediately after the latter the Diet would be opened and the address read.

Charles, after the usual exchange of civilities and a pious wish on the part of Contarini that the Holy Spirit would descend into the hearts of them all, tried to defend the omission at first. The Protestants were like wild animals which could only be tamed gradually, he argued. Patience was necessary. Contarini repeated his previous arguments with some force, and eventually the Emperor gave way and ordered Granvelle to alter the document accordingly.[46]

The legate had carried his point. It was a significant diplomatic victory. Contarini had seen the danger that the *modus procedendi* suggested by the Emperor would have given tacit approval to the Protestant doctrine of the Church: lay participation in the

---

[45] Ibid., p. 171.

[46] Granvelle took the alteration with ill grace. On Morone's attempt to thank him he replied '. . . non esser bisogno, che lo ringratij, perchè l'Imperatore gli l'haveva commandato; benchè sia stata gran difficultà a far la mutatione nel consiglio della Dieta, nel qual è presidente il Conte Federico Palatino, non perchè habbino mal animo verso la Sede apostolica, ma perchè quando hanno stabilite le loro cose, son difficili a mutarle.' 'Nondimeno io credo più tosto il primo', adds Morone. Morone/Farnese, 6 Apr. 1541, *ZKG* iii. 625.

determination of matters religious, and independence from the magisterial authority of the Roman Church. The Emperor would have come to a tolerable agreement with the Estates on the religious question with no more than a formal gesture in the direction of the Papacy. The colloquy and Diet would then have been conducted on the basis of Protestant presuppositions! That the legate managed to avert this was no inconsiderable service to the papal cause.

The Diet was now set on a middle course which appeared to endanger neither the authority of the Pope nor the conduct of friendly negotiations with the Protestants. Both the attempt of the Emperor, or perhaps rather Granvelle, to by-pass the Papacy and that of the Bavarians and their allies to prevent the colloquy taking place at all had been foiled. Contarini could be well content with the success that his mediating policy had achieved thus far. The Diet was now ready to begin.

7

Honourable and Peace-loving Persons

THE Diet was opened on 5 April with a solemn Mass of the
Holy Spirit in the cathedral. The contemporary chronicler
Widmann has given us a vivid description of the procession
which wound its way by foot from the imperial quarters in the
'Golden Cross' inn[1] to St. Peter's Cathedral.

First came a group of courtiers from the Imperial Court and the
princely households, then the Catholic dukes, Christopher of
Württemberg, Albrecht of Baden, Henry of Brunswick, Charles of
Savoy, Otto Henry of the Palatinate, and the two Bavarians,
William and Louis. After them walked six trumpeters in the imperial livery, six heralds in levitical garments, and the hereditary
marshal, von Pappenheim, bearing the sword. The Emperor
himself came next, riding on a small horse. He was clad in a simple
black garment, for he was still in mourning for his wife. Last of all
came the bishops, who for this occasion were attired in the secular
finery of princes of the Empire, not as spiritual dignitaries.[2]

The Protestants, of course, did not take part in this procession.
Nor, more surprisingly, did Contarini. He had set out for the
imperial quarters with the intention of accompanying the Emperor to the church but the Emperor requested him to go on
ahead to St. Peter's. The reason probably was that he did not want
to antagonize the Protestants by being seen publicly in such close
association with the legate.

At the cathedral itself, however, Contarini·was met with all
courtesy by the Archbishop of Mainz and conducted by him to
a prominent seat on the south side of the choir. Shortly afterwards

---

[1] The 'Goldenes Kreuz' Nr. 7 on the Haidplatz, not far to the west of the
town hall. It was a large five-storey building with an inner court and a tower at
the south-east corner. *KDB* iii. 181.

[2] Nestler quotes extensively from Widmann's account. 'Vermittlungspolitik
. . . auf dem Regensburger Reichstag'. *ZBLG* vi. 392; cf. also the slightly di-
verging report of Negri, *ZKG* iii. 627–8.

the Emperor and the princes arrived and sat opposite him. In his report to Rome Contarini stresses that he took a full part in the service, giving the benediction at the end and coming forward with the others at the offertory, for the consecration of the bread and wine.

His Majesty had requested me to intimate that I would not come forward for the offering, since this was not customary. But when I remained in my place his Reverence of Mainz and the others indicated that they would not move until I had, and when his Majesty saw this he asked me to go forward, which I did. It should be noted that the wish of the Electors that the legate share in the offertory of their Mass, as if he were a member of the Diet, is a quite unusual and remarkable event. It does the Apostolic See no little honour and enhances its authority.[3]

Thus the legate interpreted the honourable part assigned to him in the service as indicating that he, as the papal representative, was accepted as a full member of the Diet. So closely intertwined were religion and politics that a liturgical arrangement could have the weightiest political consequences. It should be noted also that there could be no question of the Diet being a neutral political occasion, a confessional no-man's-land between Protestantism and Catholicism. It began in all form with a Catholic Mass. As far as the Empire was concerned the Protestants must still consider themselves as the outsiders, whose presence was tolerated for the moment, but who were definitely something less than full participants in its life and structures.

After the service the Catholic Estates then proceeded with the Emperor to the town hall, Contarini remaining, at the Emperor's request, in the cathedral. In the imperial chamber of the town hall, the Reichssaal, the Catholics were joined by the Protestants for the civil part of the opening ceremony. The Emperor took his seat on the throne, flanked by the Electors. At right-angles to them, down both sides of the rectangular room, sat the other princes of the Empire, one hundred in number. All outsiders were expelled and the proceedings began.[4]

The imperial Proposition was read by the Count Palatine Frederick, brother of the Elector, in German. It rehearsed the endeavours of the Emperor since the last Diet of Regensburg (1532) for the settlement of the religious dispute, his attempts to have a Council convoked, his exertions against the Turks, and

---

[3] Contarini/Farnese, 5 Apr. 1541, *ZKG* iii. 172.   [4] Ibid., p. 628.

justified his long absence from Germany. It explained the purpose of the Diet and summoned the Estates to co-operate with the Emperor both in the pursuit of a religious settlement and in the coming campaign against the Turks.[5]

The Turkish situation was indeed at the moment quite unusually critical. Ferdinand seemed tantalizingly near to success. He held Pest on the east side of the Danube and his troops were besieging the Hungarian capital Buda (or Ofen) on the west bank. At the same time, however, came the news that the Turk was hastening to the relief of the besieged city. It was therefore crucial for Ferdinand to snatch a decisive victory before the reinforcements arrived, and to achieve this he hoped to set out for Hungary on Palm Sunday, 9 April, at the head of 20,000 men.[6]

The threat of a full-scale Turkish onslaught on the eastern flank of the Empire loomed over Germany throughout the summer of 1541. Hate and fear of the Turk were indeed one of the few cementing elements that still bound the Empire together. Of all the hereditary tasks of the Emperor that of directing the defence against the Turks was the one most likely to gain the support and the understanding of the territorial princes. For advantageous as the Turkish presence might be to the Protestants as a factor inclining the Emperor towards a conciliatory course, this ultimate enemy was a common one, and all knew that the threat was an ominously real one.

None, of course, more so than the border territories which were directly threatened, or had already suffered from the Turkish depredations—Hungary itself, Styria, Carinthia, Carniola, and Goerz—whose princes had already appealed to Contarini to intercede for them with the Pope that the latter aid them in their struggle against the arch-enemy of the Christian faith. Ferdinand himself made a similar plea to Contarini to intercede for papal subventions.[7] Italy itself, of course, especially after Venice had made peace with the Turk, was faced with the threat of a naval invasion by the Turks, and the Pope, as Contarini pointed out, had to throw most of his resources into the preparations to avert this danger.[8]

---

[5] Text in *CR* iv. 151–4; cf. *Zeitschrift für Schweizer. Kg.* xxviii. 57–64.

[6] D/B, pp. 590 ff.; P. Heidrich, *Karl V und die deutschen Protestanten . . .*, pp. 15 ff.

[7] Morandi, I. ii. 132–6.   [8] Ibid., pp. 136–7.

Only from the German Estates—Protestant and Catholic alike—could the resources in men and money be found to raise, equip, and support an effective campaign in the East. Nothing clamoured more urgently for the settlement of the religious dispute than the need to deal with the Turkish threat. The dynastic interests of the Habsburgs, the defence of the integrity of the Empire, the ideological campaign against the infidel—all demanded that an end be made to the internal conflicts within Germany. The promotion of a certain minimum of trust or at least mutual toleration between the two confessions was the most urgent political task of the hour.[9] For while unrest and insecurity were of the order of the day the princes, and in particular the Protestants, would never vote away monies and troops which might well be needed for their own defence.

The situation was clear. Without a guarantee of their own security—which only a religious settlement or the granting of tolerance could give—the Protestants would refuse to grant the aids without which the Empire would lie wide open to Turkish depredations. The military situation thus exerted the most direct and brutal pressure on the Emperor, limited drastically his freedom of manœuvre, and placed a most valuable bargaining counter in the hands of the Protestants. With the leverage which they possessed by virtue of their 'power of the purse' they could well hope to extract from Charles V concessions which in more favourable times he would never have dreamt of granting. To defend Christendom, it seemed, he would have to betray Catholicism.[10]

Contarini realized as well as anyone the intimate relation between a solution to the internal problems of Germany and the pursuance of the war against the Turks. When, therefore, the Bishop of Agria, sent to Regensburg on behalf of Ferdinand, told the legate he intended to advocate a postponement of the handling of the religious question in favour of the Turkish, Contarini replied forthrightly that this could only harm his own cause. For until the religious problems were satisfactorily composed Germany would not be able to act effectively against the Turks.[11] In

[9] Thus the Emperor to Contarini: '... le forze delli Turchi sono le nostre discordie; se noi fussimo concordi, non sariano grandi'. ZKG iii. 175.

[10] Note the vague terms employed by the Protestants in their reply to the Emperor: 'universa respublica christiana', 'pro communi defensione christiani orbis.' CR iv. 157 ff.

[11] D/R, p. 321.

fact, the Estates decided to leave the Turkish problem until a later stage in the proceedings of the Diet.[12]

Formally we can distinguish two main elements in the events at Regensburg. First the colloquy at which the theologians attempted to come to grips with the theological problems. Secondly the Diet proper where the politicians dealt, *inter alia*, with the outcome of the theological discussions. The first stage is characterized by the attempt to arrive at a theological concord, the second by the more politically coloured concern to establish the limits within which tolerance could be exercised.

For our purposes, however, this formal distinction is not the decisive one. The real turning-point comes long before the termination of the colloquy, namely in the failure on 4 May to come to agreement on the nature of the Church. Up to this point one can speak of a qualified optimism, above all on Contarini's part, that a concord might after all be achieved. This optimism reaches its peak with the triumphantly welcomed argument on the question of justification. Thus far Contarini's main interest was directed to the possibility of reunion—and therefore to the Protestants.

In the second period, which ends with Contarini's reception of Ardinghelli's dispatch of 31 May, the legate was primarily occupied with the Catholics, and in particular with the Emperor, first in the attempt to prevent the conclusion of a theologically impermissible concord, and then of an ecclesiastically unacceptable toleration project.

Thirdly and lastly comes the period in which Contarini's main concern was to defend himself and his actions against the Pope and the cardinals. Here his attention was directed primarily towards Rome. We can and must speak, therefore, of a progressive and necessary narrowing of his horizons. In the first stage we see Contarini's ecumenism, in the second his Catholicism, in the third his curialism. It will be our task to see all these three aspects together, in their contrariety indeed, but also in the, to us, bewildering synthesis to which Contarini brought them. First, however, we must turn to the initial stages, to the period of qualified optimism, to Contarini and the Protestants.

---

[12] e.g. the Protestant insistence that before the Turkish problem was dealt with 'natura ipsa negotiorum postulat, ut pax in Germania fiat quod ad causam religionis attinet'. *CR* iv. 160.

Before discussions could even begin, the questions of procedure and the choice of the collocutors had to be settled. In his Proposition the Emperor had suggested the formation of a small group of 'honourable and peace-loving persons' concerned for the welfare of the German nation, whom he himself would appoint, and whose task it would be to examine the disputed articles of religion with a view to putting an end to the controversies. The outcome of their discussions they would then refer to the Emperor and the Estates for their decision, and also to the papal legate.[13]

The Bavarian Dukes immediately raised the confessional issue by demanding—with the threat that they would otherwise leave the Diet—that the Protestant and Catholic Estates discuss the Proposition of the Emperor separately.[14] The purpose of this move was, of course, to hinder the development of a party of the middle which would straddle the confessional divide and steer the negotiations towards a compromise solution. They won their point. Granvelle was forced to capitulate. Procedurally, at least, the demarcation lines would be clearly drawn.

As usual the Bavarians and the Archbishop of Mainz were assiduously spreading rumours—largely groundless—about Charles's intentions. The colloquy that the Emperor was planning would, they asserted, be composed primarily not of theologians at all but of princes to whom a few highly suspect theologians such as Pflug and Gropper would be added. They hinted at dark schemes on the part of the Emperor to turn over all the Church properties into the hands of a military order.[15] More important than these allegations, which Granvelle promptly denied, and to which it is unlikely that the papal representatives gave much credence, was that dealing with the vital question of the participation of the legate in the colloquy.

---

[13] '... dass ihre Majestät ... etliche guter Gewissen ehr- und friedliebende Personen, die auch des heiligen Reichs deutscher Nation Ehr, Nutz, und Wohlfahrt zu fördern geneigt, in geringer Anzahl aus gemeinen Ständen und deutscher Nation erwählen und verordnen, die streitigen Artikel der Religion nothdürftiglich zu examiniren und zu erwägen ... wie dieselben zu Vergleichung und Einigkeit gebracht werden mögen ...' Ibid., p. 154.

[14] *ZKG* iii. 174, 631.

[15] Ibid., p. 630-1. At first the Emperor does seem to have considered having laymen among the collocutors. The Proposition leaves this possibility open, speaking only of 'ehr- und friedliebende Personen'. *CR* iv. 154. Melanchthon, in his profoundly pessimistic letter to Brenz, utters a similar suspicion. Ibid., pp. 147-8.

They interpreted the Proposition to mean that the collocutors had only to 'communicate' their conclusions to the legate while they had to 'refer' them to the Emperor and the Estates for their decision. Contarini shared their concern but was unable to gain any further clarification of the issue.[16]

The key point, however, was that of the appointment of the collocutors, on whom the main burden of finding a way to reconcile the theological differences would rest. Understandably the Emperor wanted to keep the right to select them in his hands, for on their 'moderation' everything would depend. The Protestants, anxious to gain the imperial goodwill, had, after some initial hesitation, given their assent to the whole project, leaving everything to the Emperor's good judgement.[17] A good tactical move.

The Catholics, on the other hand, were hopelessly divided in their counsels. Mainz expressed his profound mistrust of the whole scheme. The Protestants, he pointed out, had not the slightest intention of uniting with the Catholics. Indeed their aim was to win over the latter to their views. Even if an agreement did come to pass, they would refuse to recognize the authority of the Apostolic See, and the Estates would accordingly simply by-pass the latter, and the Emperor would be powerless to prevent this. Similar pessimistic statements were made by Duke William of Bavaria to the papal nuncio.[18] An index of the extent of the

[16] '. . . gli pare non esse satisfatto, quando sol si communicasse con soa Rma Sria et non ricercasse il parer et consenso della Sede apca.' Morone/Farnese, 7 Apr. 1541, *ZKG* iii. 631. The Protestants would never have tolerated a recognition of the ultimate authority of the Pope. The presence of the legate could be tolerated, as John Frederick indicated in the instructions to his representatives. Any claim, however, on the part of Contarini to be present 'von des Papsts wegen *auctoritative*, als des Haupts der Kirche' must be rejected with all vigour. He was, be it noted, afraid that the Landgrave and perhaps some other Protestants might be ready to admit this claim. *CR* iv. 126.

[17] Ibid., pp. 162–3. Dittrich's statement, 'The Protestants raised all manner of objections and recriminations and assigned the whole blame for the regrettable conditions pertaining in Germany to their opponents' is an unusually grotesque exaggeration on his part. D/B, p. 601. The two replies to the Protestants on 9 and 12 Apr. are, in fact, remarkably innocent of any acrimony. *CR* iv. 156 ff., 162 ff. His reference on p. 602, *Anm.* 2, should of course read A. a. O 631, not 531.

[18] Not, as Dittrich has it, in *ZKG* iii. 626 (D/B, p. 602, *Anm.* 1) but in Lämmer, p. 369. The near identity of William of Bavaria's statement that the Emperor would have to choose between breaking with the Papacy and coming to terms with the Protestants with the warning transmitted by Farnese to Contarini 'di bonissimo loco' confirms one's previous suspicions as to the provenance of this warning. *NB* I. vii. 15 n. 2.

disagreements is that it was not until 12 April, a whole week after the opening of the Diet, that the Catholics could agree on an answer to the Emperor. This requested for the Catholic Estates a voice in the nomination of the collocutors.[19] The Emperor being dissatisfied with this reply they finally agreed on the following day, albeit somewhat reluctantly, to commit the nomination of the collocutors to the discretion of the Emperor, still requesting, however, the right to veto the imperial nominations.[20]

That it had come eventually to this positive answer was largely due to the exertions of the papal representatives. Morone, on hearing the allegations of the rigorists—which, of course, as far as the unlikelihood of any recognition by the Protestants of the papacy was concerned, were not without their basis in truth—brought the crux of the whole matter before Granvelle—the alleged intention to by-pass the Holy See. With hitherto unparalleled vigour Granvelle rebutted the imputation. The Emperor, he insisted, would never have countenanced a colloquy which would involve a break with the old faith. Nothing would be done without the knowledge of the legate and the consent of the Pope. He himself would rather be transported to a life of destitution at the uttermost end of the earth than suffer any detriment of the authority of the Holy See. These protestations appear to have convinced the papal representatives that the risk involved in continuing their support of the colloquy was a lesser one. They needed no reminder of the dire consequences which a departure of the Emperor from Germany without having achieved any settlement would have for the faith.[21] Yet if the Catholics could not even agree on a reply to the Proposition failure seemed imminent. Some of the Catholics were already preparing to leave the city. Contarini and Morone, there-

---

[19] *CR* iv. 163–5. One of the principal reasons for the disunity among the Catholics was the traditional rivalry between the cities and the princes. The latter wanted to exclude the former, the more conciliatory group on the religious issue, from the deliberations on the Proposition, and eventually the Catholic cities made a quite separate submission to the Emperor. Like the Protestants, they left to him the nomination of the collocutors. The Protestant princes had also to take care not to weaken the Schmalkaldic alliance by alienating the cities of their confession. In the work of smoothing out these rivalries—an added complication for the imperial plans—Naves, who replaced Held as Vice-Chancellor in May, was to play an important role. Heidrich, pp. 12 ff.

[20] *CR* iv. 165–6.

[21] Cf. Negri, *ZKG* iii. 629. 'Et se l'Imperatore parte di qui, ch'el non metta qualche buono assetto, che habbia excutione, actum est de tota Germania et forsi di altri lochi vicini.'

fore, took the only course open to them and threw all their energies into the attempt to remove the obstacles that lay in the way of a beginning to the negotiations. This meant in practice bringing their influence to bear on the Bavarian Dukes and on Mainz.[22] Their response to Granvelle's appeal in this direction was certainly instrumental in making the colloquy possible. The flank attack from the papal representatives caught the rigorist party unawares and put an end to their resistance.

Thus Contarini and Morone distanced themselves, as they had intended,[23] from the schemings of the Bavarians. In an audience with the Emperor on 12 April Contarini established that the latter did, after all, intend to nominate theologians and not laymen as collocutors, though it appeared that he had toyed for a while with the notion of having a lay prince as a 'neutral' moderator. On the delicate issue of peace with France—avoided thus far by the legate lest it be regarded as a red herring to distract attention from the colloquy—the Emperor protested, pale with anger, that on his part no effort had been spared to bring it to pass. God would have to change the hearts of the others. The topic was not pursued any further. A tentative suggestion by Contarini that the Emperor might take a personal initiative in restoring the true observance of religion in Germany found an equally cool reception.[24]

Holy Week was now well advanced and as a result the course of negotiations was temporarily suspended. 'From the ecclesiastical point of view', comments Dittrich, 'Regensburg presented in these days a strange spectacle, a picture of the most tragic dismemberment.'[25] It was certainly not altogether edifying.

On Palm Sunday the Emperor had worshipped with the Catholic Estates in the cathedral. The Protestants, on the other hand, gathered, as was their daily wont, in Philip of Hesse's house to hear a sermon by Bucer. The legate participated in the service in the cathedral but had to refrain, on the Emperor's advice, from giving a solemn benediction or proclaiming the indulgence granted by the Pope for the occasion lest he rile the absentee Protestants![26] And

---

[22] Lämmer, pp. 370–1.

[23] Contarini was concerned to dispel any suspicion that 'dal canto nostro siano posti impedimenti alla concordia . . .' and the danger that '. . . tutti li disturbi, proceduti dalli Duchi di Bavera et altri, haveriano [i.e. the Imperial Court] attribuiti a noi come autori di quelli'. *ZKG* iii. 174.

[24] Ibid., pp. 175–6.   [25] D/B, p. 605.

[26] 'Your Reverence will note', comments Negri, 'to what a pass we have come.' *ZKG* iii. 633.

while the Emperor and the legate retreated to a cloister to give a godly example of prayer and fasting to the other Catholics, and— indeed—to the Protestants,[27] Philip of Hesse and the Elector of Brandenburg patronised a meal on Good Friday itself, at which at least some of the company present partook of meat. On Easter Day itself the Lord's Supper was celebrated in both kinds in Hesse's lodgings, among the fifty Regensburg citizens present being members of the council. The traditional Holy Week processions of the nuns through the city had had to be abandoned lest they become the target of Protestant abuse and insults. As Nestler comments, 'The unitary medieval outlook had collapsed in ruins.'[28]

What hope, many must have asked themselves, could there possibly be of an end to the schism if the two parties could not even pray together in Holy Week, could not celebrate together the central feast of the faith? What could all reasonableness, all good-will, all humanist moderation avail in the face of such unbridgeable differences?

Hopes were not, then, of the highest. Girolamo Negri, Contarini's private secretary, observed that the too tender concern of the Emperor for the feelings of the heretics seemed to many Catholics to indicate a lack of warmth for the true faith. Bucer's preaching was an open scandal; Melanchthon was tirelessly producing new books, the latest a bestial polemic against the celibacy of the priesthood. The other Protestant theologians were developing a highly subversive activity among the people. All in all, he lamented, the state of Germany could not be worse.[29]

Contarini himself continued cautiously to hope for the best. 'We are anxiously waiting for the outcome of this Diet', he wrote to the Venetian Consul in Sicily, '[in the hope] that some worthy settlement may be found to the religious questions in this sorely taxed land. To bring this about His Majesty the Emperor is leaving nothing undone; thus I pray God, that He will bring it to a

---

[27] The personal religious observance of the Emperor was above reproach: '. . . viene con tanta modestia et religion con tutta la sua corte, che un Monasterio de' frati Scapuzzini non saria più osservante.' Ibid., p. 635. Equally so that of the legate. At the end of the month he was still in the Benedictine monastery, at least partly '. . . per dar buon odor di se a questi lutherani'. Ibid., p. 638.

[28] ZBLG vi. 395, 410.

[29] 'Certo le cose sono molto intorbidate. Questa povera Alamagna è in un pessimo stato quanto alla fede di Christo et etiam al resto.' ZKG iii. 629.

good end.'[30] Unlike his companions, who were longing to leave Germany, Contarini, wrote Negri, was ready to stay there twenty years if he saw any hope of recovering 'this lost people'.[31]

The Protestants, for their part, were either very cautious about expressing optimism on the outcome of the colloquy or bleakly pessimistic. The Saxons in particular were in no conciliatory mood. For personal, political, and theological reasons the Elector's instructions to his representatives were rigorous in the extreme— even more sceptical about the Diet than the papal instruction to Contarini.[32] John Frederick's main concern was that there should be no weakening of the Protestant front, which, for the sake of God and conscience, must stand steadfastly by the Augsburg Confession, as had been decided by the Schmalkaldic League at Naumburg in November of the previous year. His own decision not to attend the Diet was in itself significant enough. For once there he was convinced that he would come under pressure from Granvelle to agree to a watering down of the evangelical truth, as he feared Hesse might be. There must, however, be no yielding of the truth, not even on one single point, nor should any ambiguous formulae be admitted which the Catholics could interpret to their advantage.

This was, argued Frederick, no ordinary worldly transaction in which a certain 'give and take' would be of the order of the day. Here God's Word was at stake—that is what the 'foreign potentates'—a dig, no doubt, at the Emperor—could not understand when they complained of the Protestants' obstinacy.[33] It might be that the Catholics would make certain concessions, but they would always refer them to the final arbitration of the Pope. But once this—papal authority—was admitted, all the achievements of the Reformation could be whittled away stage by stage.

[30] Contarini/Pelegrini Venier, 14 Apr. 1541, D/R, p. 169.

[31] ZKG iii. 634. He was reconciled to a long stay in Regensburg, 'perche le cose di Germania sempre son longhi . . .' Contarini/Bembo, 26 Apr. 1541, D/R, p. 323.

[32] The heresy decrees in the Netherlands, the threat to his relative the Duke of Jülich, his traditional opposition to the Habsburgs, his bitter enmity to Mainz all played a role here. Vetter, pp. 7 ff.

[33] '. . . dass es mit Gottes Worts Sachen viel eine andre Gestalt denn mit prophanen Händeln hat. Denn in denen kann ein jeder seinen Rechten wohl entweichen; aber in jenen, wenn alle Artikel erhalten und nachgegeben sollten werden bis auf einen, der nöthig (wäre), und würde begeben: so steckt man doch eben so hoch in Beschwerung und Fahr der Gewissen als sonst.' CR iv. 127.

The purpose of the Diet for the Elector was therefore twofold—on the one hand the Protestant cause would be upheld theologically and perhaps new adherents won, and on the other when it became clear that a concord was not to be achieved, the Emperor might be moved to grant the Protestants a permanent peace. It was illusory to hope for a genuine agreement, for the papal household was not in the least inclined to give way to God's Word and Truth. Negatively the suspicion must be removed that the real concern of the Protestants was not the promotion of religion but of 'discontent and rebellion against his Imperial Majesty'.[34]

The truth of the matter is that the leading Protestants never really expected that a concord would be achieved. Their main interest lay more in the political realm, in the granting of tolerance. After polemicizing against Rome for some twenty years they were hardly prepared to believe that, after all, no real differences existed! They welcomed the irenical spirit of the Emperor naturally, but with a surprise not untinged by scepticism.[35]

Philip of Hesse was undoubtedly the leading Protestant personality at Regensburg. If the jaunty livery of his retainers attracted the attention of the curious,[36] others were more concerned to speculate about his political ambitions. He had, as we have seen, high hopes for himself, if not for Protestantism from the Diet. For the moment, however, he was in an exceptional, and exceptionally uncomfortable position. On the one hand, he had to convince the Schmalkaldic League that he had no intention of deserting their cause.[37] On the other hand, he had to act in such a way that the Emperor would agree to a quiet settlement of the bigamy question.

He was, of course, a key figure in Granvelle's 'grand design'. Hesse, with Brandenburg and some of the south German cities would form, it was hoped, the core of a moderate Protestant party which would counteract the influence of the intransigent Saxons. No effort was spared, therefore, from the imperial side to reconcile

[34] WAB ix. 320–2.

[35] 'Imperator aperte nihil ostendit hostile, ut alioqui eius admiranda est in omni apparatu modestia, et in respondendo lenitas', wrote Melanchthon to Jonas at the end of March. *CR* iv. 143.

[36] The livery bore two fighting-cocks on the arms and the inscription 'v.d.m.i.', i.e. verbum Domini manet in aeternum. *ZBLG* vi. 391.

[37] 'Macedonici [Hesse] concionatores de suo domino etiam bene promittunt. Nidanus [Pistorius] nobis heri narravit, in hoc itinere Macedonem dixisse, se nec a confessione discessurum esse, nec passurum ut abstrahatur a foederatis.' Melanchthon/Luther, 29 Mar. 1541, *CR* iv. 142–3.

the differences between Hesse and Henry of Brunswick,[38] which threatened otherwise to plunge north Germany into civil war. And though—if we are to believe Contarini[39]—his first audience with the Emperor was not exactly cordial, this was no doubt at least partly dictated by the need not to scandalize the Catholics. He was accorded, however, the licence for Bucer to preach in his house,[40] which, if one remembers that the Augsburg Recess was still in force, could only be regarded as a precedent of importance—as a licensing of heresy. In the same city as Diet, Emperor, and legate, heretical sermons were being preached daily with the explicit approbation of the Emperor himself. Perhaps the first step towards a comprehensive policy of toleration? Hesse had even dared to set certain conditions—of a theological nature—for his presence at the opening Mass of the Diet, which, it is true, the Emperor had rejected.

Another key figure at the Diet was, of course, Joachim II of Brandenburg. The tragic disunity of Holy Week moved perilously near to the farcical when the Elector proceeded from the notorious meal on Good Friday to participating—with all apparent reverence—in the Catholic Mass on Easter Monday. An eloquent if ludicrous illustration of his ambiguous position. Contarini had urged the granting of his request to attend since it seemed more prudent and Christian to do so.[41] With the princes of Hesse and Brandenburg in their mediatorial position Melanchthon associates the towns of Strasbourg and Augsburg,[42] and although Morone's impression that if they were permitted to observe communion in both kinds and to dispense with priestly celibacy they would leave the Schmalkaldic League and return to the Church was a typical misunderstanding,[43] they certainly constituted one of the most moderate groupings among the Protestants. Peaceful conditions were of course particularly desirable for their commercial activity.

[38] Francesco Contarini/Senate, 6 Apr. 1541, D/R, p. 166.

[39] *ZKG* iii. 164.

[40] On the other hand Charles refused the request of the Elector of Brandenburg for the use of the Dominican church—and indeed the use of any church—for a service following the Protestant rite. Quirini iii. 254; Philip of Hesse's accommodation in the Styrer house, Nr. 5 Untere Bachgasse, running at right-angles from the south-east corner of the Rathausplatz, was itself ideal for holding services since the two bottom storeys were taken up by a chapel. *KDB* iii. 190–1.

[41] *HJ* i. 366.   [42] *CR* iv. 578.   [43] *HJ* iv. 435.

On the whole, however, as Holy Week came to an end the auspices for a favourable outcome to the Diet seemed anything but good. On Easter Monday, 18 April, Granvelle came to discuss with the legate the next step—the choice of the collocutors.

The question of their selection mirrored the difficulties of the situation for the Emperor. For their conclusions to carry weight they had to be representative personalities, recognized champions of Catholicism and Protestantism. It was clear therefore from the beginning that neither Eck nor Melanchthon could be excluded.[44] If, on the other hand, a settlement, a breaking down of the confessional barriers were to be achieved, then the moderate, conciliatory, liberal elements must predominate, men of the calibre of Gropper and Bucer, the two architects of the Regensburg Book. The plan was audacious, and yet the only possible one—to harness reaction and liberalism in the one team and to hope that somehow they could be persuaded to pull together.

The final decision as to the choice of collocutors lay of course with the Emperor.[45] Contarini, however, was kept in the closest consultation, and indeed from this point on until the failure to reach agreement on the question of transubstantiation the legate participated in every important development. This was only possible because of the mutual trust that now existed between Contarini and Granvelle, a trust that was certainly not unlimited but one which made an alliance of forces possible.

Granvelle and Contarini discussed the likely candidates.[46] Cochlaeus, it was agreed, lacked the necessary human warmth. Eck, whether warm or not, must, insisted Contarini, be included. The idea of having a lay prince present to act as arbiter was quietly dropped. It would, however, still be necessary to have a president, and it seems that it had been even thought at one time of appointing the Archbishop of Mainz to this post.[47] A more recurrent proposal was that Contarini himself should preside.[48] Granvelle believed that, were it not for fear of their princes, the

[44] Granvelle did, it is true, hope for a while that Eck could be excluded. Ibid., p. 430.

[45] '. . . pensarò et il tutto communicarò con voi', said the Emperor to Contarini when the latter inquired about his intentions. *ZKG* iii. 175.

[46] *HJ* i. 365-7.

[47] Vetter suggests, as is possible, that this suggestion came from the papal representatives. Vetter, p. 71.

[48] *ZKG* iii. 625. Morone pointed to the precedent of Worms where Campeggio had been present at the deliberations.

Protestant theologians would have no objection to this.[49] Granvelle, if he was sincere here, failed to see that for the Protestants admiration of Contarini as a person[50] would in no way have been sufficient to lead them to waive their objection to his presiding over the colloquy in his status as papal legate. As it happened, nothing came of the suggestion.

On 21 April the Emperor announced the names of the collocutors. Predictably Eck and Melanchthon, Gropper and Bucer were among those named. The number was completed by the bishop elect of Naumburg, Julius Pflug, and the Hessian preacher Pistorius: three Catholics and three Protestants. The terms in which their function was described were almost identical with those in the Proposition. They would be purely advisory, and, as Melanchthon wrote, the aim was not disputation but conciliation.[51] Of the legate and the Papacy, however, there was no mention at all, an omission afterwards explained away by Granvelle as a mere scribal error.[52] The desire to avoid a possible altercation with the Protestants is a more likely ground. Granvelle and Count Frederick of the Palatinate were to preside and six lay witnesses were added whose duty it was to exercise a calming influence on the theologians.[53]

[49] *HJ* i. 365. The text, as Pastor remarks (*Anm.* 6), is obviously corrupt here. Dittrich is in two minds as to how it should be translated. In the *Regesten* (Nr. 680, p. 171) he interprets it as meaning that, albeit unwillingly, the Protestants would accept Contarini out of respect for the wishes of their princes; in the biography (p. 607) that they themselves would gladly accept Contarini but dared not express this because of fear for their princes. The latter is probably the correct translation, being in accord with Granvelle's oft-expressed view that it was out of craven fear about possible reactions that the Protestant theologians tended to be so inflexible.

[50] The exemplary conduct of the Cardinal, wrote Negri, made the Protestants 'curdle'! (*cagliano*) *ZKG* iii. 633.

[51] *CR* iv. 178–9; Contarini/Bembo, D/R, p. 322; *ZKG* iii. 639. In his 'Historia' Melanchthon wrote: '. . .Imperator ostendit se paucos delecturum esse, non ut sententiae inter se pugnantes defenderentur, sed ut quaererentur quae dogmata conciliari possint. Ac ne quid periculi esset ex hac deliberatione partibus, praefatus est velle se non teneri quenquam his deliberatis, nec vim ea praeiudicii habere, sed omnia rursus ad consilium principum referenda esse.' *CR* iv. 330.

[52] *HJ* i. 367.

[53] '. . . acciò questi altri 6 Doctori non vengino alle villanie et perdino tempo in cose impertinenti.' *ZKG* iii. 636. They had been added at the request of the Protestants (*CR* iv. 179) and Negri suspected them all of Lutheran sympathies. Melanchthon's hope was that they would exert a favourable influence for the Protestant cause on the Emperor. *CR* iv. 331. They were Heinrich Hase, Franz Burckhard, and Johann Feige, the chancellors of the Palatinate, Electoral

The Catholic doctors, noted Negri, were all able men, independent of any man's favour, whether that of the Pope or the legate or the Emperor.[54] This had its grain of truth. Eck, for example, certainly cannot be regarded as a mere protégé of the Bavarian dukes. On the other hand there can be no denying his dependence upon them. The opposition of the latter to the colloquy had, after all, almost prevented his presence at Regensburg at all.[55] The enthusiasm of the Ingolstadt theologian for the colloquy had no Erasmian or irenical basis. He saw it rather as an opportunity for him to collapse the whole Protestant edifice by his rhetoric and scholarship. It in no wise contradicts therefore his usual intransigence.[56] He came to Regensburg, however, only when he was instructed to do so by the Bavarian dukes. The decision of the latter to invite him was, as Dittrich surmises, probably influenced by Contarini and the Emperor.[57] The dukes knew well enough, however, that his presence would hardly be calculated to improve the chances of arriving at a peaceful settlement.

Surprising, at first sight at least, is the relatively high estimate which Contarini had of Eck,[58] although he had, of course, the advantage of not knowing him very well. Eck was also, however, in his way a reformer, a scholar, a fighter for the Catholic cause, and had been in constant touch with the legate in the past few months. The comparatively cordial contacts between the two men should warn against too hasty judgements either about the spuriousness of Eck's concern for 'religion', or about Contarini's understanding of the latter. The traditionalism of the legate should not be underestimated. In view, of course, of the catastrophic dearth of able Catholic theologians in Germany he could, on the other hand, hardly afford to be overselective in his choice of allies. Of the other two Catholic collocutors, Gropper and Pflug, Gropper was without doubt the better-equipped theologian. Both, as we have

---

Saxony, and of Hesse, Count Manderscheidt, Eberhard Rude, the Steward of the Archbishop of Mainz, and Jacob Sturm, from Strasbourg.

[54] *ZKG* iii. 635.

[55] 'Cur autem non vocer Ratisbonam, miror: iniussus non venio.' Eck/Farnese, 1 Apr. 1541, D/R, Nr. 643, p. 162.

[56] A justified intransigence? Lortz, ii. 92. 'Es würde sehr schwer halten, Ecks Intransigenz für die vierziger Jahre wesentlich als verfehlt zu erweisen.'

[57] D/B, p. 608.

[58] 'Excellentissime Eccki', 'Eckio mihi amicissimo.' Contarini/Eck, 10 Apr. 1541, D/R, p. 316.

seen, were suspect to the Bavarians and therefore also to Eck as being too conciliatory.

Melanchthon, the Protestant counterpart to Eck, was profoundly unhappy in his role. Conciliatory by nature, he found himself saddled with the main weight of defending the Protestant cause. He had grave fears, like his Elector, for the solidarity of the Protestant camp, and distrusted his fellow collocutors Bucer and Pistorius on account of their dependence on Philip of Hesse.[59] As to the Catholics, he appears to have been quite unaware of any differences of opinion between the papal representatives and the Bavarians and believed that both were equally opposed to any real colloquy.[60]

He doubted therefore that the good intentions of the Emperor—to which he gave full credit—would bear any fruit though Charles might at least come to realize that the beliefs of the Protestants were not so absurd as they had been made out to be.[61] Handicapped by a very painful—and at first wrongly diagnosed and treated—injury to his hand caused by a fall from his horse on the journey to the Diet,[62] and under the strictest instructions not to budge even an inch from the Augsburg Confession, he felt himself surrounded by a myriad of dangers, real and imaginary, far more subtle than had been encountered at Worms, and was profoundly pessimistic about the outcome of the negotiations.[63]

He was subjected, moreover, to what amounted to house arrest on the instructions of the Elector. Everything was done to 'pro-

---

[59] *CR* iv. 187.

[60] 'Sed Contarenus Cardinalis multo est durior. Nulla in re discedi vult a consuetudine Romana. Ideo impedire has deliberationes de concordia sedulo conatur.' Ibid., p. 188.

[61] Ibid., p. 331.

[62] Ibid., p. 142.

[63] Ibid., p. 172; '... petimur insidiis aliquanto astutius quam in Vangionibus.' Ibid., p. 176; 'Numquam res instructa est insidiosius. Nec video nos humano consilio ex his laqueis evadere posse.' Ibid., p. 186. Melanchthon was particularly bitter about the 'levity' of Hesse, which had brought matters to this pass. (The reference, of course, is to his bigamy.) Since Hesse was now ensnared by the imperialists, Eck, expecting the Protestants to be cowed and disheartened, was behaving with intolerable insolence. More than Eck's raging, however, was to be feared, Melanchthon thought, the moderation of Aenead (Gropper?). Ibid., p. 186. On the Protestant view on Gropper, Burckhard is interesting: '... vir est satis bonus et modestus, neque etiam indoctus, sed vincetur ab uno clamoribus ab altero astutia, et fortassis ipse quoque suas peculiares proferet opiniones veritati Evangelicae non per omnia consentientes.' Burckhard/Brück, 22 Apr. 1541, ibid., p. 185.

tect' him from any fraternization with the Catholics.[64] It was, of course, an open secret that the Catholics hoped to win him over to their cause, and the protection from such intrigues was, no doubt, welcome enough. That, however, any normal friendly relationship with the 'other side' was excluded from the outset hardly boded well for the success of the colloquy. Of the other two Protestants, Bucer, heavily compromised by his co-authorship of the Regensburg Book (a carefully guarded secret), had to exercise the utmost caution in order not to lose the confidence of his co-religionists. Pistorius, a relatively unimportant figure, at no time played a decisive role in the ensuing negotiations.[65]

Apart from Eck, therefore, none of the collocutors was trained in scholastic theology, and the consensus of opinion certainly lay on the conciliatory side. Given the circumstances, the Emperor could hardly have made a better choice.

[64] Hans Hoier was ordered to accompany Melanchthon wherever he went. The councillors were to prevent anyone speaking with Melanchthon alone so that 'Wenn nun solches vermerkt, wird er unsers Versehens wohl ungeplagt werden . . . in alle Wege musste sich Philippus auch enthalten nicht zu viel auszugehen, sondern in der Herberge und bei unsern Rathen zu bleiben . . .' Ibid., p. 131.

[65] Cf. Burckhard's comment: 'homo, ut audio, non indoctus, et de quo Dom. Philippus etiam optime sentit.' Ibid., p. 184.

8

Dio Laudato!

THE preliminaries over, the colloquy could now get under way. Contarini and Morone were reasonably happy about the emerging pattern. The collocutors might do no good, wrote Morone to Rome, but at least they could do no harm, since they had no mandate to take any decisions but simply to confer together. He noted, however, with concern the lack of any mention in the instructions to the six that they should keep the legate informed of the course of the discussions. This might well have the gravest consequences. The majority of the group was irenically inclined. It could well happen that for the sake of attaining agreement the Catholics would agree to a compromise formula of dubious Catholicity. Pope and Emperor would then be powerless against this disastrous *fait accompli*, for the fact that unity had been achieved at all would have a far more profound impression in Germany than the fact that it was a unity in error.[1]

To cover themselves against this nightmare possibility Contarini insisted that he be kept informed daily of the course of negotiations. Any incipient tendency towards error could then be nipped in the bud before it was too late. Granvelle granted this request without demur.[2] This cautious move by the legate, working here as always in the closest collaboration with Morone, was to prove all-important for the course of the colloquy. In his daily meetings with the three Catholics,[3] before and after the meetings with their three

[1] *HJ* iv. 445; *HJ* i. 367; cf. also Contarini/Dandalo, 26? July 1541, Morandi, I. ii. 200 ff. The papal interests required a particularly stout defence at this time. The Colonna affair had done nothing to improve the papal image in Germany and many Catholics saw no point in the Emperor 'sacrificing' German interests for the sake of Rome. Fr. Contarini/Venice, 25 Apr. 1541, D/R, p. 172.

[2] At first it was only foreseen that Eck should report to the legate every evening on the day's proceedings. *HJ* i. 368; *HJ* iv. 445.

[3] Granvelle appears to have attended himself. The only others Contarini was allowed to admit were Morone and Badia. Thus Negri: 'Et ogni mattina dopo il principio della disputa vengono qui dal Rmo legato il Sor Nuntio Vescovo da

Protestant counterparts, Contarini was to exercise a quite decisive influence.

Somehow, as we have seen, reaction and liberalism—harnessed together in the one team—had to be made to pull together if the whole venture were not to fail miserably. The first result of Contarini's unseen activity behind the scenes was to make this concerted action on the part of the Catholics possible. Secondly Contarini's own ecumenical orientation ensured that the participation of the Catholics would be of a positive nature and that every effort would be made to come to a tolerable settlement. Thirdly, that he exercised this controlling authority precisely as the papal representative guaranteed that the concern for an agreement would not be allowed to end in a sacrifice of the papal interests.

All this was accomplished by Contarini in what was, strictly speaking, a private capacity.[4] It was unthinkable that the Diet would have empowered him in any sense to act *qua* legate, as the representative of the Pope. In fact, the Emperor did his best to keep the very existence of these conferences of the legate with Eck, Gropper, and Pflug a secret. For they meant a decisive departure from the humanistic ideal of a colloquy—of a meeting of minds which were free from all prejudice, i.e. literally from all previous decisions, and therefore open to the arguments of the other side, where reason and moderation alone would hold sway. Now, however, the actual decisions would be made, in part at least, prior to and not during the colloquy. All this meant, of course, that to an extraordinary extent all depended on Contarini.[5] On his skill would depend the unity, on his judgement the Catholicism, and on his concern for reunion the 'ecumenicity' of the Catholic collocutors.

The Protestants, for their part, acted in an analogous if more corporate manner, hammering out a concerted policy in the theological conferences which they held throughout the Diet. But because

---

Modena, Mons*or* di Granvela et li tre dottori et spesso il padre maestro sacri Palatii et stanno inchiusi insieme col Rmo legato per due hore.' *ZKG* iii. 639.

[4] '. . . li cattolici per ordine della Cesaria Maesta ogni giorno conferiscono meco come persona privata però, et non come con legato . . . ogni cosa con molta secretezza.' *HJ* i. 372. '. . . non come a legato, ma come a persona amica.' *D/R*, p. 325.

[5] The legate was well aware of the responsibility he carried. Despite the exclusion of Wauchop and Pighius from the conferences he would, he wrote to Farnese on 28 Apr., treat them with the greatest of tact, 'perchè io non voglio in modo alcuno prendermi cosi gran carico, se non cominciandolo con molti prima, et poi inviando il tutto a Sua B*ne*'. *HJ* i. 371.

of their essentially defensive attitude—the desire to conserve their revolution—and because, above all, of the Catholicism of the Emperor, the onus for taking an initiative lay primarily with the Catholics. It was the unique phenomenon of Contarini—a papal legate who incarnated the most progressive forces within Catholicism—which made this initiative possible. It was without doubt primarily from the Catholic side that the olive-branch was extended at Regensburg. Whether it was stretched out far enough or in the right direction or even with a full comprehension of the extent of the gap to be bridged[6] is another matter. But that it could be stretched out at all is largely to be attributed to the activity in Regensburg of Cardinal Contarini.

On 22 April, the day after the announcement of their names, the collocutors were solemnly sworn in, or so at least Negri informs us.[7] The Saxon representatives mention nothing of an oath of this nature.[8] At any rate the six came before the Emperor and were exhorted by him to spare no effort to find a way to reunite Church and nation. The stage was set for the theological encounter.

Hopes were surprisingly high both in the imperial and in the papal camp. Contarini, in a personal letter to Bembo, wrote: 'The spirits of these Germans are somewhat milder than is their wont and they show great respect for the Emperor; it seems that they are concerned about the disastrous state of this land, so that there is ground for hope, though whether it will come to a successful outcome or not is hard to say.'[9]

One of the grounds for optimism was the skilful tactics of the Emperor, who was making every endeavour to win over the German princes to his moderation policy. He concentrated particularly on the waverers, and went to the length, we read, of a courtesy visit to the wife of the Elector of Brandenburg. He

---

[6] Vetter comments: 'Er [Contarini] kennt die Lage Deutschlands in ihrem vollen Umfange, aber er verkennt ihre Bedeutung; die prinzipiellen Diskrepanzen sind ihm verborgen, er sieht nur die streitigen Artikel, nur den formellen Unterschied. Er vermag es nicht einzusehen, dass ess ich nich tum eine Sekte handelt ... sondern um eine neue Kirche, die den Entwicklungsgang der mittelalterlichen Kirche negierend an die alte Kirche wieder anzuknüpfen sucht.' Vetter, p. 44. That Contarini only saw the formal difference is, however, a somewhat doubtful thesis.

[7] They promised, he reported, to seek the reunification of Germany 'sotto Una fede vera et Cathca'. ZKG iii. 635.

[8] CR iv. 188–9.

[9] Contarini/Bembo, 26 Apr. 1541, D/R, p. 322.

adapted himself to whatever company he was in, being, indeed,
'all things to all men'.[10]

A grave underestimation of the determination of the Protestants
was another, more dubious ground for the optimism. Negri, for
example, described the Protestant theologians as disheartened men
who would recant at once if they did not fear the reaction of their
followers. The Elector of Brandenburg was already half con-
verted.[11] Not only had he heard the Mass with all reverence, but
had declared that he would live and die by the rite and the faith of
the Emperor, and if he had been misled up to now he was eager to
take the opportunity which Regensburg offered him of clarifying
his position and turning his back on his previous errors. He asserted
further that Hesse was of the same mind as himself. It seemed,
Negri concluded, that a divine deliverance of the poor deluded
people of Germany was at hand.

Contarini reported to Farnese on the discussions which Eck—of
all men—had held with Brandenburg and Hesse. With the latter
surprisingly much common ground had been found. Only on the
question of priestly celibacy, communion in both kinds, and the
papal primacy had Philip been found difficult. The Elector, who
had also spoken with Eck, shared Hesse's scruples about the first
two points, and also raised doubts as to the sacrificial nature of the
Mass, but was quite ready, on the other hand, to recognize the
papal primacy in view of the need for unity of faith and practice
among all Christians.[12]

The spectacle of two of the leading Protestant princes engaging
in friendly discussion with the most militant of the Catholic
controversial theologians was indeed something new, even though
one suspects that Eck probably exaggerated somewhat the success
of his persuasive powers on the princes. Granvelle's plans appeared
to be coming to fruition, the Protestant front to be crumbling, and
the winning over of the moderates to the Catholic position seemed
only a matter of time.

---

[10] '. . . et fa [the Emperor] con questi tedeschi le ceremonie tedesche benisso,
con spagnoli le spagnole, con gli italiani le italiane, in modo che fa la simia
eccellentissimamente;' *ZKG* iii. 635.

[11] 'Sapia V.S., che questi heretici sono più stanchi che non siamo noi et
desiderano trovar modo di ridursi, sed timent plebem, la qual hanno già tanti
anni sedutta. Il Marchese di Brandeburg Elettor . . . è mezzo convertito et già
confessa il primato del Papa et molte altre cose.' Ibid., pp. 635, 637.

[12] Contarini/Farnese, 28 Apr. 1541, Quirini, iii. 254–5.

It was in the context of such sanguine expectations that Contarini made his first acquaintance with the Regensburg Book, Granvelle's last and best trump card.[13] On 23 April de Praet and Granvelle, after swearing the legate to secrecy, explained that the Emperor had considered what would be the best *modus procedendi* for the colloquy and had decided against proceeding on the basis of Melanchthon's *Confession*[14] as the Protestants would not give way on the slightest point of this. He had, however, had placed in his hands a book composed by certain learned theologians in Flanders which dealt with the controverted articles, and believed that it would provide a better basis for discussion. He asked the legate to scrutinize the document and stressed anew the need for absolute secrecy. Gropper's assistance in the examination of the book was offered.[15] The next two days were devoted to the reading of the book by Contarini, Morone, and Gropper, the latter betraying his authorship of it by the close acquaintance with it which he displayed. He accepted all the twenty-odd corrections which Contarini thought necessary. On Monday, 25 April, Contarini expressed to Granvelle his satisfaction with the thus amended document, stressing however, that this was only his own personal opinion. He was careful to avoid giving any official blessing to it in his status as legate, and covered himself further by saying that a more careful reading might well reveal further errors.[16]

Granvelle, who was not unacquainted with the capacity of

[13] Its appearance put to a premature end the fifteen articles produced by some of the Catholics as a basis for the negotiations. These had placed, as Cruciger remarked, all the 'most repellent' articles at the beginning, the articles to which the Protestants were most likely to take exception: the 'venerable sacrament of the Eucharist', the authority of the Church and of the Papacy, etc. The article on justification came a very lame last and its very wording was a provocation. 'De fide iustificante et de meritis et de bonis operibus.' *ZKG* iii. 639. A slightly different version in *CR* iv. 183–4; cf. Melanchthon/Baumgart, 20 Apr. 1541, ibid., p. 178.

[14] Contarini in his report says that it was Melanchthon's *Apologia* that was to be replaced, but this is a slip. It was the *Confession* that had been used at Worms.

[15] That Contarini did not at once inquire more closely into this unlikely story about the Flanders theologians is astonishing. Diplomatic tact? One can only surmise that the legate was too occupied by his purely theological interest in the contents to spare any thought for the question of its origin. He soon remedied this, however, surmising correctly from Gropper's conduct that he was the author. *HJ* i. 368; likewise Morone: *HJ* iv. 454. The adjuration to secrecy seems to have been well kept. Even Contarini's private secretary Negri had, as late as 30 Apr., no knowledge of the existence of the book, as Dittrich points out. D/B, p. 609, *Anm.* 3.

[16] *HJ* i. 369.

theologians for discovering further errors, recommended the immediate submission of the book, again under the seal of secrecy, to Badia and the three Catholic collocutors.[17] The Catholic representatives thus had an opportunity to examine the document— unlike their Protestant counterparts—prior to the commencement of the colloquy proper.

Events were now moving fast. Granvelle was forcing the pace. Not only had much time been lost already, but a prolonged theological discussion among the Catholics at this stage could hardly further the hopes of reunion. The faster the theologians were forced to work, the less time they would have to find fault with the book. Accordingly, although Eck was still far from satisfied, the first joint meeting of the collocutors took place on the same day—the twenty-seventh—and Count Frederick of the Palatinate, on behalf of the Emperor, exhorted the collocutors once again to a collected and pious determination to pursue the end of concord, and introduced—to the Protestants for the first time—the Regensburg Book as a basis for negotiations especially fitted by its moderation to the Emperor's irenic intentions. The Protestants, who would have preferred the *Confession*, deferred to the wishes of the others lest they be 'uncivil' to the Emperor, who had suggested the book, and in view of the eminently reasonable condition that it should be altered wherever it was not in accord with Scripture.[18] Melanchthon soon recognized in the book the writing that had been transmitted to Luther and the other Wittenberg theologians by Joachim of Brandenburg.[19]

The speed and the secrecy with which the negotiations were now being pushed forward caught the Protestants by surprise, and forced them to proceed along this new tack without prior consultation with Luther and the Elector of Saxony. They were given a bare hour to read the first part of the book—too brief to allow them to have a copy of it made—and then it was given to the Catholic collocutors, likewise for an hour.[20]

[17] Vetter's statement that it was the failure to gain Contarini's official imprimatur which led Granvelle to lay it before the other Catholics has little to recommend it. Vetter, p. 77. Granvelle knew well that an approval of that kind was in the highest degree unlikely.

[18] *CR* iv. 332.

[19] *CR* iv. 253. (It was not until 5 May that the Saxon delegates informed the Elector of the intention to proceed on the basis of the book.)

[20] *HJ* i. 370. As Vetter remarks (Vetter, p. 68) Granvelle kept the book in his own hands throughout the colloquy, removing it himself at the end of every

The attitude of Eck, however, threatened to make any progress impossible. He lauched a frontal attack on the book. Its conciliatory nature led him to suspect that Witzel was its author. Both de Praet and Granvelle complained bitterly about such intolerable conduct and begged Contarini to use his influence on Eck. The legate agreed to do so, and pointed out to Eck *amorevolmente* that it was unseemly to launch such an attack on the book. The latter had, after all, been laid before them by the Emperor, and in view of the obstinacy of the Protestants it was understandable that he preferred it to the *Confession*. He had, finally, only submitted it for their scrutiny. On the particular points, such as Eck's fear that behind the description of Christ as the 'causa subefficiens', of God, on the other hand, as the 'causa efficiens' of our salvation lurked the Arian error, Contarini was able to set his mind at rest. The definition, he explained, referred to the humanity of Christ, and in this sense had ample precedent. He met and convinced Eck therefore on the level of scholarship. It was, as Dittrich says, 'no small achievement' on the part of the legate, for from this time on Eck behaved considerably more reasonably.[21]

The satisfaction of the Imperial Court at this turn of events was evidenced by the instruction which Granvelle gave at this point to the three Catholics to confer with the legate daily for a theological briefing prior to meeting with the Protestants. Any independent action by Eck would thus, it was hoped, be rendered impossible. The interests of 'moderation' were championed by the closest working alliance between the representatives of Papacy and Emperor.

Morone comments on this satisfaction with the 'goodness, sagacity, and learning' of the legate, and the total dependence of the three Catholics on Contarini.[22] He was particularly critical of Eck.

---

session. *CR* iv. 338. The aim was probably to prevent as far as possible an intervention on the part of Luther or the Elector in the form of a critique of the book. He made of course no attempt to hinder the representatives from informing their prince of the course of events at Regensburg. Ibid., pp. 255–6.

[21] D/B, p. 611. Melanchthon, who had hoped (*CR* iv. 186) that the accustomed vehemence of Eck would speedily bring the burdensome negotiations to an abrupt end, noted the change. 'Essemus iam tota hac molestia liberati, si Eccius suo more pugnaret; sed seu collegae seu alii eius impetum moderantur.' *CR* iv. 239.

[22] Similarly Negri: 'Il Rmo legato si sta con li suoi theologi, il Mro sacri palazzi, il Cocleo, il Pighio, l'Ecchio, Groppero etc. et instruit aciem da buono capitano; omnia credit, omnia sperat, omnia sustinet.' Negri/Bishop of Corfu, 27 Apr. 1541, *ZKG* iii. 635.

The latter, confident in his powers of memory and intelligence, proud of his leading role against the heretics in the past, and full of hate for the Protestants, had hoped to be the leading personality at Regensburg, although, because of his unnecessary contentiousness, this would have been palatable to no one.[23]

This success of Contarini in winning over Eck even led Morone —by an interesting train of thought—to the hope that he might have equal success with the Protestants so that they would come eventually to a recognition of his status as legate by way of an appreciation of his personal qualities. Such gleams of hope convinced him that the colloquy must be furthered with all energy. He strongly opposed the intention of the Bavarians to withdraw Eck from the colloquy.[24]

Eck, as the sole champion of the intransigents, thus found himself in an impossible position. Not only was he quite isolated among the collocutors themselves, but Granvelle's success in gaining Contarini's agreement to the exclusion of Pighius and Wauchop[25] from the preliminary conferences—in which, apart from the legate and the nuncio, only Badia was to be allowed to confer with the three Catholics—meant that he was there also in a hopeless minority of one.

The first of the conferences on the morning of 28 April showed how unenviable his position was. The doctrine of justification was discussed. Eck's obduracy only lost him something of his reputation in the eyes both of Badia and of Contarini, and got him nowhere. It was probably at this meeting that the ground for the most significant achievement of the colloquy—the agreement on the question of justification—began to be laid. Gropper,[26] Badia, and Contarini were all agreed on the issue, and the Catholics generally appear to have been hopeful of agreement with the Protestants on this point.[27]

The discussion of the book was now going steadily ahead. At

---

[23] *HJ* iv. 449, 454.

[24] Morone saw that if Eck were allowed to leave it could later be claimed that all the others were Lutherans and therefore their deliberations worthless. *HJ* iv. 449–50.

[25] To the understandable disgust of the two concerned. Contarini accepted Granvelle's judgement that Pighius was unsuitable. The Scot was rejected on the grounds of his garrulity at Worms. *HJ* i. 371.

[26] Not Poggio, as it stands in the text, *HJ* i. 371, Cf. D/B, p. 612, *Anm.* 1. The text here is very corrupt.

[27] Thus Francesco Contarini/Venice, 28 Apr. 1441, D/R, p. 174.

first—on 27 April—all went well. The pressures of time, the reluctance to show undue obduracy at this early stage, the fact that the first articles—on the state of man before the Fall, the freedom of the will, the cause of sin, and on original sin—were all briefly and unpolemically formulated, all contributed to the speedy progress.[28] Melanchthon and Eck swallowed, for the moment at least, any doubts they had[29] and although neither side was fully content[30] the differences were evidently not felt to be great enough to justify a serious conflict at this point. All were well aware that it was on the fifth article—that on justification—that the real differences could be expected to come out into the open.

From 28 April to 2 May came the dramatic discussions on article five—*de iustificatione hominis*. The secrecy in which all was shrouded at the time, and the apologetic motives which coloured all later representations make an exact reconstruction of these negotiations difficult. The main outline, however, is clear enough.

Neither Eck nor Melanchthon was disposed to tolerate the long-winded and highly ambiguous article which stood in the book.[31] Unlike Contarini, who had been content with making occasional amendments, they demanded that the book be laid aside altogether and free discussion on the nature of justification allowed between the two parties. Both hoped that they would thus be rid of the book for good. This must have been a surprise move on the part of Eck. We have no hint that even the possibility of departing from the book had been contemplated in the morning

[28] 'De his locis', wrote Melanchthon, 'nunc quidem rixae nullae fuerunt.' *CR* iv. 332.

[29] e.g. Melanchthon: '. . . und wiewohl sie im guten Verstande mögen hingehen, so habe ich doch nicht klein Missfallen gehabt, dass der Meister der Buchs, wo er das Unsre zulässet, doch also dunkel redet und verstreicht, dass es wenig scheinet . . . Nun habe ich Geduld gehabt, das man nicht sagte, ich wollte die Handlung ohne grosse Ursache umstossen.' Ibid., p. 240.

[30] 'Als hat man solch Buch vor die Hand genommen, und die vordern Artikel, bis auf den Artikel der Justification gelesen, aber nicht darinne geschlossen; denn Doctor Eck hat etliche Punkte angefochten, so haben es die unsern auch nicht allenthalben approbirt, darum es also hangend blieben, und der Artikel von der Justification vorgenommen . . .' Saxon Councillors/Elector, 5 May 1541, ibid., p. 254.

[31] Cf. Melanchthon's account: 'Und da wir in den Artikel von der Justification kommen, fochten wir beide, Eck und ich das Buch zugleich an, wie es auch sehr ungereimt Ding zusammen gerafft hat . . .' *CR* iv. 581. Then, 'Ist . . . bedacht worden, man sollte das Buch liegen lassen, und frei von der Sache reden, und so man eins würde, sollte man einen Artikel stellen.' Ibid., p. 420; cf. p. 332.

conference with the legate. Eck's deference to the latter should, therefore, not be overestimated.

In the face of this formidable alliance between Eck and Melanchthon Granvelle had to capitulate, and the book was set aside. Accounts differ as to whether in the subsequent debate the first draft to be laid before the collocutors came from Melanchthon or from the Catholic side.[32] It is in the last resort immaterial. Probably, however, Melanchthon opened with a summary statement of the Protestant position. The Catholics took exception to its terminology and it was therefore rejected. Then the Protestants in turn rejected on 29 April the Catholic draft.[33] An attempt on the part of the legate to intervene with an amended version of his own met with a derisive reception from the no doubt overwrought Melanchthon.

Melanchthon's assertion that the Catholics were visibly ashamed of their legate's intervention will be an exaggeration.[34] It could, however, point to some sign of open dissatisfaction on Eck's part. Brieger's suggestion that Contarini's draft formula referred only to the special point of certainty of justification is not without a certain probability.[35] It is highly unlikely that the legate would have attempted to draw up a complete new draft of the article himself. In view of his close collaboration with the Catholic collocutors this was unnecessary and would have been tactically unwise. A personal intervention on a particular point, on the other hand, could well have recommended itself to Contarini, though it was of course contrary to the spirit and to the letter of his instruction. An intervention of this sort could have been construed later as implying papal approval of, or commitment to, the outcome of the colloquy.

In any case Contarini's action brought matters no further. The collocutors returned to the Catholic draft, and a fierce tussle now ensued within the two parties. Melanchthon took the chance to

---

[32] According to the report of the Saxon representatives the first draft was put forward by the Catholics. *CR* iv. 254. Melanchthon's short report of 30 Apr. would seem to indicate the opposite. Ibid., p. 239. Also Cruciger's (somewhat tendentious) account, which ascribes the first Catholic formula to Contarini, probably confusing it with the later intervention by the legate. *CR* iv. 252.

[33] Eck then appears to have proposed a formula of his own. Melanchthon: 'Nostras formulas amplecti metuit [i.e. Eck] ac nunc de ipsius formula rixamur. Heri totam formulam ipsorum repudiaram, sed ita corrigunt, ut nos abrumpere negotium non sinant.' Melanchthon/Luther, 30 Apr. 1541, *CR* iv. 239.

[34] *CR* iv. 306, 582.   [35] *Pace* Vetter, p. 92, *Anm.* 2.

advocate openly the breaking off of negotiations. It would be better, he argued, for the Protestants to act now than to allow themselves to be entangled in the still more hateful articles that lay ahead. The blame for the collapse of the negotiations could easily be shrugged off onto Eck.[36] Bucer, however, supported by Sturm, reiterated his familiar argument that an acceptance of the Protestant doctrine of justification by the Catholics would be a great advance, paving the way for further reforms within the Catholic camp. As a hopeful sign they pointed to the fact that the standpoint represented by Gropper and Pflug was markedly more liberal than that of Eck. They did not hesitate to accuse Melanchthon of deliberately trying to sabotage the colloquy at the behest of his Elector. Melanchthon was forced to give way and the dispute continued. Gropper and Pflug, manifestly with the backing of the legate, allowed the Protestants to amend the Catholic draft so radically that nothing remained in it which they found incompatible with the Augsburg Confession.[37] Agreement on the doctrine of justification had been achieved!

Granvelle himself—a final histrionic touch—wrote out the agreed version of the article in his own hand, and sealed his triumph by managing to wrench even from the reluctant Eck an eventual, grudging consent.[38] It had been a great triumph for his diplomacy. How, however, would the theologians react? And how the world outside Regensburg?

The article is certainly a product of diplomacy, yet it is by no means lacking in theological substance. It is a finely balanced piece of conciliation, but it exhibits an integrity all its own. It falls outside the confessional categories certainly; its language, however, is that of conviction, not caution. It is no mere mediatorial formula, offering a crumb of theological comfort to every grouping. It

---

[36] *CR* iv. 420.

[37] In their report to the Elector the Saxon councillors refer to it as a formula which was '. . . von den Theologen dieses Theils in der Substantz mit nichten der Confession und Apologia zuwider oder ungemäss geachtet wirdet, auch an Worten klar genug, dass er zu keinem Missverstand mag gedeutet werden. Und obwohl solcher Artikel etwas kurz und weiter Erklärung bedürftig, so ist doch derselbige in der Confession und Apologia ganz wohl erklärt, welchen man dieses Theils in alleweg vorzubehalten und darinnen nichts zu vergeben bedacht und entschlossen.' Ibid., p. 254.

[38] If we are to believe Peucer he at first refused to append his signature, but was eventually pushed into doing so by Granvelle. Dedication to vol iv. of the *Opp. Melanchthonis*, quoted in D/B, p. 622, *Anm.* 7.

takes up a clear line, and it is because of this uncomfortable clarity, not because of an alleged ambiguity, that it was later rejected by Catholic and Protestant confessionalists.

The two main characteristics of the article are an insistence on the entirely gratuitous character of our justification, and secondly on the impossibility of driving a wedge between faith and love. Everything else follows from these two basic convictions.[39]

Hence it is not particularly helpful to extrapolate from the article its 'Protestant' elements on the one hand, e.g. the description of faith as confidence (*fiducia*), and the phrase 'imputation of righteousness', or its 'Catholic' elements on the other hand, e.g. the description of faith as 'active in love' or the term 'inherent righteousness'. The article should be judged rather as an attempt to provide a statement of the essential Christian beliefs on justification while leaving ample room for a continuing theological debate on the knottier issues.

The whole point, for example, of its much abused distinction between the two types of righteousness, imputed and inherent, is to exclude specifically the possibility that any virtues which we may possess can merit our justification, while avoiding the dangers of moral indifferentism. Similarly, while establishing the principle that the penitent believer can be certain of his forgiveness it does not regard a lapse from this certainty as a necessary indication that he has fallen from grace. Likewise good works are commended and promised their due reward but, in Augustinian terms, '. . . not according to the substance of the works nor in so far as they are our doing, but to the degree that they flow from faith, and are the doing of the Holy Spirit . . .'

There is no prevarication or self-contradiction here. Of course many points are left open, but this, after all, was the aim of the whole exercise: to take a firm stand where it was necessary, but for the rest to have the courage and the tolerance to let discussion proceed.

The reaction among the Protestants in Regensburg to the agreement was strangely subdued, ranging from cautious expressions of pleasure to stunned disbelief.[40] The incredulity was, after

---

[39] Text in *CR* iv. 198–201.

[40] Dittrich's assertion (D/B, p. 625) that Contarini's 'Dio laudato' also 'filled the breast of many a Protestant' gives a quite misleading impression. His sole authority is a quotation from Cruciger wrenched out of its context. Indeed his whole picture of a sudden outburst of ecumenical cordiality and conviviality on the successful conclusion of the agreement could hardly be more misleading.

all, understandable. Wittenberg and Rome had now been at odds
for two decades. Those who had been young men when the struggle
had begun had by now lived under the shadow of the schism for
the best part of their lives. Those who were now young had never
known anything else but schism. Those who had been of mature
years in 1517 and had experienced something of what a united
Christendom meant were now largely dead.

The schism had lasted too long. It had become something self-
evident, a part of the fabric of life. Men had long since made their
decision between the two possibilities that lay open to them—in
the rare event that such decisions were in their power. In any case
they had become accustomed themselves to the new order of
things. Was it now to be upset overnight by the confabulations of a
few theologians? The wall of distrust from behind which the two
parties now regarded one another, and the vested interests in a
continuation of the *status quo* (in which the economic is only one
of the many factors to be taken into account) made any such dramatic development seem in the highest degree unlikely.

To the Protestants it was as if they had been defrauded by a
confidence trick of their own most precious possession—the
doctrine on justification that was distinctively and characteristi-
cally theirs, and which by a sleight of hand the Catholics were now
appropriating for themselves. For it was generally agreed that there
was nothing in the agreed article to which one could take exception
from the Protestant point of view. It was fully consonant with the
Confession and the *Apology* although the latter were more explicit
and alone could be relied upon for a full statement of the faith.[41]

Calvin wrote to Farel:

You will marvel when you read the copy [of the article on justification]
... that our adversaries have conceded so much. For they have committed themselves to the essentials of what is our true teaching. Nothing
is to be found in it which does not stand in our writings. I know that
you would prefer a more explicit exposition and in this you are at one
with myself. But if you consider with what sort of men we have to
deal, you will acknowledge that a great deal has been achieved.[42]

---

[41] Thus Burckhard, *CR* iv. 256. One of the most friendly reactions, from
Cruciger, noted that the article '... quae etsi non est a nostris composita, sed
utrinque consarcinata, tamen a nostra doctrina, quod discrepet, nihil habet,
quare si haec de quibus inter delectos convenit accipiuntur publico consensu
doctrina nostrarum ecclesiarum approbata et recepta est'. Ibid., p. 259.

[42] Herminjard, vii. 111.

How was this undeniable fact that hitherto unthinkable concessions had here been made by the Catholics to be explained?
Burckhard reacted with the now familiar suspicion that it could
only be a Catholic dodge. The latter could not be sincere in their
avowed desire for reformation. That would be cutting their own
throats, 'for it would be all up with their power if the truth were to
prevail and a pious Christian reformation—to which the Emperor
seems to incline—were to be carried through'. Their aim might
well be to confuse the Protestants with ambiguous formulae;
and hence some of the Protestants would probably not even
accept the agreement on the fifth article until they saw whether
a genuine concord could be attained on the other points. This,
however, was an impossibility.[43] This cautious, waiting attitude
was indeed the general reaction of the Protestants.[44] The apparent 'change of heart' among the Catholics would have to be
put first to the test in the discussion of the other articles before any
one should give way to rejoicing, which at this stage would be premature.

Among the Catholics, on the other hand, apart from Eck, the
reaction was considerably more positive. Even Morone suffered a
temporary relapse into optimism. Melanchthon, it was true, he
wrote to Rome, remained stiff-necked as ever, bound by his mandate from the Elector. In Bucer, however, who was exerting himself to the utmost for the attainment of a concord, Morone set the
highest hopes, believing indeed that he was already regained for
the Church, and was only holding back from an open declaration of
his change of allegiance in order to work more effectively within
the Protestant ranks. With his help, he hoped, Melanchthon's
resistance could be overcome in the difficult negotiations that lay
ahead, as had already happened at Worms on the question of

---

[43] 'Verum non possum mihi persuadere ullo modo, quod de hac tanta causa,
in qua tam multae sunt non verbales sed reales controversiae, tam facile con-
venire possit . . . Sed fortassis vix recipietur hic articulus ab omnibus, nisi
integra fiat concordia, quae est impossibilis.' *CR* iv. 257.

[44] e.g. Cruciger, in whose breast, according to Dittrich, there was room for
nothing but joy. Cruciger does indeed show pleasure at what he interprets as a
victory for the Protestant position. 'Quare, quod faustum foelixque sit et salutare
Ecclesiis, de hoc articulo convenit eatenus, ut ad Caesarem et Principes referatur
et nostri subscribant;' Here, in mid-sentence Dittrich has closed the quotation.
Cruciger, however, continues immediately '. . . subscribant; quod tamen non
existimo prius futurum esse, quam de caeteris articulis certum sit'. Exactly,
in other words, the cautious standpoint of the other Protestants. Ibid., pp. 252–3.

original sin. For Gropper also, Bucer's Catholic counterpart, he had only the highest praise.[45]

Contarini himself greeted the news with a heartfelt 'Dio laudato!' The article, he reported to Farnese, had been adjudged by Badia, Cochlaeus, Morone, and himself, with the three Catholic collocutors, to be 'cattolica et santa'. No mention, as Dittrich points out, of the differences of opinion within the Catholic camp.[46] In his concern to win the consent of Rome the legate did not shrink from giving what amounted to a false picture of the situation at Regensburg. With his report went a copy of the article, and a renewed plea for the need for the greatest of secrecy, in view of attempts from Italy, of which Granvelle had news, to disturb the work of reunion.[47]

A further attempt to gain backing among his friends in Italy for the agreement was his sending of a further copy, again with the strictest injunction to secrecy, to his friend Ercole Gonzaga, the Archbishop of Mantua. He asked him to show it to Cortese and Messer Angelo, his own theological adviser (and to none other), and to inform him with all speed of their judgement upon it. He enclosed an explanation on two of the points which he considered most controversial.[48]

How far, then had Contarini contributed to the achievement of the agreement on the fifth article? His moderating influence on Eck, his approval of Gropper's mediatorial work, his excellent relations with Granvelle we have already noted.

As far as the Protestants were concerned Contarini had begun to break down some of the distrust with which any representative of the Papacy had automatically to contend. Even to have attained the point, as he himself put it, where he was '. . . not ill regarded by the Protestants'[49] was in this context a considerable achievement. Concrete evidence of the new atmosphere was the visit of Johann Sturm to the legate which, however—since the legate did not think it opportune—did not deal with the theological controversies. It ended, all the same, on the friendliest of terms, Sturm showing the legate all due reverence and resolving, as Contarini heard afterwards from Wauchop, to repeat the visit at a later

[45] *HJ* iv. 453–4; similarly Contarini, *HJ* i. 374.   [46] D/B, p. 620.
[47] *HJ* i. 371–2.
[48] Contarini/Archbishop of Mantua, 3 May 1541, D/R, pp. 324–5.
[49] '. . . non mal visto da protestanti.' Contarini/Dandino, 1 May 1541, D/R, p. 323.

opportunity.[50] Equally cordial was a meeting arranged by Veltwyck with Bucer in which the latter responded to Contarini's
exhortation to do all in his power to promote concord in a way
which filled the legate with the highest hopes. Bucer also, he
thought, would be repeating his visit.[51]

A further initiative on the part of the legate was the sending of
his greetings to the Elector of Brandenburg, after an initial sound-
ing of his relation, the Cardinal of Mainz. Joachim received
Contarini's emissaries with great courtesy and replied with a
lengthy profession of his desire for an end to the religious discord.
Contarini drew in particular the attention of Farnese to the fact
that the Elector had addressed him in his reply as 'the legate sent by
our most reverend lord Paul III', for this seemed firm evidence that
these friendly contacts were bearing the desired fruit—a more
amenable temper on the part of the Protestants.[52] A picturesque
touch was added by the Elector sending his instrumentalists to
serenade the cardinal, for which Contarini did not fail to express
his cordial thanks.

The significance of all this activity one should neither overestimate nor underestimate. Morone had already conducted personal conversations with Sturm, Bucer, and Melanchthon in
Worms. In itself, that was nothing new. Nor can the so frequently
cited remark of Jacob Sturm that five or six papal councillors of
the stamp of Contarini would be enough to persuade him to abandon any doubts as to the correctness of the papal decrees be taken
with such gospel seriousness.[53] One can, moreover, ask oneself
what Bucer thought of Contarini's promise that his efforts in the
interests of reunion would gain for him the gratitude not only of
God but of the Pope and the Emperor. For the Strasbourg reformer
such co-operation of God, Pope, and Emperor was not perhaps
quite such a self-evident proposition as for the legate. The world
in which Contarini moved was truly a very different one from that

[50] Contarini/Farnese, 3 May 1541, *HJ* i. 373.

[51] Contarini makes no mention of Bucer's remark, reported by Beccadelli, that
there was fault on both sides, the Protestants having defended many things too
stubbornly, the Catholics having left many abuses uncorrected. Morandi, I. ii.
34. He may have feared that the Curia would take this amiss. Cf. D/B, p. 617,
Anm. 2.

[52] '. . . il che ho voluto significare a V. Sig. Rev*ma.* perchè vegga come questi
animi danno qualche segno di humiliarsi, il che a Dio piaccia segua in effetto.'
HJ i. 374.

[53] Morandi, I. ii. 35.

of the German Protestants, and personal contacts, however friendly, would have to reach a much deeper level if the cultural, not to speak of the theological gap were to be bridged.

On Melanchthon he had totally failed to make any impression, or if anything, only a negative one. The cloistered seclusion of the latter, and his almost neurotic fear of the subtleties of Roman and imperial diplomacy kept the two men apart. They never met. This in itself points to the superficiality of the encounter between the two sides at Regensburg. Special circumstances, of course, played a role in Melanchthon's case. Calvin, however, was equally sceptical. He does not spare us the cheapest of polemic against the legate[54] and apparently believed that the latter was opposed to any genuine discussion and that the support for it which he professed was only a sham. The aim of the papal representatives, he argued, remained now as before the reduction of the Protestants. Contarini only differed from his predecessors in preferring this, if possible, to be a bloodless business. Which, of course, was not without a certain element of truth.

The truth is that, at best, Contarini's tentative gestures of friendship in the direction of the Protestants were only a modest step forward. Foundations had been laid on which, given time, a structure of confidence and goodwill could have been gradually built up. The dialogue at Regensburg, however, never reached any depth. To ask whether, given more favourable circumstances, it could ever have done so is to speculate. We can only observe that even from the modest beginnings that were made the practical and psychological conditions had been created in which a breakthrough on the question of justification became possible. On the human level, Contarini's achievement at Regensburg was not inconsiderable, especially when we bear in mind how minimal his actual potentialities for action were, how limited his room for manœuvre, how pessimistically the chances of success had been adjudged. For a moment of time divided Christendom had seen a flickering of hope. The visitation was brief. Its fascination remains.

[54] 'Contarenus Cardinalis [adest] pro suo pontifice: qui nobis primo ingressu tot cruces aspersit, ut biduo post brachium illi ex fatigatione laborasse arbitrer . . .' Calvin/Farel, 29 Mar. 1541, Herminjard, vii. 58.

9

On the Authority of the Church in the Interpretation of Scripture

THE success of the colloquy thus far had been pre-eminently Contarini's success.[1] Yet ultimately the colloquy was to fail. Should not this final failure also be laid at the door of the legate?

Contarini had come to Regensburg with a twofold aim: to restore the unity of the Church and to defend the inviolability of the Catholic faith and the interests of the Papacy. The success of his mission rested on the presumption of the compatibility of these two aims. At no point had he entertained the idea of purchasing unity at the cost of 'the truth'.[2] The agreement on the article on justification had only been acceptable to him because he believed in its genuine Catholicism.

If, in the negotiations which followed, his attitude appeared to undergo an abrupt change this was, in fact, not the case. He remained as concerned for unity as ever he had been. What had changed, however, was his conviction that agreement was possible without a sacrifice of the orthodox position, that his ecumenism need not endanger his Catholicism. His two aims no longer appeared to be compatible.

We can, and indeed must, attribute to Contarini part of the responsibility for the failure of the colloquy. This is, however, only another way of saying that his concern for 'Catholicism' was as passionate as that for 'unity'. The point at issue here is what he

[1] Others had, of course, played their part—Gropper, Bucer, and not least Granvelle—yet without the lead given by the legate, their efforts would have had little hope of succeeding.

[2] 'Et come per l'altre mie scrissi a V.S., quella li faccia pur ampia fede per mio nome, ch'io sto con l'occhio aperto et mai non consentiro a cosa, che non sia in honor di Dio et della sua santa fede, ne N.S. mi ha mandato qui ad altro effetto se non per questo.' Contarini/Dandino, 1 May 1541, D/R, p. 323.

understood by this 'Catholicism'. As we have already seen it was an understanding flexible enough to permit the acceptance of a statement on justification which satisfied many Protestants. Where, however, did this flexibility find its limit? At what point did Contarini come to believe that the substance of Catholicism was threatened? The following two chapters will attempt an answer to this question.

Agreement having been reached on justification, discussion proceeded on 3 May to the next section of the Regensburg Book,[3] that dealing with the Church. Article VI dealt with the 'notes' of the Church and its authority, Article VII with the 'note of the Word' (*de nota Verbi*), Article IX[4] dealt with the authority of the Church in regard to Scripture.

Predictably, Article IX gave most trouble.[5] The others occasioned little dispute, being drafted in general and conciliatory terms.[6] The reference in Article VI to the damnation of heretics and schismatics did arouse a certain amount of unrest among the Protestants, though it could, of course, be interpreted in different ways.[7] In general the Protestants were, if not content with these articles, at least ready to postpone open dissent until the discussion of the ninth article. Accordingly, it was soon possible to dispose of

[3] Or rather returned to the book again. Both Melanchthon and Eck had argued for a continuation of the previous free discussion. Cf. Melanchthon's report: 'Da wir von diesem Artikel [i.e. on justification] kommen meineten Eck und ich, wir sollten nun des Buchs lose seyn, und nach Ordnung der Confessio fortschreiten. Aber Granvel wollt haben, dass wir das Buch wiederum vor die Hand nehmen sollten. Dazu trieben auch Groperus und Bucerus, sagten, dieses wäre der bequemste Weg zu handeln und zur Concordia.' *CR* iv. 582. Apparently Pistorius supported Melanchthon. Ibid., p. 441.

[4] Article VIII, apparently out of place here, asserted, against the Novatians and the Cathari, the need for 'poenitentia post lapsum' to deal with mortal as well as venial sin. Le Plat, iii. 20–2; *CR* iv. 205–8.

[5] 'Hora trattano l'articulo de Ecclesia nel quale gli adversarii sin qui non vogliono admettere l'autorità delli concilii, come doverebbono.' Morone/ Farnese, 3 May 1541, *HJ* iv. 545, quoted in D/B, p. 628, *Anm.* 2.

[6] Cf. the reports of Pistorius and Melanchthon in *CR* iv. 441, 582; also the comment of the Zürich theologian Rudolf Walthart: 'Darnach hat man das buch wider lesen müssen in folgenden artiklen, von der kirchen, von der kirchenzeichen, nemlich von Gottes wort hat man passieren lassen, dann es sind generalia gewesen, die nit besonder zu streiten, dann sy in ires wesen selb christlicher liebe nit entgegen sind.' *Zeitschrift für Schweizer. Kg.* xxviii. 99.

[7] Melanchthon comments: 'Res in genere dicitur, ne nobis contradicere liceret, sed tela ex insidiis emissa haereret in nobis.' *CR* iv. 414. Concerning this point the Protestant Estates remarked in July: 'Quod autem damnat idem articulus eos, qui discedunt a recte docentibus.' Ibid., p. 487.

them, and on the same day, 3 May, discussion could move on to Article IX.

This handled the questions of the interpretation of Scripture and the authority of the Councils with great restraint.[8] There was no trace of anti-Protestant polemic or of an exaggerated *theologia gloriae*. The treatment was predominantly historical. Both Scripture and the authority of the Church in regard to it were interpreted as divine ordinances to prevent the distortion of the original tradition. The Church was given authority to determine the canon and the true understanding of Scripture. It was not claimed that the Church stood above Scripture, and indeed Scripture was ranked far above any human authority.[9] It was futile, the article argued, to dispute whether Church or Scripture had the greater authority, for both were directed and inspired by the one Holy Spirit, working in both through the instrumentality of men.

Further, many doctrines—those of the Trinity and of the Person of Christ—were implicit rather than explicit in the Scriptures. The latter needed interpretation, the Church's interpretation. One might have expected a reference here to the teaching office of the Papacy, but there is at least no direct mention of this. The stress was laid instead on the whole Church, the consensus of all believers as against the individual Christian. It was this consensus which was recorded in the first councils and orthodox Christian writers of every age; the decrees of the first ecumenical councils in particular, in so far as they refer to the dogmas which are necessary for salvation, were infallible.

So much for the content of the article. It will hardly be denied that, if the 'Catholic' position were to be retained at all, it could not have been framed in a more conciliatory manner. Yet it met with the instant and vehement opposition of Melanchthon. It could scarcely have been otherwise.

True, in deference to the expected Protestant objections, nothing had been said about the mystical or—in contemporary thought closely allied[10]—the hierarchical nature of the Church. Was, however, the organic, corporate understanding of the Church,

---

[8] Text in *CR* iv. 208–12.

[9] Note the ambiguity. It was a matter of dispute whether the Church was, in fact, a human authority in this sense.

[10] Note the recurrent mention of the mystic writing *De ecclesiae hierarchica* of Dionysius the Areopagite in the Catholic writing of this period.

the stress—so typical of Gropper—on the historical continuities, really any more acceptable? It was all more than vaguely disquieting to Protestant ears, accustomed to the note of the Church 'under the Word'.

Disquiet became, however, implacable opposition at the point where concreteness could no longer be avoided—on the question of the infallible authority of the orthodox Councils. The assertion of this was only the logical consequence of Gropper's whole doctrine of the Church. Any system of thought which understands the integrity or orthodoxy of the faith in terms of an ideological continuity must necessarily posit infallible instances, or at least an infallible instance whose decisions ground and constitute that continuity. In Gropper's thought—for all the freedom his positive theology and critical scholarship accorded him—the Word was bound not only to Scripture but also to the dogmatic tradition of the Church. The alternative 'Church under Scripture' or 'Scripture under Church' became here abruptly actual.

Bucer, in accepting the article originally, had apparently not seen this, and at Regensburg too, he argued for the acceptance of this article.[11] His attempts, however, to gloss over the differences do him no credit. To Melanchthon, on the other hand, assent here would have been a betrayal of his conscience, and of the truth itself.[12] As he saw it, a concession on this issue would have meant a capitulation all the way along the line, in effect a surrender of the whole Lutheran position.

If the principle of *sola scriptura*, with its ultimate basis in the absolute polarity of the divine will and human 'traditions' were sacrificed, the whole Protestant front could be rolled back and Catholic faith and practice defended at every critical point. Here there could be no retreat. Since, however, this applied equally to the Catholics, deadlock seemed imminent and the whole colloquy threatened to grind to a halt. For the moment a tactical rescue operation by the politicians saved the day.

Granvelle tried at first—a grotesque irrelevancy—to urge

---

[11] Melanchthon's reference to 'mein Gesell' who 'mir den Artikel viel glossiren wollt' is obviously a reference to Bucer. *CR* iv. 582.

[12] 'Denn sich die Theologen dieses Theils standhaftig und wohl bis anhero gehalten, und insonderheit hat sich Magister Philippus auch in Gegenwärtigkeit der verordneten Theologen und der andern vernehmen lassen, dass er eher sterben, denn ichts wider sein Gewissen und Wahrheit einräumen wollte . . .' Saxon Councillors/Elector, 5 May 1541, ibid., p. 255

Melanchthon to read the articles 'more industriously'. The discussions had led nowhere, he seemed to be indicating, because Melanchthon had not properly digested the content of the article. Indignant at the imputation that he had been neglecting his homework, Melanchthon retorted that he had studied the book thoroughly both in Wittenberg and in Regensburg. He was neither willing nor able to approve of the articles, and that was an end to it.[13]

Count Frederick of the Palatinate, the other President, then proposed that the Protestant collocutors submit their own views in an irenic alternative or counter-draft and this was duly presented.[14]

Like the original article this Protestant draft was unpolemical, and went far to meet the Catholic position. Not only was the interpretative role of the Church readily admitted. As far as its authority in determining the limits of the canon were concerned, the Protestants could say in conscious continuity with Augustine, 'Evangelio non crederem, nisi me ecclesiae catholicae commoveret auctoritas'. Further they agreed that the true understanding of Scripture was to be found in the Church alone.

On the other hand, however, they protested that this gift of interpretation was not bound to particular persons or places, but pertained to those pious men whose teachings were at one with the testimonies of Scripture and the general consensus of the Church.[15] Authority was not bound to office.

It was true that the Church had also to decide on doctrinal matters. While, however, the witness of the early Church, derived as it was ultimately from the apostles, could be a guide here, the final authority must always be the Word of God. The Councils must be obeyed where they had interpreted the Word of God aright, but there had also been synods—such as that of Sirmium—which had erred. On historical, therefore, as well as theological grounds the infallibility of the Councils and of the early Church Fathers could not be accepted.

The new Protestant article brought the two sides no closer to one another, and Granvelle, seeing that a prolongation of the discussion at this stage would only mean that the two sides entrenched

[13] Ibid., p. 582; similarly Cruciger pp. 253, 432–3.
[14] Ibid., pp. 583–4; text of counter-article, ibid., pp. 349–52.
[15] Ibid., pp. 350–1.

themselves even more deeply behind their established positions, reluctantly decided to postpone the settlement of the conflict to the end of the colloquy. According to Melanchthon he did not want it said that the colloquy had foundered on the attitude of the Catholics to the Councils.[16]

Contarini does not seem to have been aware of the gravity of this failure to come to terms on the nature of the Church. He could make the strange statement that on the whole agreement had been reached, and only on the question of the infallibility of the Councils in the interpretation of Scripture did differences remain.[17] Is this a hangover from the euphoria about Article V?

Melanchthon, on the other hand, saw it as portending the collapse of the colloquy[18] and in retrospect we must admit that his judgement was the better. On the question of authority neither side would surrender, and neither the urgent desire for an accommodation, nor the common respect for the Church's patristic heritage, could bridge the chasm. The parting of the ways had already been reached—only three days after the agreement on justification. The postponement of the issue may have been politic; theologically it was a confession of bankruptcy. From now on the advocates of reunion would be in the invidious position of having to paper over the ominous cracks that were beginning to appear, but which had not been squarely faced. The evasion of the issue of authority had already settled the doom of the colloquy. The later debate on transubstantiation would only provide the occasion for its demise.

The uncertainty in the Catholic camp on the question of authority may well have contributed to the decision to postpone its discussion for the moment. Contarini had, of course, accepted the formulation of Article IX about the infallibility of the Councils. He was, however, only too well aware that this was a disputed point among Catholic theologians. Pighius for example argued that the Papacy was the sole infallible instance, and that the Councils were not infallible. Contarini, while himself inclined to the anti-Parisian school, which placed the Pope above the Councils, felt it

---

[16] 'Dieweil wir unverglichen blieben, und Granvel sahe, dass sie wenig Glimpfs haben würden, so man sagt [sagen würde] dass sich die Handlung in diesem Streit von den Concilien gestossen: haben sie eine Höflikeit geübet, gesagt, man soll diese materia suspendiren, und fort schreiten.' Ibid., p. 583.

[17] Contarini/Farnese, 4 May 1541, *HJ* i. 375.

[18] 'Hic sperabam finem totius actionis fore . . .' *CR* iv. 414.

would be the part of wisdom to avoid too close a definition of this theoretical point.[19]

These differences were, of course, of quite secondary importance to those with the Protestants, who rejected any infallibility of the Church, whether attributed to Councils or to Pope. However, it would be embarrassing if in the attempt to prove the historical validity of this infallibility, the differences within the Catholic camp should come to light. The historical arguments (Sirmium) used by the Protestants had a startling resemblance to those which Pighius himself had brought to play.[20]

Certainly Contarini's hesitation here prevented him from coming forward with any initiative of his own. He had to rest content that the Catholic theologians had rebutted the Protestant errors. Above all, Contarini was concerned—with German Catholicism in its present state and the *mana* of the Papacy at a nadir—to avoid a discussion on the authority of the Roman See. Although Article IX had side-stepped this point, the precision of the differences which a longer debate would have brought about must inevitably have raised it. It followed on logically from the question of the authority of the Councils and, indeed, Eck suggested that the collocutors should now occupy themselves with the Papacy,[21] instead of with the sacraments. The legate firmly resisted this suggestion.

It would, he believed, almost of necessity lead to the total breakdown of the discussions. If the colloquy were to fail, 'quod Deus avertat', let it be on the nature of the sacraments rather than on the Papacy, for it would be disastrous for the papal cause in Germany if the colloquy were to founder precisely on the question of Rome's authority.[22] It would be better to tackle the other less contro-

---

[19] Contarini/Farnese, 9 May 1541, *HJ* i. 379–81; for Pighius cf. Walter Friedensburg, 'Beiträge zum Briefwechsel der katholischen Gelehrten Deutschlands', *ZKG* xxiii. 110–55; esp. p. 144: 'Stupendum profesto est quam absurda invenerimus etiam nostrorum theologorum, quos Parisensis nobis schola subministravit, his in rebus judicia, eorum presertim quos Cesar magnis alit et ditavit stipendiis et facit maximi, ut in multis iisque precipuis adversariorum non paulo quam illorum tolerabilior sit sententia.' Cochlaeus was also impressed by Pighius's arguments, but felt that his book, *Hierarchiae Ecclesiasticae Assertio*, had appeared at an unpropitious time. Cochlaeus/Morone, 12 Jan. 1538, *ZKG* xviii. 279–80.

[20] Cf. Vetter, p. 111.

[21] Contarini/Farnese, 9 May 1541, D/R, p. 179.

[22] Morone believed that this was what the Protestants were hoping for. Morone/Farnese, 9 May 1541, *HJ* iv. 459.

versial articles first, for if agreement were reached on them the chances of the Protestants accepting papal authority would be greater.[23]

In a sense this was, again, only a postponement of the evil day, and yet Contarini had done well to avoid a discussion. With the Catholic camp split, there was no telling what the outcome of a debate about the Primacy at such a time, in such a situation, would have been. Certainly claims to papal infallibility would have been swept aside by many a Catholic; if, however, other Catholics doubted conciliar infallibility the Protestants could have asked very pointedly: just where did the infallibility of the Church lie?

To say the least the Protestants would have been in a strong bargaining position. Rome, the one-time symbol of the unity of the Church, could have been represented as a stumbling-block in the way of recovery of unity. Not a few would have been willing to purchase that unity at the expense of papal claims and powers.

What, however, the German Catholics had to say about the Papacy never came to utterance. Since the Catholic theologians at Regensburg were not in a position to define their views exactly, neither side emerged from its established position, and the debate had to be broken off prematurely. A debate comparable with that on justification could not develop. A descent into detail would have embarrassed the Catholics, while a continued tussle on the level of general principles could only lose time and exasperate the Protestants. Contarini was left little choice but to agree to the suspension of the debate on 4 May, and a transition to the question of the sacraments.

[23] Contarini/Farnese, 9 May 1541, *HJ* i. 376.

No Compromising of the Truth

THE turning-point of the Regensburg colloquy was the failure to reach agreement on the nature of the Church; the death blow was given by the controversy over transubstantiation. This was really most surprising. Why should the boundary between the confessions have been drawn at this particular point? Was this not a relatively new dogma, promulgated as recently as 1215 at the Fourth Lateran Council, and one pertaining to the realm of scholastic theory rather than to the substance of the Faith? It seems decidely out of character that Contarini should dig in his feet on this particular issue, especially when he knew that the success or failure of the colloquy depended on his attitude. It seems ironic that the ecumenical endeavours of the sixteenth century should have foundered on a teaching which today seems to be dropping slowly but steadily below the Catholic horizon.

We would do well, however, to avoid a premature judgement that the sixteenth-century theologians had sadly misread their priorities. The controversy about transubstantiation at Regensburg was genuine enough. To understand its crucial role we must see it in the context both of the doctrinal discussions which preceded it and of the non-theological factors at play in the situation. In the last resort the transubstantiation debate was concerned not with words or theories but with the nature of authority in the Church and with the right and indeed obligation of the Church—whatever the unfortunate political consequences—to be content with nothing less than the truth. This, at least, was the conviction of Contarini.

The discussion of the sacraments began on 4 May. At first, all went harmoniously. Agreement was reached on Article X, an exceedingly innocuous little discussion of the sacraments in general.[1] Based on the Augustinian distinction between *res* and

---

[1] *CR* iv. 212–13.

signum it managed to avoid every controversial point.[2] It comes as a perhaps salutary surprise to see that there were points about the sacraments on which Protestants and Catholics still agreed.

Even more surprisingly, agreement was also reached about the sacrament of ordination, as explained in Article XI.[3] Lest individuals should arbitrarily take the preaching of the Gospel into their own hands, it explained, God had established a certain order. In this way any uncertainty about the truth, any vaunting of the personality above the office, would be avoided. This power of ordination, and indeed this order was a sacrament.[4] The 'word' of the sacrament was Christ's command to preach and baptize, its 'element' the laying on of hands, its 'power' (*vis*) embraced the *potestas ordinis*—the ministry of the Word, the administration of the sacraments, and the governing of the Churches—and the *potestas jurisdictionis*—the power of binding and loosing. In the final paragraph a distinction was made between the four principal sacraments: baptism, ordination, the Eucharist, and absolution 'sine quibus Ecclesia non consistit' and those which, though sacred symbols and useful for strengthening man's infirmity, were not necessary in the same way.

The Protestants were even ready, as Melanchthon had been at Augsburg, to recognize the right of the bishops to ordain the clergy, providing they first took in hand the long-promised programme of reform. As Bucer pointed out, the Protestants did, in any case, regard their pastors as bishops.[5]

The 'moderation' of the Protestants on this question was largely a matter of tactics.[6] We see the same in the following two articles, on baptism and confirmation, to which they also agreed. Melanchthon added a caveat to the effect that he did not accept the dominical institution of confirmation, but, rather than raise controversy over these 'lesser ceremonies', would stipulate only

[2] The number of the sacraments was not specified and the 'opere operato' controversy was avoided. The sacraments are described as 'non signa, ut tantum signent, sed ut sanctificent . . .' Ibid., p. 212.

[3] Ibid., pp. 213–14.

[4] 'Hanc ordinationis vim, atque adeo ordinem esse sacramentum . . .' In Melanchthon's text we read 'ordinem esse sacramentorum'. Ibid., p. 213.

[5] Ibid., p. 422. Contarini understood this to mean that the Protestants conceded to the bishops the right to reordain their clergy. *HJ* i. 376.

[6] Melanchthon explains that they had shown themselves 'ganz gelinde . . .', 'dass man uns nicht Schuld kann geben, wir haben nichts nachgegeben'. *CR* iv. 422.

that the abuses connected with them be abolished.[7] The Protestants, in other words, reluctant to attract the Emperor's wrath for 'obstinacy' on their part, concentrated their fire on a few major articles, and were prepared to let the others slip by, relatively unscathed by their criticism. The next article, however, the fourteenth, which dealt with the Eucharist, was bound to raise controversy, and in fact did.

The discussion of Articles VI–IX on the nature of the Church had lasted one day, that of Articles X–XIII even less. The debates that raged around Article XIV, however, continued for a record nine days, twice as long as the time taken to agree on justification. In view of Granvelle's parsimony in the allocation of time for discussion, this indicates—perhaps better than anything else—how desperately anxious he was to arrive at agreement on this subject. If the colloquy were to have any chance of success at all, agreement simply must be attained.

At no point did the political pressures on the theologians become so overt as here. The failure in the event to reach agreement was, therefore, a signal victory for the theologians at the expense of the statesmen, above all for Melanchthon on the Protestant side, and for Contarini on the Catholic. In the debate on justification the impulse to unity had not lacked a genuinely theological element; now a mediate position was being urged for purely political reasons. Neither Melanchthon nor Contarini, conciliatory as they might be by inclination, could have been expected to give ground under such auspices. We are confronted not by an authentic theological debate—for the critical issues were not really aired—but with a tactical juggling of diplomatic formulae in which considerations of truth and falsehood threatened to become altogether irrelevant.

One is pushed back again to the fundamental question: what was the colloquy meant to achieve; what was the Regensburg Book itself meant to be? Should it represent a confession of faith of purely theological character, or merely a unitary formula, the highest common denominator of agreement possible in the circumstances? Granvelle consistently furthered the latter alternative, a formula which, admittedly, would not clarify all the issues, would leave much unsaid, and satisfy neither side entirely, but yet would provide a workable basis of unity for a joint attack on what

[7] Ibid.

Granvelle regarded as the real problems before Germany—the reform of the Church, restoration of law and order, a united resistance against France and the Turk. Here was truly grandiose, far-seeing thinking. The Emperor's determination to force this statesmanlike programme through was understandable.

And yet, this scheme had one fatal flaw. It assumed that the differences between the confessions, great and bitter though they might be, were not in the last resort fundamental to the Faith itself. They were due either to semantic misunderstandings or to particular doctrinal points which could be 'frozen', or put into suspension until the Council finally met. For the rest it was a matter of setting aside the stubbornness, pride, wilfulness, hate, and fear, the personal antagonism and ambitions which perpetuated the schism. Disunity, to Granvelle, was an indication of the moral immaturity of the theologians, and we will not deny his diagnosis its measure of truth.

At heart, however, it was false. It failed to recognize that Protestantism was in its very essence, by origin and intention and ethos, protest, and protest against the very heart of Catholicism. Protestantism existed to protest. It could only make its peace with the object of its protest by denying its own most inmost being.

The situation was, of course, complicated by the emergence of a reformed or reforming Catholicism, which could not be immediately and unambiguously identified with the traditional object of Protestant protest. If it is true that Protestantism existed to protest, it is equally true that where and when and in so far as its protest had been recognized and met it must cease not only to protest but to exist at all. A Protestantism which has lost this readiness to desist seeks itself alone. Its continued existence can be justified only by the continued and clamant need for protest.

The Protestants at Regensburg believed that such a need was only too distressingly present. The 'reform' the Catholics promised was not radical enough. Despite the irenic language of the Regensburg Book, despite the reform enthusiasm of a Gropper or a Contarini, despite the agreement on justification the Protestants remained suspicious. In the coming few days their suspicions were to be confirmed.

Granvelle's scheme also failed to recognize the impossibility of Catholicism's coming to terms with a movement which threatened to destroy the very bulwarks on which it rested—the authority of tradition and of the bearers of tradition, the priestly mediation of grace, the primacy of the sacramental. If it were not to cut its own throat Catholicism dared not give any ground. For both Catholicism and Protestantism the substance of their self-understanding was at stake. No reason—humane, political, or whatever—could justify to them their yielding here. The stage was set for a head-on collision.

Contarini himself was in no position to avert this. He had, at his very first reading of the book, insisted on the insertion in the article of a reference to transubstantiation.[8] It is not immediately obvious why Contarini should have laid such stress on this point. There were other far more glaring omissions in the article from the point of view of Catholic orthodoxy—the sacrificial nature of the sacrament, the participation of the priest, the communication of habitual grace. On the other hand, the article leaves no doubt as to the true and substantial presence (*vere et substantialiter*) of the body and blood of Christ after the consecration, which is then distributed to the faithful 'sub specie panis et vini'. This formulation neither explicitly affirms nor denies transubstantiation. It would be open to both sides to understand it as they wanted. Possibly, however, Contarini was concerned to avoid any suggestion of doubt in the Catholics' camp about a teaching which had figured so prominently in the interconfessional polemic.[9]

What is clear is that Contarini was not so well informed about the Protestant understanding of the sacraments as he had been on the question of justification. On 9 May he wrote to Farnese that the collocutors had 'entered upon the discussion of the sacraments in which these Protestants have expressed gravely erroneous views and on the question of the holy sacrament of the Eucharist I have been surprised to find the worst errors of all, none of which are to be found in the Augsburg Confession or their Apology'.[10]

It may be significant that even before it came to disagreement about transubstantiation the collocutors had disputed about the reservation of the Host, and its ceremonial circumgestation.[11] The abandonment of the doctrine of transubstantiation would make

---

[8] 'A questa parte de sacrament. altaris, quando io la lessi insieme al Nontio et il Groppero, per quella prima acchiata notai, che in questa parte mancava questa transubstantiazione et la feci aggiungere in margine con circa venti luoghi che coressi . . .' Contarini/Farnese, 9 May 1541, *HJ* i. 377.

[9] Text of the article *CR* iv. 216–17.   [10] *HJ* i. 376.   [11] *CR* iv. 256.

the defence of these practices exceedingly difficult. Contarini's conservatism as far as Catholic practice and ritual were concerned would thus be an added ground for his defence of transubstantiation. The Protestants certainly believed that the aim of their adversaries was to defend their Catholic practice and, above all, their 'idolatrous Masses'.[12]

Even after the first day of discussion doubts were felt on the Protestant side as to whether any further progress in the colloquy would be possible; Burckhard echoed the general view when he opined that a cessation to the proceedings would be 'to the glory of the Evangel'.[13] The 'steadfastness' of Melanchthon, and Philip of Hesse's support for this, found universal favour. If the Catholics remained obstinately by their views a continuation of the discussion would, Cruciger thought, be scarcely possible.[14]

Prior to the discussions, which began on 5 May and were to last until 13 May, the Catholic collocutors had met, as usual, with the legate, together with Veltwyck.[15] Then they gathered again in the evening with Contarini, Morone, and Badia. There 'someone'[16] suggested that it would suffice to declare that Christ was present 'realiter et personaliter', and to defer the other questions to the Council in view of the probable obduracy of the Protestants. This course Contarini rejected at once. The aim of the Catholics must be to stand by the truth, and to arrive at an agreement on the basis of the truth.[17] There was clear testimony to the truth of the doctrine in the words of Christ and Paul, in the interpretation of all the Church's teachers ancient and modern, Greek and Latin, and in the decision of the celebrated Council under Innocent III. Hence he could not tolerate any doubt being cast upon it. If agreement could only be reached by the use of ambiguous formulae

---

[12] Cruciger/Menius, 5 May 1541, 'Scis enim quam mordicus pontificii in omnibus nationibus opinionem illam transsubstantiationis retineant, unde isti abusus adorationis inclusi sacramenti et circumgestationis.' Ibid., p. 259. Similarly Burckhard and the Saxon delegates, ibid., pp. 257, 261.

[13] Ibid., p. 257.　　[14] Ibid., p. 259

[15] Contarini/Farnese, 9 May 1541, *HJ* i. 377. The chronology is not absolutely clear from Contarini's dispatch, but he discusses the meeting and then says 'et cosi partirono da me et il giorno seguente, che fu Venere alli 6, furono insieme li Cattolici et Protestanti ...' Ibid., p. 378. Dittrich sets it in the morning of 5 May, but does not specify when the previous meeting with Veltwyck took place. D/B, pp. 629–30.

[16] Probably Gropper. The suppression of the name is hardly accidental, an attempt to shield the individual from the wrath of the Curia.

[17] 'Di far concordia nella verità,' *HJ* i. 377.

the Catholics must stand by the truth and reject them. Contarini had no doubts either about the truth or about the importance of the doctrine, and his stand evidently convinced the others.[18]

On 6 May the collocutors decided to abandon the discussion of the article in the book, as had been done so successfully in the question of justification, and to seek another basis for agreement. The two parties retired to compose their separate drafts. The Catholic one was laid before Contarini by Pflug and Gropper and found his approval.[19] This much is clear. For the rest, however, we are confronted by a series of riddles. First of all, what was this formula?

If, as Pastor and Vetter suggest,[20] it is the short statement 'De transsubstantiatione'[21] then this merely deepens the mystery for it is scarcely an exposition of the traditional Catholic standpoint. While affirming the real presence, the permissibility of the adoration, and reservation of the sacrament, and of the term 'transubstantiation', it interprets the latter in, to say the least, an unusual way. The bread is still present after the consecration, but as a mystical, supernatural bread.[22] The term 'transubstantiation' is used to define not the mode but only the fact of a mutation. 'Both the ancient and the modern doctors admonish us to abstain from inquiry into the manner in which transubstantiation takes place.'[23] The scholastic explanation of the transaction in terms of substance and accidence has, in fact, been thrown to the winds. The traditional term has been retained but the thought categories are quite different. It can come as no surprise that in the final para-

---

[18] 'Mia riposta fu laudata.' Ibid., p. 378.

[19] 'Dopo lungo tempo, havendo gia desinato, ritornarono da me il Groppero et il Fluch et mi portarono una scrittura fatta fra loro, la quale stava benissimo, onde pensai, che dovessero essere d'accordo.' Ibid.

[20] Vetter suggests that it was composed on 5 May, but all the evidence would point to the afternoon of 6 May. His further comment that Bretschneider offers no evidence for his view that only part of the formula has survived appears to overlook Bretschneider's belief that the following document (CR iv. 262–3) was the Protestant reply to this Catholic formula. Bretschneider then had to explain the fact that the Protestant statement cited phrases not found in the latter, and did so by saying that the copy we possess is an incomplete one. Ibid., p. 261. Vetter, p. 112, Anm. 2.

[21] CR iv. 261, 262.

[22] 'Convenit, quod ubi verba Christi deprompta sunt, iam esse et dici corpus Christi. Et interim etiam panem, sed non communen, verum supernaturalem et supersubstantialem.' Ibid., p. 262.

[23] '. . . doctores, nedum veteres sed et recentiores iubeant abstinere a scrutatione, per quem modum fiat transsubstantiatio . . .' Ibid.

graph the postponement of any discussion of the exact understanding of transubstantiation to the end of the colloquy is
suggested, and the avoidance of such terminology in preaching is
advocated. The simple folk should merely be exhorted to believe
in the real presence.

Could this possibly have been the formula of which Contarini
approved? It certainly seems to stem from Gropper and Pflug.
Eck, who took a very vigorous part in the discussions on this
article,[24] is not even mentioned in Contarini's report.[25] Gropper's
own treatment of the Eucharist in his *Enchiridion* is primarily patristic; he shows no great interest in the scholastic interpretation,
and the stress on preaching the essentials would suit him and Pflug,
with his catechetical concerns, very well.[26] On the other hand,
quite apart from any considerations of content, we know that
Contarini was later strongly opposed to the deferment of the
question of transubstantiation to the end of the colloquy. Would
he have been likely to agree to it here?

The formula we must deal with next is, if anything, even more
mysterious.[27] It has inscribed on the back, 'The judgement of the

---

[24] 'De conversione panis in coena domini magnam tragoediam excitavit
Eccius.' Thus Melanchthon. Ibid., p. 415. It appears that Eck had accused the
Protestants of misrepresenting the Church Fathers on the subject. 'Wir hören
aber, dass Doctor Eck gegen Ew. Gnaden uns nach der übergebenen unsrer
confessio beschwerlich dargegeben, und crimen falsi aufgelegt haben soll, dass
wir zu unserm Vortheil etlich allegata verkehren, auch Bastard-Schriften
anziehen, und mit solcher Auflage uns beschweren will, dass man unsern
angezognen Gründen nicht soll Glauben geben.' Ibid., p. 274.

[25] Cf. note 19 above.

[26] Gropper does not, of course, deny the change of substance; to deny this
would be for him to doubt the omnipotence of God's word and he gives a
traditional account of the doctrine of transubstantiation. His main interest, however, is in the union of the believer with Christ. 'Unde id consequitur, . . . nempe
nos virtute huius tam eximii sacramenti non solum spiritualiter . . . sed et corpo-
raliter Christo uniri . . .' Johann Gropper, *Enchiridion Christianae Institutionis*
(in *Canones Concilii Provincialis Coloniensis;* Cologne: 1538), p. 110. It is Christ
who is both the priest and the victim: '. . . in hoc sacramento nihil proprium est
sacerdotis, sed totum agit Christus.' Ibid., p. 103. In so far as the Church offers
itself as Christ's mystical body, this is a true but spiritual sacrifice. 'Immolatur
ergo Christus in altari, sed sacrament aliter et mystice.' Ibid., p. 105. The real
Presence is thus a spiritual one; 'missa non tantum representativum, sed
praesens etiam ac verum, sed spirituale sacrificium . . .', and one in which faith
plays the primary part. 'In missa primas partes tenet fides, hoc est, fiducia
remissionis peccatorum per Christum . . .' Ibid., p. 107. On Pflug cf. Wolfgang
Offele, 'Julius Pflugs Irenik im Spiegel seines Katechismus', *Theologisches
Jahrbuch*, 1966, pp. 545–59.

[27] *CR* iv. 262–3.

theologians belonging to our side on the recently transmitted articles', and is regarded by Bretschneider as the Protestant reply to the document we have just been studying. Incredibly Dittrich accepts this hypothesis.[28]

It begins, conventionally enough, by accepting the teaching of the real presence and by protesting that 'the real presence has been defended in the writings of numerous members of our churches'. But it then proceeds to accept a 'mystical mutation' of the elements, and suggests again that the closer definition of 'transubstantiation' be left until the end of the colloquy. The adoration of Christ as present in the sacrament is not rejected, provided the abuses which have arisen in connection with this are remedied.

This draft article could not possibly have been that which Melanchthon laid before the collocutors on 7 May as the official statement of the Protestant position, for this omitted any reference to transubstantiation and appears to have been a strong statement of the normal Lutheran position. Melanchthon's own statements and those of his colleagues all point to his having taken a firm stand at this point.[29]

Much more probable is that the formula stems from Bucer, who was working in close collaboration with Gropper in the attempt to arrive at a compromise solution. It may even be that we have here the explanation for Granvelle's puzzling statement to Morone that Bucer had declared himself ready to preach transubstantiation if agreement were reached at Regensburg.[30] For by 'transubstantiation' he would have meant no more than the explanation of our Catholic formula that after the consecration it was a 'spiritual' bread which was present.

These two formulae may well, therefore, represent the attempt of a mediating party to bridge the differences by stressing the common ground (the real presence) of both Catholics and Lutherans, the 'spiritual' or 'mystical' character of the change in the elements, and the need for practical reform. In the unlikely case of the first formula being the one which Contarini accepted, his hope that it would form a basis for agreement becomes somewhat more

[28] D/B, p. 630, *Anm.* 7.

[29] 'Volunt mutari panem et repositum adorari. Nolui assentiri, fuique durior quam meus parastetes, qui olim maxime oppugnavit illam adorationem.' Melanchthon/Camerarius, 10 May 1541, *CR* iv. 281.

[30] Morone/Farnese, 11 May 1541, D/R, p. 180. Vetter suggests that this may well have been a convenient diplomatic lie. Vetter, p. 116.

intelligible. Such flexibility on his part would have been made possible by the imprecision of his understanding of transubstantiation. If he found it attested in Basil and Chrysostom and even in Christ's own words, then he presumably cannot have meant by it the relation of the substance of the elements to their accidents. The second formula, however, cannot possibly be the 'official' Protestant answer, which has unfortunately been lost.[31] Its composer will probably have been Bucer, and it may be related to the talks with Gropper on a possible compromise formula to which Granvelle had commissioned him on the seventh.

Melanchthon's unbending attitude alarmed Granvelle, who threatened him with the disfavour of the Emperor.[32] Granvelle's concern was understandable, for with the original article rejected, and the alternative articles of the Protestants and the Catholics unacceptable, deadlock seemed not far away. It may well have been to meet this situation that Bucer's mediating formula, if it was his, was composed.

Melanchthon's reaction to this heavy pressure was, however, the opposite to that of Bucer. Instead of bowing before the storm, he sought the backing of the Protestant Estates for his position. The theological 'opinion' they commissioned from the other Protestant theologians at Regensburg was a complete vindication of Melanchthon's stand. On Sunday, 8 May, they reported to the Protestant Estates that neither transubstantiation nor adoration nor reservation of the elements could be tolerated. It had come in the meantime to a hefty dispute between Bucer and some of his colleagues.[33]

On the 10 May the Protestant collocutors, following the command of their Estates, presented Granvelle with an account of the reasons why they could not accept the Catholic position.[34] Granvelle, understandably, refused to receive this statement. Not only had the recourse to the other twenty-one theologians been a breach of the pledge of secrecy which the collocutors had given,

[31] As Vetter remarks. Vetter, p. 113, *Anm.* 2.

[32] Contarini/Farnese, 9 May 1541, *HJ* i. 378.

[33] *CR* iv. 279. Gropper reported to Contarini, '. . . che in dicendis sententiis il Melantone et il Bucero sono stati molto modesti, ma il Brencio, Musculo, et Capitone sono stati veementissimi, et che fra loro sono in grandi dispiaceri et controversie'. *HJ* i. 379.

[34] This text was in Latin, *CR* iv. 275–8; a German text (ibid., pp. 271–5) was submitted to the other president, Count Frederick, who agreed to accept it. Ibid., p. 279.

the involvement of the Protestant Estates had brought about exactly what the colloquy had been intended to avoid: the head-on collision of 'official' representatives. Yet Granvelle could hardly complain. He himself had sought to bring political influence to bear on Melanchthon and could have expected that the latter would defend himself as best he could.

Gropper presented another Catholic draft[35] and Granvelle exerted all his influence to secure its acceptance. With the departure of Eck, who had been stricken down by a fever,[36] Pistorius had also had to leave for the sake of parity. Melanchthon was now therefore the sole one among the five present who was opposed to a compromise agreement, and was under very considerable pressure. Gropper himself was ready to omit the word 'transubstantiation', but when he showed the draft to Contarini in the evening the legate enforced its reintroduction.[37]

11 May saw the presentation of a further article by the Protestants, which the Catholics retired to discuss with Contarini, while the Protestants conferred about Gropper's draft. Contarini's attitude to the Protestants had now hardened considerably. In his dispatch on 9 May he had spoken of new and dangerous errors in the Protestant position. Their opposition to the adoration of the Host, and denial of the continued presence of Christ in the sacrament after communion were to be attributed, he thought, to an inner-Protestant attempt to conciliate the Zwinglians.[38] The denial of transubstantiation had apparently become confused in his mind with the denial of the real presence.

Hence it was not enough for him that the Protestant draft of 11 May lacked any explicit errors. Now that he knew the mind of the Protestants he realized that these errors lurked behind the formula, and he was not prepared to turn a blind eye to this in the interests of unity.[39] The word 'transubstantiation' had become for

[35] Vetter, p. 115.

[36] *CR* iv. 280; the dispute about this article was, from all accounts, one of the bitterest in the whole colloquy, and Melanchthon suggests that it may have taken a toll on Eck's health. 'In diesem Gezänk ward Eck krank, mocht sich vielleicht zu hart bewegt haben, und darnach sehr getrunken, dass ein febris folget.' *CR* iv. 583.

[37] Contarini/Farnese, 11 May 1541, *HJ* i. 382.

[38] *HJ* i. 376–7; the Protestants, he said, 'non hanno nè ragioni nè dirò vere nè verisimili, ma dirò etiam nè pur sofistiche nè autorità nè cosa alcuna se non la sua mera voluntà'. Ibid., p. 378.

[39] He would have had no doubts about accepting it, 'se io non sapessi il suo errore . . .' *HJ* i. 382.

him a shibboleth, a pointer to the real intentions of the Protestants, to the vital differences between the parties which must not be papered over with a glib formula. Unlike Bucer, Melanchthon, and Pflug, Contarini had had no previous experience of a colloquy of this nature. No doubt he felt that the ground was slipping away from under his feet, that he was getting out of his depth, that the bartering over the formulae was endangering the substance of the Faith. Nothing is more understandable in such circumstances than the resort to a fixed point of impeccable orthodoxy. Between the world of dogmatic tradition and the relativities of committee theology Contarini's preference was emphatically for the former.

Lest the whole colloquy grind to a halt over this one issue Granvelle suggested despairingly that the entire question of the Eucharist be deferred to the end of the colloquy. Contarini, however, refused to countenance this if it implied casting any doubt on such a central issue. He could only allow it, he said, if it were explicitly declared to be on the wish of the Protestants and not to any uncertainty or need for clarification on the Catholic side.[40]

On 12 May, therefore, the discussions were continued. The Protestants demanded amendments to Gropper's draft of 10 May, concentrating on the reference to transubstantiation, and Gropper and Pflug advised the legate to accept this. They reported that Melanchthon and Bucer, due to the influence of the other Protestant theologians, were unable to yield, and that if the Catholics did not concede the point deadlock would ensue. Each side would have to lay before the Emperor their own separate article. Contarini remained adamant. The breakdown of the discussions, and the possible collapse of the colloquy would be preferable to what would be regarded in Rome as apostasy. The Protestants, as he read the situation, were intent on smuggling in their dogmas under the cover of a false concord.[41]

13 May saw the continuation of the debate, held this time in Granvelle's own lodgings. The crucial discussions were no longer, however, between the collocutors, who were agreed that the term 'transubstantiation' could be dispensed with, but between the Catholic collocutors and the legate, to whom they brought two draft articles, one from each party, Gropper's own

---

[40] Ibid., p. 383.
[41] The Protestant amendments made it clear, Contarini argued, that 'sub involvere verborum volevano nascondere li loro dogmi e fare una concordia palliata'. Contarini/Farnese, 13 May 1541, *HJ* i. 384.

draft, as Contarini saw at once, omitting the reference to transubstantiation.

This was by now, of course, an overt and deliberate defiance of the legate's wishes by Gropper and Pflug. The Catholic front was irreparably broken, and a Protestant victory seemed on the cards. Contarini's decisiveness managed to avoid this, but at a high cost. By refusing his assent to the amendment he sealed the fate of the colloquy.

It was the most critical moment of the whole colloquy. Granvelle, informed of Contarini's intentions, appeared on the scene at once and remonstrated with the legate. He described his untiring efforts in the last eight days to win over the Protestants to an agreement, and begged Contarini not to bring about the failure of the colloquy.

Contarini retorted that he wanted no such thing, but that he would never surrender one point of Catholic truth or allow it to be obscured. Otherwise he, with the Emperor, would be regarded as a heretic by the whole of Christianity. At the instance of the Protestants he was ready to permit the postponement of further debate until the end of the colloquy, but on no account could the reference to transubstantiation be omitted from the Catholic draft.[42]

On the human level, Contarini sympathized with Granvelle, 'because he certainly spares himself no exertion, but there can be no compromising of the truth'. His last word had obviously been spoken. Granvelle had to give way. In the evening he returned to the legate after a further session with the collocutors on the two drafts. In the Catholic draft the clause in which the 'transformatio' involved in the sacrament was described as 'transsubstantiatio' had been restored. The Protestants insisted that the substance of the bread remained after the consecration of the elements. It was clear, Contarini concluded, that the differences were genuine, not merely verbal.[43] He was ready to meet the Protestants' request that he clarify some points, but Granvelle explained that they meant at the close of the colloquy. In the meantime any further discussion of the question was suspended.

Any hope of a successful outcome to the colloquy was now, of

[42] Ibid., p. 385.
[43] Gropper and Pflug had claimed previously that Melanchthon and Bucer agreed with the Catholic formula 'per il senso'. The Protestants' insistence that the substance of the bread remained after the consecration proved, however, said Contarini, 'che noi differentiamo nel senso et però si faceva difficoltà nelle parole'. Ibid.

course, almost totally extinguished. As Contarini put it, 'unless God brings about a miracle, I shall not see concord between us'.[44] He feared that Granvelle would try to shrug off the responsibility for its failure on to the Papacy, but was determined to present the Holy See positively not as the disturber of ecumenical endeavour but as the 'guardian of Christian doctrine'.[45] His concern for Catholicism was beginning to merge into his concern for the Curia.

[44] '. . . nè spero, se Dio non fa miracoli, verrà concordia fra noi.' Ibid., p. 386.
[45] 'Conservatrice delli dogmi christiani.'

II

To Emerge Honourably from this Labyrinth

THE discussions which followed the deadlock on the sacraments continued for another ten days, but they were no longer animated with any real hope of success. It was rather a matter of going through the prescribed motions, of pursuing the delicate task of finding the scapegoats and allotting the blame. Contarini himself had begun to speak of the Protestants in moralizing terms, as 'highly obstinate and stubborn'.[1]

The transition on the next day, 14 May, to the article on penance and absolution[2] brought little relief. As might have been expected, the Protestants refused to agree that the enumeration of all mortal sins was necessary. On the question of satisfaction Melanchthon stoutly resisted with biblical arguments the 'auctoritates patrum et ecclesiae' which the Catholics adduced to support their case. Since he was having to bear the brunt of the struggle for the Protestants, he would gladly have seen the colloquy broken off. His inflexibility won him Burckhard's cordial praise, while Bucer's behaviour was described as 'irresolute'.[3]

The Protestants' refusal to recognize the necessity for auricular confession, while conceding its utility in many cases, prompted Contarini to energetic intervention. On 15 May he presented himself before the Emperor.[4] His driving concern was to avoid the compromising of the Catholic position.

The emergence of the new errors about penance, together with their previous attitude to the Eucharist, made it evident, he

[1] 'Ostinati molto e pertinaci.' *HJ* i. 386.
[2] *CR* iv. 217–18.
[3] 'Fast wankend.' Ibid., p. 291. The unflattering epithet seems to have been applied to Bucer fairly generally in the Protestant camp. Cf. the report of the Saxon delegates: 'Und da gleich Bucerus etwas wankend wollt werden, wie denn seine Reden gemeiniglich mit halben Munde gehen, so werden doch die andern, ob Gott will, nichts begeben, das der Confession und Schmalkaldischen Rathschlag entgegen.' Ibid., p. 293.
[4] *HJ* i. 388; the memorandum he presented to Charles V in D/R, pp. 325–6.

explained, that a reunion with the Protestants was out of the question. The central doctrines of the Christian faith were the Trinity, the Incarnation, and the Eucharist.[5] Without a recognition of them all no union was possible. The sole remedy he could suggest was that the Emperor exert his authority over the Protestant princes and theologians, and thus induce them to depart from their erroneous ways.

Charles replied that while he was no theologian, he had been informed that the difference was only the single word 'transubstantiation', and the Protestants were ready to reintroduce the practice of auricular confession. This being the case the best policy seemed to be not the abandonment of the discussions but the extraction of a maximum of concessions from the Protestants. At the end of the colloquy an attempt could then be made to resolve all outstanding disagreements.

Contarini's answer is interesting. He compared the term 'transsubstantiatio' with the Nicene 'consubstantialis'. Just as in the latter case it was not a dispute over a mere word so in the article on the Eucharist it was not a matter of terminology but of the substance of a central article of the Faith.[6] This had been promulgated by a Council attended by patriarchs, archbishops, and between eight hundred and a thousand bishops which had chosen that term 'transsubstantiatio' in order to explain exactly the mutation of the bread and of the wine into the body and blood of Christ. On such key articles there can be no wavering; we must be ready to sacrifice our very lives for them. Worldly, political considerations must be subordinated to religious ones, Contarini argued. At the time of the martyrs Christians had no temporal possessions, and then the Faith, whose body and substance are the articles now being dealt with, was at its most effective. Compared with this the temporal welfare of Christendom is a mere external good. This argumentation makes it quite clear that for Contarini the debate is not a theological one at all, for the Protestants have no genuine basis for their views, but a struggle of the true faith against mere indifferentism.

[5] Only on the Trinity, on Christology, and on this sacramental issue had the Church made dogmatically binding pronouncements; hence Contarini could say that the sacrament of the Eucharist, together with the other two, constituted the three principal articles in the Christian faith, 'nelli quale bisognava l'intelletto a veramente essere Christiano'. *HJ* i. 388.

[6] 'Quella parola importava il tutto . . .' Ibid., p. 389.

Meanwhile Melanchthon was showing an equal disinclination to compromise his principles. In the conference on 15 May Melanchthon declared that he was no more willing to make concessions on auricular confession than on private masses, the adoration of the saints, or the primacy of the Papacy.[7] He was firmly committed to a completely unconciliatory position. The displeasure with which the agreement on justification had been greeted in Wittenberg had led to a new instruction by the Elector John Frederick, that nothing was to be agreed on in future without Luther's prior consent.[8] The other Protestant theologians in Regensburg also tended to influence Melanchthon towards a more rigorist approach. It would all the same be foolish to deny that Melanchthon's opposition to Bucer's mediating course had its basis in his own very personal convictions. Granvelle's rather ham-handed attempt to bring pressure on him had the very opposite effect from that intended. On 16 May he threatened that unless freedom of speech were granted him, he would absent himself from all future deliberations. This threat produced an apology from Granvelle, but the discussions made no progress.[9] Gropper being ill, Pflug affirmed his determination to abide by the Catholic viewpoint, and Melanchthon produced a Protestant counter-article.[10]

In his audience with the Emperor on 15 May Contarini had suggested that the sole way out of the impasse might be for pressure to be brought to bear on the Protestant princes and theologians. The resort of Melanchthon to the Protestant Estates on the question of transubstantiation had been the first hint that the Erasmian theory of an independent colloquy of the learned was proving hard to realize in practice. Contarini's suggestion was a further vote of no confidence in the colloquy method, and an even more important one, for in his desperation Granvelle gave it his support.

On 17 May Philip of Hesse was summoned before the Emperor. His reply to complaints about the extremism and stubbornness of the Protestant theologians was to propose—presumably with a straight face—that Luther be invited to participate. He might well prove more amenable than some of his followers.[11]

---

[7] *CR* iv. 300.   [8] Ibid., p. 282.   [9] Ibid., pp. 584, 300, 305.
[10] Contarini/Farnese, 18 May 1541, *HJ* i. 390; text in *CR* iv. 354–63.

[11] The Emperor complained that he had heard 'wie doctor Lauter Philippo Melanthoni ein instruction zugeschickt habe, daruber Philippus nicht schreiten dorfe . . .'; Philip replied, 'Philippus sie ane zweivel wedder an Francreich noch

On 18 May it was the turn of the representatives of Electoral Saxony to appear before Charles. The Emperor protested anew his desire for the unification and reform of the Church, and urged that the Protestant theologians show themselves more conciliatory and keep the secrecy of the negotiations better so that this end could be achieved.[12] The Margrave of Brandenburg and the representatives of the free cities were also treated to similar expostulations.[13]

All this activity, however, availed little. For the third time an article had to be set aside as unresolved. Granvelle could only hope to force through agreement on the other articles, and by bringing political pressure to bear on the Protestant princes to force them to accept the Catholic point of view on the Church, the Eucharist, and confession.[14] A forlorn enough hope.

The next article, that on marriage, which was discussed on 19 May, occasioned no great controversy, although marriage was described as a sacrament. The question of divorce was deferred until later.[15] The Protestants also allowed the seventeenth article on Extreme Unction to go through, provided the abuses connected with it were abolished, and the minuscule eighteenth article on Charity as the third note of the Church raised no objections.[16] They were without doubt saving their energy for the major rumpus which was to be expected over the following article, 'On the hierarchical order of the Church, and its authority in determining Church polity'.[17]

The very title was a provocation for Melanchthon, who launched a frontal attack on the whole article, although it had obviously been framed with exquisite care. Any language offensive to Protestant ears had been excised, many noble things were said about the diversity of gifts, the bond of charity, and Christian freedom. The quotations were drawn from Irenaeus, Tertullian, Cyprian, and

---

Lutherum gepunden, sonder sehe ane zweivel auf Got; So mocht s.f.g. ires teils leiden, das Lutherus hie were; derselb, wan er das gut gemut sehe, das die notwendigen artigkel nachgelassen wurden und ein christlich ehrlich reformation furgenomen, so wurde [er] schidlicher sein dan der andern keiner; man hat zu Schmalkalden von artigkeln, was man thun konte, geredt, darine sei lutherus nicht unschidlich gewesen.' Lenz, iii. 75, 78.

[12] *CR* iv. 293–8.
[13] Contarini/Farnese, 23 May 1541, D/R, p. 326.   [14] *HJ* i. 391.
[15] *CR* iv. 219.   [16] Ibid., p. 317.   [17] Ibid., pp. 221–4.

Augustine, from Paul and the Gospels; not one from the scholastics.

The article argued that Christ had ordained that Peter should be the chief of the apostles for the sake of the unity of the Church, although he possessed no more power or honour than any other of the apostles. The followers of the apostles were the bishops, archbishops, and patriarchs. Of these the Roman bishop, who held the chair of Peter in vicarious succession, was adjudged the Primate, excelling the others by the extent of his compassion and— that the unity of the Church might be preserved—by his powers of jurisdiction.

This order is maintained by the legitimate episcopal succession, and by the power committed to the bishops of administering the ecclesiastical polity, both as regards ceremonies and discipline, in neither of which, however, rests our hope of salvation, which lies 'in the grace of our Lord Jesus Christ'.[18]

The major part which the discussions on this article played in the reports of the Protestant theologians showed the importance which they attached to it.[19] It is the logical continuation to the article on the Church, and is dealt with in the context of the third note of the Church, the bond of charity. Melanchthon detected an intention to extract generalized concessions from the Protestants in the former article which would then be twisted to their disadvantage in the nineteenth.[20] He distrusted profoundly the whole tenor of the article.

The term 'hierarchy' displeased him—he would have preferred 'Church order'—as it smacked of domination. He drew unflattering comparisons between the claims of the bishops to be the followers

---

[18] 'Sic tamen, ut hae Ceremoniae et disciplina hoc fine in Ecclesia insituantur et administrarentur, non ut in illis fiducia salutis, quae in gratia domini Iesu consistit, reponatur ... Sed tantum ut sint incitamenta et retinacula pietatis, ut omnia in Ecclesia pie, decenter, honeste et ordine fiant ...' Ibid., pp. 223–4.

[19] e.g. Ibid., pp. 422–4, 442–3, 584.

[20] 'Darnach ist ein tückischer Artikel gefolget, den sie nennen: von Ordnung der Kirchenherrschaft. Der Dichter dieses Buchs hat gethan wie ein listiger Hauptmann, der die Haufen hin und her versteckt. Also in diesem Buch siehet ein Artikel auf den andern, und sind die Tück mit grossem Fleiss versteckt ... Droben hat das Buch gesagt, die Kirche sey die Versammlung der Heiligen und Unheiligen; nur kommt dieser Artikel und erkläret dasselbige, nämlich: unter Einem Haupte, dem römischen Bischoff; und sagt weiter: zusammengefügt mit dem Band der Liebe, das ist, mit Gehorsam in Menschensatzungen.' CR iv. 422–3.

of the apostles and the actual conduct of the German bishops, and pointed to the abuses which had arisen from the episcopal jurisdiction over ceremonial and disciplinary matters. He opposed the recognition of the papal primacy.[21]

Melanchthon was alone in this attack on the article, for Bucer joined with Gropper and Granvelle in urging him to accept it. Granvelle pointed to the critical state of the deliberations. If this article were not agreed upon the whole colloquy would fail and the hope of a reformed and unified German Church would vanish. Feige, the Hessian chancellor, and Joachim II, Elector of Brandenburg, also attempted to win Melanchthon over.[22] Master Philipp was, however, not to be shaken, and so yet another article remained unresolved.

Contarini had long foreseen that the question of the hierarchy and in particular of the Papacy was bound to cause trouble. While the article on the Church was being discussed he had drafted two statements with which he hoped to secure an agreement, and at the same time avoid bringing to light the difference of opinion within the Catholic camp on the relative standing of Papacy and Councils. On the Councils he simply pointed to the historical fact that in the past General Councils had been summoned to settle disputed points in the understanding of Scripture, and that where these had been duly called and assembled in the Holy Spirit, their authority had never been challenged. As to the Papacy he derived its institution from Christ who had set the Roman bishop over the other bishops for the sake of the Church's unity by according to him the general jurisdiction over the whole Church.[23] Not only are none of the controversial questions resolved here; there is also a distressing lack of any theological insight into the issues involved.

This impression of superficiality can only be strengthened by the reactions of the legate to the debates on the hierarchy. To the Protestant criticisms of the German bishops he had nothing better to offer than the rather trite distinction between office and office-

---

[21] Cf. Contarini's dispatch of 23 May: '. . . qui hanno detto che laudano tutto quest'ordine, ma che non sanno, come li loro Vescovi qui in Germania possano essere Vescovi, che significa sopraintendenti, non attendendo essi punto ad alcuna sopraintendenza del suo grege . . .' D/R, p. 327.

[22] CR iv. 584. Philip of Hesse was already engaged in secret negotiations with the Emperor through Gerhard Veltwyck in preparation for their treaty of 13 June. Lenz, iii. 78 ff.

[23] Contarini/Farnese, 9 May 1541, HJ i. 379–81.

bearer, and with it a childish play on logic. The Protestants should be asked if the German bishops had or had not sinned by the negligent execution of their duties. Either the Protestants must admit that they had not sinned, because they were not real bishops in any case, or that they *had* sinned, which latter alternative would however be an admission that they were genuine bishops.[24] Can Contarini really have imagined that a Melanchthon would be impressed by such logical gymnastics? Did he have any understanding at all of the Protestant standpoint on this issue? As compared to his understanding of justification his appreciation of this issue certainly seems deficient.

The discussion of this article had lasted into 20 May, and on the same day the next article, the twentieth, was read. We are now in the dying stages of the colloquy. The last few articles were dealt with in less than three days. Both Catholics and Protestants aimed at a speedy dispatch of the outstanding business since it was obvious that a successful outcome was out of the question.

The twentieth article dealt with certain 'dogmata'—the adoration of the saints, the Mass, celibacy, monasticism—which were derived not from the Scriptures but from the authority of the Church. It admitted the existence of abuses in connection with them, but adhered to the traditional Catholic position throughout.[25] No genuine meeting of minds took place on any of these questions. According to Contarini Bucer was ready to accept the canon of the Mass, and the Elector of Brandenburg spoke in similar terms to Gropper,[26] but these were isolated voices. To every one of the disputed points Melanchthon handed in a counter-article.[27]

The following article on the use of the sacraments compared the Catholic and Protestant position to the disadvantage of the latter, and the celebration of private masses, the limitation of the cup to the clergy, and the use of Latin in the liturgy were declared at least as justified, if not more so, than the Protestant practice. Again the Protestants submitted a counter-article.[28]

On the question of ecclesiastical discipline much common

---

[24] D/R, p. 327.   [25] CR iv. 224–31.

[26] 'Hanno poi conferito della messa et del canone, dove si parlo etiam dell' Invocatione de Santi. Il Gropperio certamente ha satisfato bene, et sciolse loro obietioni talmente, che il Bucero disse; Io per me admetteria il canone.' D/R, pp. 326–7.

[27] CR iv. 369–71.

[28] Text of article in CR iv. 231–33; counter-article, ibid., pp. 371–4.

ground was found. The twenty-second article urged, for example, the reform of the clergy and the founding of schools at cathedrals, collegiate churches, and monasteries.[29] Melanchthon, however, insisted on an explicit recognition of the right of priests to marry, and did not hesitate to remark that the best reform for the monasteries would be their abolition.[30]

The final article dealt with the reform of the laity, and also with other lesser questions. Without coming to any agreement the colloquy, to the relief of all concerned, ground to a halt on 22 May. The collocutors gathered together the revised articles on 24 and 25 May, and on the last day of the month they were presented to the Emperor, together with the nine counter-articles of the Protestants.[31] The colloquy was over.

The speed with which these last articles were dispatched, and the end to the dramatic possibility of a reconciliation, meant that Contarini's role decreased in importance. His reports tend to be generalized and to obscure the real depth of the differences. At times, one wonders if he has not lost all grip on reality. When, for example, Granvelle asked him whether he thought Luther should be invited to participate in the negotiations he replied, 'Do what the Holy Spirit leads you to do; but without doubt it would be a matter of the greatest importance if Luther could be won over.'[32]

Contarini still hoped that—although there seemed to be conflict on many articles—many of the differences might yet be resolved.[33] Without doubt he set his main hope now on the authority of the Emperor. He was, of course, bitterly disappointed at the sorry end of the colloquy. The Emperor and Granvelle seemed deeply perturbed, and at a loss as to how they 'can emerge honourably from this labyrinth'. The sole gain that could be registered, he thought, was that it must now be clear to the Emperor, and indeed to all, that the Pope had placed no hindrance in the way of the

---

[29] Text in CR iv. 233–7. [30] Ibid., p. 376.

[31] Ibid., pp. 337–8; D/R, p. 327; Fr. Contarini/Senate, 31 May 1541, ibid., p. 191.

[32] Ibid., p. 332.

[33] He noted the lack of any reference in the book to monastic vows, to fasting, and of any explicit treatment of the question of purgatory, and added that '. . . vedo, che siamo molti lontani d'accordo'. Contarini/Farnese, 29 May 1541, ibid., pp. 333–4; but he could also say: 'A me pare, che la differentia, ancorche pare essere in molti articuli, pure molti si potriano accettare, ma quelli dui de eucharistia et de confessione sono li importantissimi.' Contarini/Farnese, 23 May 1541, ibid., p. 331.

attempt at reconciliation, and that the articles on which they disagreed did not relate to the Primacy or any papal interests.[34] He was as determined as ever not to countenance any agreement which would allow the preaching of falsehood.[35]

On every point his analysis of the situation was faulty. There was neither hope of a future resolution of the differences, nor of the Emperor's authority being of any avail, nor that the Emperor or anyone else was likely to be impressed by the exertions on the papal side. If the imperial wrath was to a large extent directed towards Melanchthon, it also fell in large measure upon the Papacy, whose legate's direct intervention had forestalled any hope of agreement on the Eucharist and on penance. Contarini's well-meant crusade had failed, and as the search for scapegoats for the collapse of the colloquy became more avid, he was to find himself one of the most eligible of the contestants.

[34] 'A me pare di vedere etiam la Cesarea Maestà et esso Mons. di Granvello in grandissimo travaglio di animo, non sanno come possono uscire da questo laberinto con honor sue . . . Mi dispiace sino al cuore che le cose vadino alla rovina, si come vanno. Pure fra tanto male ci è quel bene. Prima che Cesare e tutti conoscono che da noi et da quella santa sede non è stato posto impedimento alcuno alla concordia.' Contarini/Farnese, 2 June 1541, *HJ* i. 477.

[35] *ZKG* iii. 509–10.

12

For Me it Suffices to Obey

T HE colloquy had not been a complete failure. Bucer even believed that all the essential points of Christian faith and life had been covered by the agreed articles, and that a genuine basis for a lasting concord had been laid.[1] It is certainly true that a beginning had been made, and this itself, in view of the long-standing differences between the confessions and the exclusively negative attitude of some of the principal parties involved, is astounding enough.

Yet Granvelle's hopes had been irremediably shattered; his 'grand design' lay in ruins. He had hoped, after the conclusion of the private theological discussions, to be able to present the Diet with an amended version of the Regensburg Book, agreed upon by the collocutors from both sides, which would serve as a blueprint for a lasting religious settlement. Instead he had to lay before the Estates two very different documents: the Regensburg Book itself, and no less than nine Protestant counter-articles. The 'professionals' had failed to reach theological agreement. Was there much hope that the politicians would do any better?

The Catholics had proposed no counter-articles, partly because they had been afforded an opportunity prior to the colloquy of amending the book, partly because the book had been found, in substance, more favourable to a Catholic than a Protestant interpretation. Yet by no means all of the Catholics were satisfied

---

[1] In his account of the colloquy he affirmed that the agreed articles contained, '. . . alles das jenige so dazu von nötten sein mage das wir vor gott und in seiner gemeyn gotseligklich gerecht und heilig leben. Und was nit verglichen das selbige ist auch nit not zu wissen noch zu gebrauchen und mag on alle gefahr des heyls onerkant und ongehalten bleibem.' *Alle Handlungen und Scriften zu vergleichung der Religion durch die Key. Mai. Churfürsten, Fürsten und Stände aller theylen Auch den Päbst. Legaten auf jüngst gehaltenen Reichstag zu Regensburg verhandlet und einbracht* (Strassburg: bei Wendel Kihel, 1541), p. 133.

with the book. The gap between the confessions seemed un-bridgeable, and the hoped-for theological consensus on which a religious settlement could be built evidently did not exist. A quite radical change of policy seemed to be called for.

Granvelle read the signs of the times and drew the consequences. He scrapped the 'grand design', the hoped-for reconciliation of the confessions based on a genuine theological concord, and substituted a much less ambitious project, the promotion of a policy of tolera-tion. The measure of agreement achieved thus far must be consolidated, and if possible extended by the extraction of further concessions from the Protestants. Where, however, complete agreement could not be reached the two confessions must agree to disagree, at least until the next General Council. Differences which could not be bridged must be overlooked. If unanimity were unobtainable tolerance of the other side's point of view on certain issues must take its place. This would enable a reform programme to be carried out, peace and order to be restored, and a united defence against the Turks to be mounted. Not the Edict of Worms, it appeared, and not the Recess of Augsburg, but the Respite of Frankfurt was to set the future pattern for the religious policy of the Empire.

The opposition of the Papacy and its allies to any such plan was, of course, to be anticipated. The stern resistance of the Protestants to any attempt to tie tolerance to theological concessions was to be expected. These obstacles might, in happier circumstances, have been circumvented. The situation after the failure of the colloquy, however, gave no ground for hope.

The unwelcome addition of the nine Protestant counter-articles was the least of the difficulties. They only symbolized the 'negative' spirit which now dominated the deliberations of both parties. The relative optimism of the earlier period had wholly vanished. The 'moderates' among the theologians had lost the initiative—Bucer on the Protestant side, Gropper and Pflug on the Catholic side had both been signally rebuffed by their colleagues. With the loss of the concern for a genuine reconciliation—in any case never very prominent on the Protestant side—the main concern of both parties was to defend their own positions, to avoid losing face or prestige, to capitalize on the weaknesses of their opponents. The secrecy of the discussions had been breached; intrigues had developed on both sides. Granvelle's hope that a 'third party' would develop—astride the confessional differences—had not been realized.

Granvelle's chances of success for his new toleration party were, therefore, minimal from the outset. Yet he unleashed an almost frantic activity in the pursuit of his aim. Nothing was left untried. Pressure was put on Catholics and Protestants, princes and theologians alike, secret treaties were signed, a delegation sent off to the arch-heretic Luther, a new set of conciliatory articles brought forward, a reform programme drawn up. Whatever could be retrieved from the wreck, Granvelle was determined to retrieve.

One factor, at least, was in his favour. With the transfer of the religious discussions from the academic realm of the theological colloquy to the political forum of the Diet, the negotiations moved into a sphere in which Granvelle's competence was unrivalled. Hitherto he had been attempting to further his essentially political ends by rather dubious theological means—to produce a concord *de jure* where none existed *de facto*. Now, however, he was defending his right as a politician to meet the immediate situation with a compromise settlement, and it was the churchmen who were attempting to further their essentially theological or 'religious' ends by rather dubious political manœuvres. The real conflict at Regensburg is not between theological and political interests as such, but between theologizing politicians and politically minded churchmen. It is one thing to defend one's concern for the truth as such against the pragmatism of the politician. It is another to demand that the pragmatic tools of the latter be laid at the sole service of the particular understanding of the truth one happens to represent.

On 22 May the colloquy had ended. The Diet itself, however, was to continue for another two months, until the ceremonial reading of the Recess on 29 July. The two main mile-stones in this period of hectic political activity were the presentation of the Regensburg Book to the Estates on 8 June and the Emperor's draft suggestions for the Recess which began to appear as early as 12 July.

Granvelle's first move was a renewed attempt to extract further concessions from the Protestants. Pressure was brought on Philip of Hesse to change his standpoint on the controverted articles, but he had remained firm to the general Protestant position that they were unacceptable.[2] Doctrinally, if not politically, he refused to be detached from his fellow religionists.

On 3 June the Elector of Brandenburg and Johann von Weeze, the former Archbishop of Lund, used Philip's mediation to enter into negotiations with the Protestant Estates about the controverted articles, but their plea for a compromise solution won no favour on the Protestant side.[3] Philip did, however, agree to continue to co-operate with them in their endeavours, a promise which was of little worth in view of his declared intention to leave Regensburg in the near future.[4]

Joachim II then launched another attempt to coax the Protestants away from their counter-articles, by presenting them, again through Philip, with six mediating articles. Hesse summoned the Estates on Saturday, 11 June, to discuss these.[5] The latter declined to comment on these new articles, on the pretext that they had not yet received their copies of the Regensburg Book, which was still being copied. Instead they referred them to their theologians, some of whom were impressed by the Elector's stress on the need for flexibility on both sides for the sake of peace and a joint programme of reform.[6] Melanchthon, however, carried the majority with his argument that the mediating articles were too ambiguous to merit discussion.[7]

While these attempts were still being made to bring the Protestants to further concessions, Granvelle had already begun to concentrate on his main aim—to persuade them to accept the already agreed articles, and to tolerate for the meantime the Catholic views on the controverted ones. Here the opinions within the Protestant camp varied widely. There is some evidence of a substantial grouping being ready to accept Granvelle's suggestion that the two sides coexist with their differing views. It appeared,

[2] *CR* iv. 340. He told Veltwyck on 24 May that, 'Was wir auch mit Got und gutem gewissen thun konten, das wolten wir gern thun, dise sach aber stehe an uns allein nit, sondern an Gott, wie der den andern leuten einen synn gibet.' Lenz, iii. 80.

[3] *CR* iv. 584–5.   [4] Lenz, iii. 84.

[5] The articles dealt with the authority of the Church and of the Councils, the Eucharist, the enumeration of sins in auricular confession, the Roman primacy, holy days, and fasts. Herminjard, vii. 204–5; cf. *CR* iv. 401–2.

[6] Ibid., pp. 403, 574–5, 585.

[7] As Calvin reported, 'Hosce cum perlegissemus, Melanchthon, nostrorum omnium corde et ore, responsionem germanice conscripsit, in qua petiit ut finem imponerent nostri fucosis illis conciliationibus.' Herminjard, vii. 205; cf. *CR* iv. 402.

after all, a highly realistic policy. The Protestants had safeguarded their point of view by the counter-articles, and these they would be allowed—by the highest court of the Empire—to profess. Protestantism would be legalized, and its existence and views recognized —at least until the Council. The need for peace and unity would be met.

Wolfgang of Anhalt, on the other hand, led on behalf of the Elector of Saxony the party which was resolutely opposed to the acceptance of the agreed articles. The Elector wanted tolerance for Protestantism, but a tolerance which was not tied to theological concessions, a purely pragmatic and political agreement. His reaction to the agreement on the fifth article had been anything but favourable, Both he and Luther had rejected the article as ambiguous.[8] Hence he refused his imprimatur to the agreed articles, and thereby to Granvelle's whole plan.[9]

It was the attempt to outflank this Saxon inflexibility which led to one of the most bizarre episodes of the Diet. Immediately after the colloquy had concluded Melanchthon, under strong criticism from Granvelle for his pugnacity, had suggested, either tongue-in-cheek or to shake off the burden of responsibility from himself— that it would be best to deal directly with Luther, who was himself very much concerned for the reunification of the Church. Luther could be contacted and invited to Regensburg. Informing Contarini of this proposal, Granvelle remarked that it seemed an excellent one. Even the Emperor, it seems, approved of it.[10]

The hope was a desperate enough one, and indicates that by this time Granvelle was clutching at any straw that came his way. An actual invitation of Luther to the Diet was, however, out of the question. Instead Granvelle dispatched a secret delegation to him, through the mediation of the Brandenburg Elector. This arrived in Wittenberg on 9 June, led by John and George of Anhalt, and including the Scot Alexander Alesius. Both the Elector and Luther, however, got wind of what was intended—to their great indignation. Alesius informed Brück secretly of the ambassador's instructions, which were written in the name of the Elector Joachim and the Margrave George of Brandenburg. They were to argue that agree-

---

[8] Ibid., pp. 283 ff; Luther referred to it as '. . . diese weitleulfftige geflickte Notel . . .', and only cautioned John Frederick: 'E.k.f.g. wotlten M. Philipps und den unsern Ja nicht zu hart schreiben, Damit er nicht aber mal sich zu tod greme.' WAB ix. 406, 409.

[9] *CR* iv. 346.   [10] *CR* iv. 385–6; WAB ix. 433–6.

ment had been reached on the central articles of the faith, i.e. on the doctrinal questions. Disagreement centred more on matters of usage and ceremony, on which Luther himself had said there could be liberty of opinion.[11]

Luther's written answer of 12 June was not wholly unfavourable. It bound, however, the acceptance of the agreed articles on original sin, free will, faith and works, and justification to the installation of preachers who would expound them 'purely', and only under certain conditions could the controverted articles be tolerated. Luther, at this stage at least, was not quite so totally unsympathetic to the project as his Elector.[12]

If Granvelle had found but scant encouragement among the Protestants, he was to be given even less by the Catholics. There was no question of extorting further concessions from them, of closing the gap between their views and that of the Protestants' counter-articles. Granvelle had enough to do to secure their commitment to the agreed articles, and to convince them of the virtues of tolerating what they themselves could not accept.

The failure of the colloquy had, of course, greatly strengthened the hand of those elements among the Catholics who had predicted this from the beginning. The moderates, who had invested their prestige in the colloquy, were correspondingly weakened. They lacked in any case the aggressive political leadership which the rigorists—in the persons of the Archbishop of Mainz and the Dukes of Bavaria—possessed. The moderates might have the backing of the Emperor, their opponents had that both of France and the Papacy.

The aim of the militants was to precipitate the Emperor into an armed confrontation with the Protestants, which meant that the policy of toleration must be abandoned, the Catholic League strengthened, and the Regensburg Book finally repudiated. Their immediate tactics concentrated on driving a wedge between the papal legate and the Emperor, for as long as Rome could be persuaded to support the conciliatory policies of Charles and Granvelle their own plans had no chance of success.

Albert of Mainz therefore sought to convince Contarini that if the Emperor refused to lead the Catholics in a war against the Protestants it would be as well for the Germans to choose a new

---

[11] CR iv. 394–9.   [12] WAB ix. 442.

Emperor.[13] When Contarini queried the expediency of a war in view of the degree to which Germany was infiltrated by Protestantism the Archbishop replied that it was only the weakness of the Emperor which had made other princes hesitate to join the League. Contarini, asked by the Elector what his own view on the matter was, side-stepped the question.[14]

The rigorists also sought to cast doubt on the loyalty of the Emperor to the old faith and to the Roman See. The Bavarian dukes attempted to convince the papal representatives that the Emperor intended to concede the Protestants complete tolerance for their heretical views.[15] The Archbishop of Salzburg reported that Charles had attributed to the Papacy less concern for Germany than for the prevention of the granting of tolerance.[16] Contarini carefully avoided identifying himself with their views, but he was soon to be forced into a much closer association with their position.

On 8 June, the same day on which Granvelle laid the Regensburg Book, together with the Protestant counter-articles, before the assembled Estates, there arrived in Regensburg a dispatch from Rome for Contarini, signed by Niccolò Ardinghelli on Cardinal Farnese's behalf.[17]

It was a fateful document for Contarini, for Regensburg, and for future papal policy. Contarini had requested in his reports to Rome that the progress of the negotiations be kept as secret as possible, since he had heard that there were forces in Italy which were seeking to sabotage the colloquy. The dispatch began by complaining, however, that Contarini himself, or his household in Regensburg, had preserved this secrecy very ill. From Venice and elsewhere copies of the article on justification and of letters describing the course of events in Regensburg had been circulating throughout Italy. Contarini was asked to document his references to the opponents of the negotiations so that action could be taken against them.

[13] Contarini/Farnese, 8 June 1541, D/R, p. 337.

[14] He did *not*, as the summary of Pastor states, speak emphatically against the proposal of an offensive against the Protestants 'Der Erzbischof will Krieg gegen die Protestanten. Contarini spricht nachdrücklich gegen diesen Vorschlag.' *HJ* i. 477; Vetter also claims that the legate '. . . sich sehr bestimmt gegen jede kriegerische Aktion aussprach . . .' Vetter, p. 152; D/R, p. 336.

[15] Morone/Farnese, 23 May 1541, *HJ* iv. 464.

[16] Morone/Farnese, 28 May 1541, ibid., p. 465.

[17] Ardinghelli/Contarini, 29 May 1541, Quirini, iii. 231–40.

The agreed article on justification was described as ambiguous,[18] and he was instructed henceforth not to accept any article or part article, either explicitly or implicitly, directly or indirectly, nor to let it pass after only slight resistance unless it corresponded quite clearly both in substance and terminology to the Catholic position. Whatever he did, he was not to 'approvare cosa alcuna', either as a private person or as papal legate, but must refer everything, as his instruction stipulated, to the Apostolic See. It would cause great harm if the Protestants even seemed to be justified in citing his opinion as favourable to their views. He must therefore take care that his concern for peace did not lead him to make harmful concessions to the Protestants.

His suggested formulae on papal and conciliar authority aroused particular displeasure on account of their ambiguity 'which does not do justice to the substance of such articles'. His postponement of discussion on the Papacy was criticized, for 'the entire agreement would be rendered abortive if differences remained on this point'. The Curia took grave exception to his failure to stipulate that General Councils must be summoned by, and have their decrees ratified by the Papacy, and to make it clear that the Papacy was of direct dominical institution. The fear here was that the Protestants might capitulate in all the other articles, in order, at the end, to gain their point on the Papacy.

As if to rub salt into the wounds, Farnese praised Eck for his excellent learning and knowledge of the German situation, but above all for his loyalty to the Holy See. Polite pleasure was expressed at the good bearing of Gropper, 'especially as they had been given a very different report on him from that given in his [Contarini's] dispatches, which had caused His Holiness grave displeasure, since it seemed that more deference had been shown to the Protestants than to the Catholics in the choice of collocutors'.[19]

Finally Contarini had brought to his notice the complaints of the French King that in his deference to the Emperor, the legate had neglected not only the interests of the other Catholics, but also of the Catholic faith itself.[20]

[18] '. . . presupposto che il senso sia cattholico, le parole potessero esser più chiare.' Ibid., p. 232.

[19] Cf. Wauchop's critical report to Paul III on the conduct of Gropper and Pflug. 7 June 1541, Le Plat, iii. 116.

[20] Quirini, iii. 240; Dandino, the papal nuncio at the French Court had

The language of the dispatch was restrained, but its barbs were none the less effective for that. It was a considered and sustained reproof unprecedented in Contarini's long experience. His previous diplomatic missions had not always been successful, but never before had his own performance, judgement, and even loyalty been questioned. Coming on top of the failure of the colloquy, a dressing down of this nature—to a man of his seniority —could have been expected to have an almost traumatic effect upon Contarini, and in fact it did.

This proved, however, to be more than a mere personal tragedy. It was not only that Contarini had got himself too far out on a limb, and that he had the limb cut down from under him for his pains. The vote of no confidence in his conduct of affairs in Regensburg meant the defeat of his party in Italy, and with it the loss of any hope of a Catholic ecumenical initiative for decades, if not centuries to come. It meant more than the replacement of one faction by another in the Curia, more than a different conception of the tactics best suited to the German situation. For what was at stake was Contarini's whole understanding of the faith, of Catholicism. It had been the legate's successes, not his failure, which had alarmed Paul III and his advisers on the German situation— Farnese, Caraffa, Aleander—and which led them to a decisive rejection of Contarini's brand of evangelical Catholicism.

The dispatch had its immediate and drastic effect on the conduct of Contarini. It effectively forestalled any future attempts by him to develop a personal initiative of his own. From now on he had no room at all to manœuvre. In his letter to Farnese of 9 June, for example, he mentions Morone's view that the less controversy there was about the papal primacy the better and adds, 'and I would have been of the same opinion, if I had not been advised otherwise, but for me it suffices to obey'.[21] There was only one role he could play now, one for which he was, fortunately, eminently qualified, that of the professional diplomat.

In his official actions at the Diet he became henceforth the submissive tool of papal politics, and lost all independence from the Catholic opposition. His relations with the Emperor became more

---

already informed Contarini that the King had accused him of exercising '... troppo modestia, rispetto et taciturnità ...' in defence of the Catholic cause at Regensburg. 17 May 1541, ibid., p. 278.

[21] *HJ* i. 479.

than cool, and he was soon to be the butt of enthusiastic Protestant polemics. His original optimism had allowed Contarini to adopt an offensive stance, to take the initiative, to steer, or help to steer, the course of events. Increasingly he had been pushed back on to a purely defensive position, at first in relation to Catholic orthodoxy, and now to the papal cause. He was no longer the man on whom 'all Germany' set their hopes, nor even primarily the defender of the Catholic position, but the representative of the papal and curial interests in Germany, just one more papal legate. As such, the weeks from the conclusion of the colloquy to the end of the Diet were to bring him nothing but trials.

The dispatch, however, certainly did not mean a total reversal of policy on Contarini's part. He himself had long since recognized that, barring a miracle, the colloquy had failed. Where, on the other hand, he believed it had succeeded—above all on the question of justification—he stuck to his guns.

As far as the article on justification was concerned, not only his personal honour but his orthodoxy itself was at stake. To gain support for his position he decided to submit the book to a further reading, in company with the papal theologians at Regensburg, to establish its orthodoxy. The Emperor readily agreed to this provided the imperial theologians could join Badia, Pighius, and Wauchop in their scrutiny of the book.[22] On the first day[23] the errors of the Protestant counter-articles were noted, and then, on the Emperor's request, it was stated where their views *were* consonant with Catholic teaching. It was noted that some articles in the book required further explanation, and Contarini introduced a new article on the Papacy which he had drafted to meet the objections from Rome.[24] The theologians were unanimous that there could be no piece-meal acceptance of the 'agreed articles'. Unless the Protestants were at one with the Catholics in the main articles (by which those on the Church, the Eucharist, and penance were certainly meant) none of the 'agreed articles' could

---

[22] Contarini/Farnese, 9 June 1541, *HJ* i. 479; D/B, pp. 724 ff.; Contarini/Farnese, 14 June 1541, *HJ* i. 481.

[23] Not later than 13 June; cf. Vetter, p. 170, *Anm.* 2.

[24] He complained to Farnese that it was the tardy reaction of Rome to his formulations on the primacy which had made it impossible to amend the article in the book. Now that the colloquy was over his attempt to insert the new article in the margin of the book had been rejected by Granvelle, on the grounds that it would appear to be a forgery. Contarini/Farnese, 9 June 1541, *HJ* i. 479.

be accepted, for this would then be regarded as legitimizing at least some of the Protestants' beliefs.[25]

This uncompromising attitude was obviously conditioned by the receipt of the dispatch from Rome. On the other hand the firm opposition which the legate offered to Granvelle's advocacy of toleration was quite in line with his previous viewpoint. At no stage had Contarini considered the possibility of toleration—even as a temporary measure—for the Protestants' erroneous views. Contarini's standpoint here was impeccably traditionalist, unsullied by Erasmian relativism. He consistently regarded tolerance to error as a betrayal of the faith and tolerance to schism as an open affront to the authority of Rome. The lesson to be drawn from the colloquy, he believed, was not that the Catholics should be more conciliatory, but that they should stand much more firmly by their beliefs. In a dispatch sent to Rome on 29 May he had recommended the strengthening of the Catholic League and a reform of the episcopate, of instruction, and preaching. Catholicism should be reinforced from within and from without. The sole concession which he contemplated was the granting of Communion in both kinds.[26]

His relations with the Emperor had already been deteriorating. On 31 May, more than a week before the dispatch from Rome arrived, Contarini had rejected the imperial proposal that a limited toleration be granted the Protestants. Charles had pointed out that since there was no hope of securing further concessions from the Protestants, and since a war against them was unthinkable, some measure of toleration was inevitable. Contarini replied that he wanted neither war nor civil unrest, but that a feigned agreement of the Apostolic See and the Emperor to the false teachings of the Protestants—or even the turning of a blind eye to them—would only precipitate a still worse schism, for others would use such an agreement as a pretext for teaching falsehood instead of the truth. If peace had to be made without any agreement having been reached on the religious issue then the Catholics must distance themselves emphatically from the Protestants, not only by withholding their consent to their doctrines, but by denouncing the

[25] Contarini/Farnese, 14 June 1541, *HJ* i. 482; his letter to Farnese on the following day points to a certain amount of disagreement among the Catholics, for some felt that if the Protestants agreed on the essential points, no further difficulties should be made. Ibid., 482–3.
[26] Contarini/Farnese, 29 May 1541, *HJ* i. 474–6.

latter, albeit charitably.[27] Unlike the Archbishop of Mainz and the
Bavarians, however, Contarini wanted to avert war, and was
remarkably free from bitterness against the Protestants.[28]

Thus there is continuity as well as discontinuity in the policy
pursued by Contarini before and after the receipt of the dispatch.
We should not overestimate its importance. Yet the bitterness
which occasionally creeps into his reply shows how uncommonly
painful it must have been to the proud Venetian to be suspected of
coldness in the defence of the Catholic faith and to have to defend
himself in this way.[29] Previous to Regensburg it would have been
unthinkable that he should find himself in a position such as this.
The price he was paying for his championship of reconciliation
was to be cruelly high.

[27] Morone/Farnese, 2 June 1541, Lämmer, p. 272.

[28] He attributes the failure of the colloquy to human sinfulness generally
rather than to that of the Protestants in particular. Contarini/Cardinal of Burgos,
9 June 1541, Morandi, I. ii. 175–6.

[29] He rejected as groundless some of the particular criticisms, e.g. that his
household had been indiscreet. Contarini/Farnese, 9 June 1541, *HJ* i. 478 ff; he
blamed the Bavarians for spreading rumours about his undue deference to the
Emperor, '. . . li quali senza volersi dimostrare voluto rompere questa concordia
et non paresse che venisse da loro, ma voleano usar me per instrumento . . .'
D/R, pp. 338–9.

13

Peace in Germany at Any Cost

ON 8 June Granvelle laid the Regensburg Book, together with the Protestant articles, before the assembled Estates.[1] It was in an atmosphere of frustration, bitterness, and mutual recrimination that he tried to launch his new toleration policy. It was clear, as the Venetian ambassador wrote on the following day, that there was disagreement on many articles, and particularly on the most important[2] It was certainly an ill omen for the outcome of the negotiations that Philip of Hesse chose this critical moment to leave Regensburg, despite the entreaties of Granvelle.[3] He had, of late, been rather stouter in his profession of Protestantism, but he lacked the full-blooded bigotry of the Elector of Saxony, whose influence among the Protestants now increased. Philip left Regensburg on 14 June, after having secured a conditional amnesty from the Emperor for his bigamy, in exchange for an undertaking not to conclude alliances with France, England, or Cleves, and to oppose the admission of the latter to the Schmalkaldic League.[4]

His departure was the signal for many of the Protestant theologians to leave Regensburg.[5] Melanchthon himself was instructed by the Elector, on Luther's wish, to return to Wittenberg, but the

---

[1] *CR* iv. 389–91, 392.

[2] On 19 June he added that there was little hope of any agreement, '. . . ma si tiene per certo, si trovera qualche via et modo di qualche assettamento . . .' Fr. Contarini/Senate, D/R, pp. 196–200.

[3] 'Sovil s.f.g. abzyhen betrifft, bleib sie bei voriger meinung, wissen das nu nicht mehr zu endern, etc.' Lenz, iii. p. 84.

[4] Ibid., pp. 91–6; cf. Fr. Contarini/Senate, D/R, p. 199; Vetter, pp. 156 ff.

[5] 'Putat Calvinus pacem solidam minimè expectandam a Caesare, imò talem numquam posse sperari, nisi in religione conveniat et in reformationem consentiatur. At quando id futurum existimas? . . . Redierunt domum Brentius, Musculus, Frechtus, Vitus Norimbergensis; abiturit etiam Cruciger.' Bédrot/Grynaeus, 25 June 1541, Herminjard, vii. 157, n. 2.

express command of the Emperor forced him to remain in Regensburg until the Diet was over.[6]

The Estates had been requested to state their opinion on the book. In his address to them the Emperor had reported on the progress of the colloquy. A good number of disputed points, and by no means the least important ones, had been agreed upon by the collocutors. Let the Estates show their Christian concern by a careful consideration of the articles and the Protestant counter-articles, and then inform the Emperor what they believed would be a good and rational course to follow. They were also asked to suggest the measures they considered necessary for a reform of the abuses in the spiritual and the secular estates. The papal legate, the Emperor was confident, would gladly give his assistance in this matter.[7]

Neither the Protestants nor the Catholics were of one mind about the book. We have already noted that the Protestants had reacted in different ways to Elector Joachim's six articles. On 13 June they received their copies of the Book, and at once disagreements made themselves felt. Bucer argued that the book should be viewed favourably by the Protestants. Melanchthon, who dubbed it the 'hyaena', wanted it rejected *in toto*.[8] The Saxon Elector had, of course, consistently recommended an unwavering allegiance to the Augsburg Confession and Apology.[9]

On 25 June the deliberations of the Protestant theologians on the book began in the presence of their princes. First Melanchthon gave his judgement on the book. This took the form of an account of the negotiations throughout the colloquy. From the beginning, he avowed, he had been suspicious of the ambiguity of the articles; they obscured the full meaning of the Protestant views, and decked out Catholic opinions in a seductive manner.[10] He rejected the claim that the acceptance of the book would be a step towards the reform of the German Church; on the contrary, it would encourage the maintenance of false teachings and practices, and it might even encourage the development of a third party and thus extend

---

[6] *CR* iv. 408; *WAB* ix. 430 ff.; *CR* iv. 565.

[7] Ibid., pp. 389–91.

[8] Herminjard, vii. 157; *CR* iv. 409, 410.

[9] '... wer sich vergleichen will, der vergleiche sich mit Gott und seinem Wort...' Ibid., p. 346. He bitterly criticized Philip of Hesse for his approval of the article on justification. Ibid., p. 400.

[10] Ibid., pp. 420, 437–40.

the schism still further. Nor should true doctrine be mutilated for the sake of securing order and peace.

Bucer rejoined that it was necessary to take account of the men of goodwill on the other side. Charity demanded that something be done for them. He then defended, evidently at some length, his own conduct against the criticisms of some of the theologians. It seems, however, that he was alone in his defence of the book. After prolonged discussions the Protestants eventually agreed, given certain amendments, to accept the 'agreed articles', while their adherence to the counter-articles remained firm. As Vetter says: '... under the appearance of a complete acquiescence in the Emperor's intentions in fact the plans of the latter were stymied and rejected.'[11]

How, meantime, were the Catholics reacting? They, too, were divided in their counsels, the Electoral council being amenable to the acceptance of the 'agreed articles', the princes opposing it.

The princes tended to be dominated by the Dukes of Bavaria and the Duke of Brunswick who accepted Eck's contention that the book, being full of errors, was unacceptable, and that, instead of using the language of the Church and the Fathers, it 'Melanchthonized'.[12] Not until 5 July were the Catholics able to agree on a compromise answer to the Emperor. Even this, however, evaded the issue, by refusing to deliver any independent judgement on the book, and by requesting instead that the Emperor, together with the legate, should examine the 'agreed articles' and determine whether or not they were in accord with the Catholic faith.[13] The Emperor expressed in no uncertain language his disappointment at this answer, and while agreeing to refer the article to the legate, voiced the desire that the Estates themselves would continue to consider ways and means of arriving at a peaceful settlement. He also had to spring to the defence of Gropper and Pflug, to whom Eck, while denying for himself any association with the book, had ascribed all the blame for its 'insipidity'.[14]

The Catholics were, therefore, hopelessly divided. Hitherto, during the course of the colloquy, Contarini had at least been able to prevent the rents becoming visible. Courted by all sides, he had

---

[11] Op. cit., p. 193.   [12] CR iv. 475.
[13] Ibid., pp. 455–6; Contarini/Farnese, 5 July 1541, HJ i. 489; for dating cf. Vetter, p. 182, Anm. 3.
[14] CR iv. 459–65.

been able, by skilful conciliation, to direct the Catholic viewpoint
and to hold the different factions together. He was no longer able
to do this. The failure of the colloquy, the lack of firm support from
Rome, the growing alienation from the Emperor had knocked
away, one by one, all the props on which his mediatory platform
rested. He found himself alone, isolated, and powerless, trapped
between the upper and nether mill-stones of imperial and papal
displeasure.

Already by mid-June the papal representatives were complaining
that they were not being properly informed by Granvelle of the
course of events. Contarini, like Morone, believed that the reason
was the determination of the Emperor to pursue 'peace in Germany
at any cost'.[15] Willy-nilly he found himself forced to ally with the
Bavarians, Albert of Mainz, and their party. He had urged on
Charles the impossibility of a piece-meal acceptance of some of the
articles, the need to check any further Protestant expansion by a
strengthening of the League, and his bounden duty as Emperor to
put the interests of God and the Faith before all others. He had
complained further about the activity of the Protestant preachers
in the town.[16] But while Charles had given him an attentive
audience his impression was that in fact he would not act decisively
to meet the danger of the situation. Contarini was forced, therefore,
to consider an approach to the Catholic princes. It was now he who
had to go begging for support.

He told the Bavarians of his position on the book and the need
to strengthen the League, which they approved, and urged that no
conditions should be set for entry to the League which would
repel the Emperor from joining it. He was now committed to the
anti-imperial party, which was already involved in negotiations with
France. The Archbishop of Mainz hinted that Charles's sole
concern was for the arrangement of an external peace. If he did
not demonstrate his readiness to defend the true religion Albert
and his supporters would make an approach to France.[17]

Charles, on the other hand, now declared that if the Bavarians

---

[15] Morone/Farnese, 14 June 1541, Lämmer, pp. 373–4.
[16] Contarini/Farnese, 19 June 1541, *HJ* i. 483–6; cf. Wauchop's similar
complaint about the Protestants' activities. Le Plat, iii. 116–18; Fr. Contarini
reported that the Regensburg citizens attended Protestant services in six places
while even on feast days the (Catholic) churches were empty except for some
Catholic princes and their following. D/B, p. 550.
[17] Morone/Farnese, 21 June 1541, *HJ* iv. 620.

did not change their tune, he would come to an accommodation with the Protestants. He was unimpressed by Contarini's news that the Papacy had decided to lift the suspension of the Council and to give its support to the League. Why this sudden enthusiasm of the Papacy for the Council at this stage?[18]

Contarini, understandably, was in deep depression. Even if the Emperor and he were to remain in Regensburg for another three years he was doubtful if any remedy would be found. The Protestants appeared to be immovable in their opinions.[19] By now a further dispatch from Rome had arrived which warned in the strongest terms against any support to a policy of toleration.[20] No wonder Contarini longed to return to Italy.[21]

He had been requested, as we have seen, by the Catholic Estates to give his opinion on the book. There was no doubt in Contarini's mind what his answer must be. The toleration policy, with its postponement of the theological issues to the Council, was totally unacceptable, for it implied that essential articles of the Faith were in doubt. This was not the case, and not even a future Council could submit the dogmatic definitions of the Church to a new scrutiny in this way. Moreover an interim peace was unacceptable as long as the Church lands had not been restored. This view when he communicated it to the militants found a predictably enthusiastic reception. Like the bishops, whom Contarini had summoned before him a few days previously, they urged that the Pope should convoke the promised Council as speedily as possible.[22]

[18] *ZKG* iii. 178.

[19] '. . . perchè già i popoli sono persuasi et gli par buona cosa viver in questa licenza e senza alcun freno . . . Luterani addimandano, non sia innovata cosa alcuna circa la religione, sin tanto non siano decise le differenze per guidici non sospetti, li quali non si troveranno mai . . . Ho parlato con diversi protestanti dottori, col Melanthone e altri, parmi siano risolutissimi nelle opinioni loro, nè cessano ogni dì seminar' il mal seme con li predicationi, col scrivere e in ogni modo possibile.' Thus Contarini's secretary Hier. Negri/Marcantonio Michieli, 28 June 1541, D/R, pp. 206–7.

[20] The granting of toleration to Germany was out of the question for if the Papacy were to allow this, the rest of Christendom would take the chance to follow suit, '. . . e lasciare di pigliar da qui innanzi la norma della Fede et Religione sua da questa S. Sede, come per l'addietro ha fatto, poiche la vedesse variar da se stessa . . . essendo la tolerantia nel Papa vero consenso, e statuto . . .' Ardinghelli/Contarini, 15 June 1541, Quirini, iii. 240–9; for the various drafts of this dispatch cf. *ZKG* v. 595 ff.

[21] 'Non invenio spiritum caritatis, sed spiritum aemulationis et discordiae, il quale mi dubito, che mandera in ruina tuta questa provincia. Mi duole nel core, ma non si puole fare altro.' Contarini/Bembo, 4 July 1541, D/R, p. 344.

[22] Morone/Farnese, 4 July 1541, D/R, p. 209; the bishops had urged that

In an icy audience with the Emperor on 10 July Contarini explained that since the Protestants had shown their divergence from the received opinion of the Catholic Church the whole matter should be referred to the Supreme Pontiff and the Apostolic See, which would deal with it either by the General Council shortly to be held, or in another expedient way.[23] The book, in other words, was rejected *in toto*; the colloquy might as well never have taken place.

Charles expressed his bitterness and disillusion about Pope, Council, and princes. He had wasted his time at Regensburg. He had gained neither a subsidy against the Turks nor an agreement on religious matters. And now he heard that the Pope was planning to enter the League without him and was allying with Venice and the King of France. Groundless as this rumour appears to have been, the legate's proposal that the disputed articles should be referred to the Pope was hardly likely to commend itself to Charles in his present mood, especially since Contarini himself had been one of the most effective opponents of the conciliatory programme on which he had staked all his hopes.

Almost the sole concern which the legate and the Emperor now had in common was that for reform. Here for Contarini was at least one issue on which personal inclination, official instructions, and imperial policy were in harmony. Yet it is perhaps significant that even in this matter the initiative for the convocation of the bishops to hear an address from Contarini on this subject had come not from himself but from the Emperor.[24] The time for initiatives on the part of Contarini was long since past. Eventually, after repeated requests by Charles, he addressed the assembled prelates on 7 July, and his exhortation appears to have been well received.[25]

It began with the usual admonition to sobriety and simplicity of life, which should afford no ground for scandal, and set a good example to the people. The primary note, however, is that of pastoral concern.

Contarini stressed the need for the bishop to reside in the most populous places of his diocese, so that he could at once take appro-

---

'presto, presto e piu che presto celebrasse il concilio senza fallo alcuno . . .' Contarini/Farnese, 10 July 1541, *HJ* i. 491–2.

[23] Ibid., pp. 492–5.   [24] As Vetter points out; Vetter p. 186.
[25] *HJ* i. 492; the text in Le Plat, iii. 91–3; *CR* iv. 506–9.

priate action if any decline from the Faith were detected. He should set up an information network for the other parts of the diocese, and conduct frequent visitations, as generals inspect the defences of cities besieged by the enemy. He should pay particular attention to the conduct of worship and the equitable distribution of diocesan funds.

He referred to the urgent need for learned preachers to propagate orthodox doctrine and sound morals by word and example, while eschewing bitter polemic, which neither edified the faithful nor won over the adversary. They should rather work lovingly for the salvation of their opponents.

Equally important was the foundation of Catholic schools to counteract the influence of the new Protestant schools, to which the future nobility of Germany was streaming, attracted by the renown of the Protestant teachers, imbibing not only secular learning but Lutheran doctrine. Parents must be warned against such schools, and every support given to the erection of Catholic institutions of equal standing where orthodox doctrine would be upheld.

These, Contarini concluded, were the guide-lines for reform, which he had submitted to them at the express wish of the Pope. They, the bishops, would be able to draw the necessary conclusions, and to devise the measures required to meet the actual situation as they knew it.

This was a realistic enough assessment of the situation. It surrendered the myth of a Catholic Germany, and recognized that Protestantism, far from being a bizarre sect, admittedly seductive and dangerous but essentially a transient, peripheral phenomenon, now threatened the existence of Catholicism itself. Not only did it boast an immense popular following and a heterodox theology. That in itself would not be so disturbing; Church history, after all, was littered with the wrecks of such movements. But it was recognized as having penetrated into the very fabric of national and social life, rooting itself so deeply in the political and ecclesiastical and educational structures that the only realistic policy for Catholicism to adopt was the preparation for a hard, long-drawn-out struggle in which, initially at least, the old Church would find itself very much on the defensive. Catholicism faced the uneasy future of a beleaguered fortress.

Contarini's use of the military metaphor is not accidental. His

programme breathes the spirit of the counter-reformation. This is
the language of Aleander and Caraffa in Rome, of Loyola's new
movement, of St. Theresa in Spain. Hitherto Contarini had seen
reform in the perspective of reunion. It had been his hope that a
reformed Catholicism would prepare the way for the return of the
Protestants to the true Faith. Now, however, the keyword is
consolidation, reform seen as a weapon *against* Protestantism. The
future lies with the Council of Trent, the Jesuits, and the Inquisition.

Accordingly Contarini now joined Eck in denouncing or at
least renouncing the book, joined the Bavarians and their allies in
resisting the Emperor, joined the authoritarian elements in the
Church and the particularist elements in the Empire. The shattering of his dream of a renewed and reunited Christendom was not,
then, the end for him. He still had his functions to fulfil, his work
to do. He still had his obedience.

The toleration policy had failed. Neither Protestants nor
Catholics seemed prepared to accept the 'agreed articles' as a
workable basis to a long-term settlement, but were falling back on
the traditional bulwarks of the authority of Rome and of Wittenberg respectively. Yet despite this total lack of success some sort
of working arrangement had to be devised, at least a temporary
settlement patched up, the most urgent needs of the Empire met.
However unthinkable toleration might be to the theologians,
politically it remained the only option open.

A clash of interests was therefore inevitable when, on 12 July,
having received the Protestant verdict on the book, Charles laid
before the Estates his proposals for the Recess, together with
Contarini's judgement on the book and his admonition to the
bishops.[26] The full extent of the Emperor's alienation from the
Curia and its representatives was now revealed. The promised
Council rated a mention but little more; the whole emphasis was
on the need for an immediate settlement. The Estates were requested to consider giving their approval to the 'agreed articles'
as an interim statement of belief, at least until the General Council

---

[26] Ibid., pp. 509–13, 506; Contarini had strenuously objected to the submission of his reform proposals to the Diet lest the bishops be offended, but his
objections had been brushed aside. Contarini/Farnese, 13 July 1541, D/R,
p. 344; Morone/Farnese, 13 July 1541, ibid., p. 213. Charles had already requested from the Catholic Estates on 7 July their proposals for a lasting peace.
Vetter, p. 195.

should decide on the matter, or failing this another imperial assembly. For the meantime the Nuremberg Peace should remain in force. With brazen effrontery the proposal claimed that the papal legate was in favour of a provisional acceptance of the 'agreed articles'.[27]

On 14 July the first of the replies to the imperial proposal arrived—that of the Protestants.[28] Despite their theological qualms and Luther's scepticism, they agreed to the acceptance of the 'agreed articles' provided they were given a proper Christian interpretation, and hoped that they would serve as the basis for a full concord and pave the way to a Christian reformation of the churches. They were willing to make their contribution to the immediately needed (eilend) subsidy for the Turkish campaign, but made no mention of any regular contribution.

All in all these statements showed a certain community of interest between the Protestants and Charles; at least it would afford him some support for the campaign against the Turks and establish a temporary *modus vivendi*. The answer from the Electors, where moderate opinion was in the majority, was still more favourable, in fact they were ready to go further than the Emperor himself.[29] They not only supported the acceptance of the 'agreed articles' for the meantime, but insisted that the future Council be free, Christian, and held in Germany. If this were impossible, a National Council or imperial assembly should be held.[30] The answer of the free cities was also generally favourable.[31]

On the other hand the Catholic princes, under the leadership of the Bavarians and the bishops, rejected the conciliated articles, and demanded that the Augsburg Recess remain in force as the one real remedy for the heresies rampant in the land until a General Council was convoked. Even they, however, insisted that the Council be held in a location suitable to the German nation. Following the lead of the memorandum by Eck[32] they accused the

---

[27] '. . . zum wenigsten bis auf das nächst künftige gemeine Concilium, dem die endliche Erörterung dieser und der andern Puncten vorbehalten seyn solle, dieweil der Päpstlichen H. Legat das auch selbst für gut ansieht . . .' *CR* iv. 511.

[28] Ibid., pp. 516–20.

[29] Dittrich's comment that the emperor's proposal displeased all parties ('missfiel auf allen Seiten') is therefore quite misleading. D/B, p. 753. Among the Electors opposition to any acceptance of the 'agreed articles' came from the Archbishop of Mainz and Trier. Contarini/Farnese, 19 July 1541, *HJ* i. 497.

[30] Submitted on 17 July; *CR* iv. 524–6.   [31] Ibid., pp. 552–3.

[32] Ibid., pp. 459–60.

Catholic collocutors of having made inadmissible concessions in the 'agreed articles', which would have to be thoroughly revised. In any case everything would have to be deferred to the General Council.[33]

Contarini's position was anything but enviable. Not one major grouping in Germany supported the full papal position. Even the rigorists were ready to contemplate a National Council. He had come to Regensburg to mediate between Catholic and Protestant, Pope and Emperor, Italy and Germany. His actions had already earned him a humiliating rebuke from Rome. Now his isolation in the Curia was duplicated by that in the German situation.

On 16 July he eventually secured an audience with the Emperor. He made it clear that he regarded the latter's willingness to approve the conciliated articles, with the apparent claim that he had agreed to this, the delay in granting him an audience, and the lack of any mention of the Papacy in reference to the Council, as part of a deliberate policy to make Emperor and Diet the judges on matters pertaining to religion, to the complete exclusion of the Pope and the papal representative. The Emperor's presentation to the Diet, contrary to Contarini's express wish, of the legate's private admonition to the bishops was another example of the misuse of religious matters for political ends. Even the Pope himself, who, unlike Emperor and Diet, did have the right to legislate on such matters, would never have acted in such a cavalier way, but would have first consulted the other nations of Christendom.

Charles, not a whit abashed, retorted that he had carried out his duty before God, and would not hesitate to accept the responsibility for what he had done. He had not sought the approbation of the Estates for the articles, but only their opinion, after which everything would first be referred to the Council. A mention of the Pope in connection with the Council would only have triggered off a violent reaction, which would not have been confined to the Protestants. If the Council were preceded by the carrying out of reforms he would be convinced that it had been convoked in the Holy Spirit. Otherwise he would not know what to believe.[34]

[33] Submitted on 17 July; ibid., pp. 526–9; their decision had been preceded by a hefty debate, in which Duke Otto Henry and the Bishops of Augsburg and Constance argued the case for a more conciliatory approach. Calvin/Farel, 25 July 1541, Herminjard, vii. 194.

[34] Contarini/Farnese, 17 July 1541, *HJ* i. 495–7.

The clash of interests was now quite clear. Contarini's policy of reform, League, and Council offered no help to Charles in his present predicament. The Emperor could not afford to use the Diet for the consolidation of specifically Roman or even Catholic interests, and now that the wider hope of reunion was shattered his only thought was to patch up a reasonable peace and arrange as speedy a conclusion to the Diet as possible. He planned his departure for 22 July.[35]

Of all the answers to his proposal of 12 July that of the princes alone had totally rejected the acceptance of the 'agreed articles'. But the Archbishops of Mainz and Trier had advocated the same point of view in the Electoral Court, and to alienate the majority of the German bishops and princes would only be playing into the hands of France, especially when they had the backing of Rome, as represented by Contarini. It would be a dangerous game to provoke the Curia too far.[36]

While, then, the Emperor, anxious to draw the Diet to a close and to leave for Italy, was now setting the pace, it was the Catholic opposition who had the initiative firmly in their hands. The bishops felt that the Emperor was betraying their hopes of a restitution of the Church lands, and were correspondingly uncooperative.[37] Mainz and Trier, outnumbered in the Electoral Court, secured from Contarini a second statement on the conciliated articles.[38] This new writing, while denying that there was any ambiguity in his previous declaration of 10 July, interpreted the latter as neither approving nor tolerating *any* articles until the Council, but referring the whole negotiation, and all the articles to the Pope and the Apostolic See. Nothing could have been more explicit.

It is an exaggeration to say that Contarini had now no mind of his own, that he was merely a tool in the hands of others.[39] It was his own conviction that the Emperor had embarked on a completely wrong policy and was, as a result, forfeiting the goodwill of

[35] Fr. Contarini/Senate, 16 July 1541, D/R, p. 213.

[36] Cf. Morone/Farnese, 21 June 1541, *HJ* iv. 620 ff; there were also Charles's Italian interests to be considered. Cf. Vetter, p. 200.

[37] Leopold von Ranke, *Deutsche Geschichte im Zeitalter der Reformation*, iv. 159.

[38] *CR* iv. 554–5; written on 17 July; on 18 July Contarini agreed to a further emendation suggested by Mainz and Trier. Contarini/Farnese, 19 July 1541, *HJ* i. 497.

[39] Vetter describes him as the '... willenlose Werkzeug anderer ...' Vetter, p. 201.

the German nation. Having brought about nothing but chaos, Charles now wished that he had never come to Germany. 'I would never have thought', concluded Contarini, 'that His Majesty would let himself be influenced to act in this way with such slight justification.'[40]

Contarini and Morone were deeply troubled by the determination of the Emperor to take up a 'neutral' standpoint above the competing confessions, by his threat to leave the Diet even before the Recess was negotiated, and by his reluctance to join the Catholic League.[41] Above all his support for the holding of a Council in Germany alarmed them. To this was added the cold disdain with which he now greeted their repeated requests for an assurance that no toleration would be granted.[42] The Archbishop of Mainz increased their unease by confidentially informing them that the Emperor was sending troops to Italy in far greater numbers than he had disclosed, and that he intended nothing less than the forcible submission of the Curia to his will. In view of the anti-clerical feeling at the court Morone believed it was possible that this might be true. He was even ready to attribute to the Emperor designs on the Church lands.[43]

Under such heavy pressure from the rigorists, Charles had no alternative but to present on 23 July a new draft for the Recess which met almost all their demands.[44] Nothing was said about an approval of the 'agreed articles'. The whole negotiation was to be referred to a General Council, or National Council, which the Emperor would request Paul III to summon. Should this fall through he would himself call another imperial assembly to deal with the religious question. In the meantime the Protestants were to abide by the 'agreed articles' and the bishops to carry out a thorough reformation.

This provoked, in turn, an angry reaction on the part of the Protestants, especially against the one-sided stipulation that they, but not the Catholics, should abide by the conciliated articles and should refrain from further proselytizing.[45] A refusal by the

[40] *HJ* i. 497.

[41] Morone/Farnese, 19 July 1541, *HJ* iv. 638.

[42] 'Io parlai poi a Soa M. tà circa le cose della Religione, pregandola, che non comportasse, che qui si facesse tolerantia alcuna ... Quella mi rispose, che si faria, quanto Noi volevamo, et mostrò di dirlo con alquanto di sdegno.' Contarini/Farnese, 22 July 1541, *ZKG* iii. 182.

[43] *HJ* iv. 639.   [44] *CR* iv. 586–9.

[45] Submitted on 25 July; ibid., pp. 589–94.

Protestants to subscribe to the Recess now seemed on the cards. This, however, carried with it the danger of civil war, and possibly a Protestant alliance with France, such as the Duke of Cleves had already concluded while the Diet was being held.[46]

Through the Elector of Brandenburg, with whom he had made a secret treaty only two days earlier, the Emperor suggested a compromise solution, which offered tolerance on the 'cuius regio' principle, and proposed that the Catholics tolerate married priests and Communion in both kinds.[47]

This solution, however, while acceptable to the Protestants, was rejected out of hand by the Catholics, who, with some minor qualifications, were well content with the proposals of 23 July.[48] Not so Contarini! He had been kept deliberately in the dark about its contents by Charles, and when by means of his own he discovered what they were and hurried to the Emperor, he was refused an audience, and had to resort on 26 July to a direct appeal to the Estates.[49] He urged them to reject any suggestion of a National Council, whose decisions on matters of doctrine would have no authority whatsoever, and might well set off a chain reaction of seditious movements, in Germany and out of it.

The answer of the Estates—and this at a time when the hard-liners were in the ascendant—was sharp. The best way to avoid a National Council would be for the Apostolic See to convoke the General Council it had so often promised. If, however, this were not done, the logic of the situation demanded that the controversies be settled by a National Council or imperial assembly.[50]

Contarini had already had to hear from the German bishops that the Papacy was to blame for the repeated delay of the Council. Now the entire Catholic Estates dismissed his contention that the decisions of a National Council were void, and, to add insult to injury, insisted that the General Council, if it were held, should meet in Germany. Contarini was treated even by the Catholics as the representative of an alien power with but little understanding of the German situation, whose pretensions could, if necessary, be ignored. The anti-Protestant was by no means necessarily a pro-Papalist.

The legate's humiliation was extreme. As the Diet wound to a

---

[46] Ranke, iv. 161.   [47] *CR* iv. 594-5.   [48] Ibid., pp. 595-600, 634.
[49] Ibid., p. 600; Contarini/Farnese, 26 July 1541, *ZKG* iii. 183.
[50] *CR* iv. 601-2.

close he found himself regarded as a nonentity, uninformed by the
Emperor, ignored by the Estates, the target of vicious abuse from
the Protestants. His attempts to gain exacter information from
King Ferdinand on the form which the Recess would take were
brushed aside with the remark that it would give little pleasure to
anyone—Pope, King, or Protestant—a not inaccurate forecast.[51]

The problem of the Emperor was how some sort of settlement
could be arranged with the Protestants without alienating the
Catholic party. In view of the rejection of Brandenburg's proposals,
he laid before the Estates yet another draft on 27 July, which
differed little from that of 23 July, and therefore immediately led
to a protest by the Protestants, in effect a repetition of their
objections to the previous draft.[52] In one last desperate effort to
gain an agreement Charles summoned the Estates to his quarters on
28 July, and in marathon negotiations which lasted from early
morning well into the night managed to satisfy many of the
Protestant objections by a secret Declaration on how the Recess
was to be interpreted. Further objections from the Protestants
on the following day led to a final amended Declaration by the
Emperor.[53]

The Protestants were allowed to interpret the conciliated articles
in a wholly Protestant way. They were given virtually a free hand
in the reformation of the monasteries and the financing of their
churches and schools from the income of the Church properties.
Protestantism was given a certain juridical status by the guarantee
of the Protestant as well as the Catholic clergy in their possessions,
the Augsburg Recess was to have no validity in religious matters,
and the ban pronounced upon Goslar was expressly included in the
general suspension of the law suits and imperial bans directed
against the Protestants.

At the same time Charles pacified the Catholics by joining the
League, but a League from which any commitments liable to
involve him in a premature war against the Protestants had been
removed. On 29 July the Recess was formally read and after a last
fierce skirmish between the two confessions was finally accepted.[54]
The Emperor left Regensburg at once. The Diet was over.

---

[51] *ZKG* iii. 183.   [52] *CR* iv. 612–16, 616–19.
[53] *CR* iv. 622, 623.
[54] *CR* iv. 625–30, 632; accepted by the Protestants on the condition that it be
interpreted according to the imperial Declaration. Ibid., p. 631.

14

The Catholicism of Contarini

On Corpus Christi Day, 16 June, four hundred citizens in gleaming armour and armed with halberds lined the route as the solemn procession left the Regensburg Cathedral by its main entrance, crossed the cathedral square, passed along the western and nothern sides of the episcopal palace, and then returned to the cathedral again via the Lower Minster.

Since Luther's denunciation of it the Corpus Christi processions had been tending to become demonstrations of Catholic militancy. That in Regensburg was no exception. It was led off by pipes and drums, then came citizens in armour, fifteen deep, the pupils of the cathedral school singing in harmony, the canons, Spanish clergy in their distinctive garb, the cathedral chaplains with the reliquary, and the choir of the cathedral accompanied by a portable organ carried by the corn dealers. Then came Spanish priests bearing candles, chaplains with more relics, the German Catholic princes, an Italian cleric bearing the high silver cross of the papal legate, boys with cymbals, then the sacred sacrament itself, borne by Cardinal Contarini, a reverent appearance in his flowing, greyish-white beard. The cardinal was assisted by the Archbishop of Salzburg and the High Master of the German Order; immediately behind the sacrament walked the Emperor, bareheaded and holding a white wax candle in his right hand like the other princes, in his left a 'paternosterlein' (rosary). For the chronicler Widmann he was the very model of devout piety.[1]

This, then, is the 'other' Contarini, the churchman and prelate, and it is salutary that prior to a reassessment of his Catholicism we should keep this perhaps rather triumphalist scene in mind. The 'authentic' Contarini is not to be found by stressing his views on reform or on justification by faith at the expense of everything else. The conviction lying behind this final chapter is that an under-

[1] *ZBLG* vi. 393–4.

standing of Contarini's activity at Regensburg is not without relevance for the understanding of his theology. Its purpose is to urge the need for a reassessment of Contarini's theology in the light of the events of Regensburg, and to suggest some of the new perspectives from which this reassessment will have to be conducted.

It is not merely that research in the Reformation period has progressed considerably since Brieger,[2] Dittrich, and Rückert[3] dealt with the subject. The incredible changes both within and without the theological world since the Second World War have shattered the old perspectives and the old securities. The ecumenical theologian in a secular world is constrained to ask different questions from those posed by a Dittrich.

Above all, the hermeneutical problem has to be faced. For Dittrich it was enough to give a résumé of Contarini's arguments, to interject these with the odd pious comment, and to append a cautionary tale.[4] However misplaced, there can be no doubting his conviction of solidarity with Contarini across the centuries in the defence of the Catholic cause. From a totally different standpoint, Brieger also believed that he had identified the genuine beliefs of Contarini—but this time as essentially Protestant.[5] Both could indulge in this confessional shadow-boxing because they were not conscious of any alienation from the language and thought of their hero. Their Catholicism or Protestantism was his. He was 'their man in Regensburg'.

[2] Theodor Brieger, *Gasparo Contarini und das Regensburger Concordienwerk des Jahres 1541*, Gotha: 1870; 'Die Rechtfertigungslehre des Cardinal Contarini', *Theologische Studien und Kritiken*, xlv. (1872), 87–150.

[3] Hans Rückert, *Die Theologische Entwicklung Gasparo Contarinis*. (Arbeiten zur Kirchengeschichte, vi.), Berlin: 1926.

[4] On specific points Dittrich can describe Contarini's view as incorrect or incompatible with the later definitions of the Council of Trent. e.g. D/B, pp. 657–9. Egelhaaf comments that Dittrich's monograph offers less a critical appreciation of Contarini's life and work than a presentation of this life from the point of view of Contarini himself. Review in *Historische Zeitschrift*, lviii. (1887), 120–4.

[5] 'Mag daher die Rechtfertigungslehre unsers Cardinals *den Worten nach* in diesem oder jenem einzelnen Punkte eine halbirende, nach rechts und links Concessionen machende sein, *der Sache*, der Tendenz oder, sagen wir lieber: der Stimmung, ihrem eigentlichen Herzschlage nach ist sie *echt* protestantisch.' Brieger, *Theologische Studien und Kritiken*, xlv. 141–2. Under the influence, perhaps, of critical reviews by W.M. (Maurenbrecher?) in the *Historische Zeitschrift*, xxiv. (1870), 160, and of Tourtual in the *Göttingische Gelehrte Anzeigen*, 1870, pp. 1436–7, Brieger modified his views, and agreed with von Druffel (ibid., 1882, p. 1056) that 'Contarini katholisch zu sein und zu bleiben gedachte.' *ZKG* v. (1882), 578–9.

The denizen of the modern theological world, however, furiously engaged in demythologizing his God-talk, is confronted with the almost total incomprehensibility of Contarini's language and thought-patterns. At best the purely formal analysis of his theological writings has a certain technical interest. Origins can be traced, source-material compared and contrasted,[6] linguistic divergencies from the Catholic or Protestant norm recorded. But this, of course, is at best only a first step towards an understanding of Contarini's thought, and the code, it appears, has yet to be cracked.

This is most obviously the case with the formal theological writings which, to tell the truth, exhibit a profoundly unoriginal mind.[7] His arguments are generally second hand, second rate, and stilted. They move in a creaking Aristotelian framework, philosophical axioms jostling with Biblical proof texts and papal decrees. To read them is to doubt whether Contarini ever had an original thought in theology.

Now this is, to say the least, surprising. Why should Contarini's systematic theological work be so uninspired and uninspiring when the man himself, his life and work, is so full of interest?

It is not as if Contarini were a man of action who was uninterested in such theoretical matters. As the very considerable number of his theological writings demonstrates, he was passion-

---

[6] The publication by Jedin of thirty letters from Contarini to the Camaldolese monks, Tommaso Giustiniani and Vincenzo Quirini, between 1511 and 1523 has been the most important find here. Hubert Jedin, *Contarini und Camaldoli*. Edizioni di Storia e Letteratura. Estratto dall'Archivio Italiano per la Storia della Pietà, ii. (1953). His interpretation of the material in 'Turmerlebnis des jungen Contarini', *HJ* lxx. (1951), 115 ff. Lenz's initiative in providing a critical edition of the Regensburg Book (Lenz, iii. 31–72) has been followed up by the theological evaluation of Robert Stupperich in *Der Humanismus und die Wiedervereinigung der Konfessionen* (SVRG No. 160), Leipzig: 1936; and in his article, 'Der Ursprung des "Regensburger Buches" von 1541 und seine Rechtfertigungslehre', *ARG* xxvi. (1939), 88–116.

[7] Contarini's main philosophical and theological writings were gathered together by his nephew, Luigi Contarini: *Gasparis Contareni Cardinalis Opera*, Parisiis: 1571. Friedrich Hünermann has reissued four of the controversial works: *Confutatio Articulorum seu Quaestionum Lutheranorum, Epistola de iustificatione, De potestate Pontificis*, and *De praedestinatione* in, *Gasparo Contarini: Gegenreformatorische Schriften (1530 c.–1542)* (Corpus Catholicorum, vii.), Münster: 1923; Jedin has provided a German translation of the *Confutatio* in *Kardinal Contarini als Kontroverstheologe* (Katholisches Leben und Kämpfen im Zeitalter der Glaubensspaltung, ix; Münster: 1949); pp. 19–48; cf. also Felix Gilbert, 'Contarini on Savonarola: An Unknown Document of 1516', *ARG* xlix. (1968), 145–50.

ately concerned for the doctrine as well as the reform of the Church. Yet of the few, for example, who have ventured on the reading of his *De Predestinatione*[8] the number who have plodded through to the end must be small indeed, and the number who would claim to have received any illumination thereby infinitesimal.

Considerably less obscure, on the other hand, are Contarini's letters. Where they deal with theological matters we approach that coherence of thought and personality so characteristic of Luther, and encounter something of the spontaneity and freshness which Contarini's action would have led us to expect. Partly, of course, this is because of the more immediate and personal appeal which all correspondence has, partly also, however, because he is relatively free here from the conventions of scholastic argumentation.

The most promising point of departure would appear, then, to be his correspondence, where the air is somewhat less rarified, where he writes in the immediate context of a situation familiar to us. Contarini, the amateur theologian, has too long been left to the somewhat disembodied treatment of the professional historians of doctrine.[9] Valuable as the work of the latter has been, it has left many of the most important questions unasked, and has tended to overlook the diffidence with which Contarini moved in the purely doctrinal field. It was at Regensburg, where doctrinal and diplomatic issues were scarcely to be disentangled, that Contarini, the professional diplomat, was at his most natural. Hence the value of interrogating him as to his theology within this setting.

One of the most immediate problems which the confessional confrontation at Regensburg sets us is that of the adequacy of our understanding of 'Catholicism' or 'Protestantism'. Just where is the line to be drawn between the two when a Calvin and a Contarini can both be convinced of the essential correctness of the Regensburg formula on justification—'faith which is active in love'. We have already noted that both Rome and Wittenberg

---

[8] Hünermann, pp. 44–67.

[9] Hugo Lämmer, *Die Vortridentisch-Katholische Theologie des Reformations-Zeitalters* (Berlin: 1858), pp. 63 ff., 192 ff; Reinhold Seeberg, *Lehrbuch der Dogmengeschichte* (3rd edn. Leipzig: 1920), IV. ii. 732–53; Friedrich Hünermann, 'Die Rechtfertigungslehre des Kardinals Gasparo Contarini'. *Tübinger Theologische Quartalschrift*, cii. (1921), 1–22; J. Rivière, 'Justification', *Dictionnaire de Theologie Catholique*, VIII. ii. 2159 ff.; P. C. Gutierrez, 'Un Capitolo de Teologia Pretridentina: El Problema de la Justificacion en los primeros Coloquios religiosos alemanes', *Miscelanea Comillas*, iv. (1945), 10–30; Giuseppe Agosta, *Il Card. Gaspare Contarini e il Luteranesimo*, Trapani: 1950.

later rejected the article as ambiguous. But what does this mean? Does it necessarily follow that it was neither Catholic nor Protestant, or not 'fully' so? Do we accept a purely positivist criterion: whatever Rome accepts is Catholic, whatever Wittemberg (or Weimar) accepts is Protestant? This would be to cast doubt both on Contarini's Catholicism and on Calvin's Protestantism.

But we must not restrict our discussion to this single article. We have already indicated the many similarities between the thought of the Catholic Gropper and the Protestant Bucer. Even the expert in the field of theological archaeology would have difficulty at times in distinguishing their utterances from one another. Distinctions can be made, and on certain points obviously must be made. Very often, however, one does not seem far from hair splitting. It is assumed *a priori* that a difference must exist, and by looking long enough and hard enough one is indeed found. The exercise, however, carries little conviction, and certainly does not establish that the differences were grave enough to justify the continued division of the Church.

The whole Regensburg Book raises, then, in the sharpest manner, the question as to the adequacy of our interpretative categories. We have seen how the book was conditioned through and through by its character as a response to a personal and ecclesiastical crisis. Does this make its articles any less 'Protestant', or more 'Humanist'? Does Bucer necessarily stand condemned as an opportunist because of his support for them?

Certainly for the modern Catholic and Protestant treatments of the Diet these questions do not appear to arise. The Regensburg Book is written off as an unhappy compromise which could never succeed,[10] or as an exercise in self-deception.[11] Does this not,

[10] Thus Agosta, p. 43.

[11] Speaking, e.g. of the welcome given Article V by both sides at Regensburg, Stupperich comments, 'An dieser Stelle zeigte sich aber, wie sehr man sich auf beiden Seiten durch Worte hatte täuschen lassen . . . Der Fortgang der Verhandlungen zeigte, wie wenig man sich tatsächlich verständigt hatte.' *Der Humanismus und die die Wiedervereinigung der Konfessionen*, pp. 100–1; Jedin even assigns to Regensburg, 'eine geradezu providentielle Funktion. Denn in Regensburg ist versucht worden, das Unmögliche doch noch möglich zu machen . . .'; its failure demonstrated once for all the futility of such attempts and prepared the way for the Council of Trent. 'Geschichtlich betrachtet ist nicht einzusehen wie ein anderer Weg hätte gefunden werden können.' 'Das Konzil von Trient und der Unionsgedanke'. *Theologie und Glaube*, xl. (1950), 503, 513; Gutierrez describes it as more of a treaty between the two confessions than a doctrinal agreement. *Miscelanea Comillas*, iv. 23.

however, seem to indicate a rather unrealistic theological purism? What else could a public theological document like this be but a compromise? How were the decrees of the Council of Trent arrived at if not by a series of compromises? Who would care to argue that the creeds of the early Church descended straight from heaven, or dispute that they were often catapulted into existence by the painful necessity to clarify imperial policy on matters religious if political disorders were to be avoided? The theological purist tends to be impelled here by confessional imperialism rather than by any clear appreciation of the situation.[12]

What, then, of Contarini's Catholicism? The question has been posed before now. Indeed the legate's activity at Regensburg, and the attention which the Inquisition later devoted both to his works and his friends were bound to encourage speculation about his orthodoxy.[13] Jedin's view that his inherent goodness and his concern for the unity of the Church may have led him to make some imprudent concessions to the Protestants, but that basically he remained always 'unquestionably Catholic'[14] can be taken as representing the attitude of the great majority of Catholic scholars.[15] Protestant historians have tended to lay somewhat more emphasis on the Lutheran colouring to his understanding of

[12] Rivière, e.g. speaks of the danger to Catholic orthodoxy and concludes that, 'le protestantisme menaçait évidemment d'introduire la confusion dans bien des esprits. Il était temps pour l'Église d'intervenir.' *Dictionnaire de Théologie Catholique*, VIII. ii. 2164.

[13] The amendments made by the Inquisition to the Venetian editions of 1578 and 1589 of the *Opera* are collected in Hünermann, *Gegenreformatorische Schriften*, pp. xxxiv–xxxvii.

[14] 'Einwandfrei katholisch'. *Contarini als Kontroverstheologe*, p. 16; Jedin rejects on dogmatic grounds the possibility that Contarini's views on justification were an admixture of orthodox and unorthodox thought, 'for in the sphere of faith there can be no middle course, that is, there is no half-truth but only truth and error'. *History*, i. 383 n. 2.

[15] Referring to Contarini's statement that without the authority of the Church he not only could not accept any doubtful statements but could not even accept the Gospel of John, Agosta exclaims: 'In un uomo che pensa così, ogni vena è cattolica.' Agosta, p. 44; Joseph Lortz speaks of '. . . so absolut kirchen-und papsttreue, religiös und sittlich so wertvolle . . . Männer wie Kardinal Contarini und Gropper . . .', *Reformation*, ii. 228; Hünermann, however, speaks of Contarini slipping gradually 'in eine immer grössere Annäherung an die reformatorischen Ideen . . .', *Tübinger Theologische Quartalschrift*, cii. 21; Wilhelm Braun, a modernist, uses terms reminiscent of those of Brieger. He concludes that '. . . wenn auch der *Theologe* Contarini katholisch gelehrt hat, doch der Mensch, der Christ evangelisch empfunden hat'. *Kardinal Gasparo Contarini oder der 'Reformkatholizismus' unserer Tage im Licht der Geschichte* (Leipzig: 1903), p. 69.

justification, but Rückert's analysis of his teaching has discouraged any from following Brieger's rash example in claiming him for Protestantism.[16]

It will be seen that on the question of Contarini's Catholicism a certain consensus of opinion has been arrived at, but one based rather narrowly on a consideration of Contarini's teaching on justification. It was natural enough that attention should be concentrated on this one issue, for it was Contarini's approval for the controversial Article V which, both at the time and later, attracted the suspicion that he held unorthodox views,[17] and the Council of Trent, of course, explicitly condemned the doctrine of 'double justice'. In determining the nature of Contarini's Catholicism an examination of this article and his statements on it obviously has a central place. It should not, however, as it unfortunately has, have usurped the place of all other considerations.

Above all it should have been complemented by an examination of Contarini's conduct at Regensburg, for it is the latter which affords the key to Contarini's understanding of justification. It is not enough to know the origins and trace the development of this doctrine in Contarini's thought; we must also know the intentions with which he furthered it, and this we can only learn from the proceedings of the Diet itself. There is one further point. It is as important for an appreciation of Contarini's Catholicism to see where he did not diverge from the trodden path as to note where he did, as illuminating to examine his attitude to the articles on the Church and on the sacraments—the ones on which the colloquy foundered—as to pore over the article on justification which seemed to pave the way to its success.

[16] Seeberg believes that the main element in Contarini's double justice theory remains that of inherent righteousness and that '. . . die Eigenart der imputierten Gerechtigkeit ist nicht klar erfasst, weil sie eben ein übernommenes fremdes Element in dem Begriffsgefüge war'. *Lehrbuch der Dogmengeschichte*, IV. ii. 749; Philip McNair believes Contarini '. . . accepted the doctrine of Justification *ex sola fide* not so much because it was taught by Luther as because it seemed to him to be supported by the sturdiest pillars of the Catholic doctrinal tradition'. *Peter Martyr in Italy: An Anatomy of Apostasy* (Oxford: 1967), p. 13.

[17] Pole's ecstatic welcome for the agreement was quite untypical. Pole/Contarini, 17 May 1541, D/R, p. 185. The first reaction in Roman circles was deep suspicion of the Lutherans', though not of Contarini's motives. Priuli/Beccadelli, 21 May 1541, Quirini, iii. 46–9; in the lively controversy which ensued opinion soon hardened against the formula though care was taken not to implicate Contarini personally in the criticism. Bembo/Contarini, 29 May 1541, D/R, p. 188.

If we do this we shall discover that the question as to the nature of Contarini's Catholicism is falsely, or at least too narrowly, posed. Contarini was a many-layered individual, and his concern for Catholicism was only one side to his character. Throughout this study we have attempted to demonstrate that at least three different factors determined his decisions at Regensburg—his ecumenism, his Catholicism, and his Curialism. We would suggest that the clue to Contarini's theology lies here, in the coexistence, in rather unstable equilibrium, of these three elements.

The question as to whether Contarini was 'basically' a Catholic or a Protestant is thereby revealed as inappropriate. It is certainly true that in some situations his 'ecumenical' concern, for example, could become so dominant that all other considerations seemed to disappear, as happened during the successful negotiations over the fifth article on justification. In fact, however, it was only because he was convinced that his other loyalties—to the traditional teaching of the Church, and to the Papal See—were not endangered that he could act as he did. Even in this instance, far from acting as a Protestant, Contarini did not even act exclusively for 'ecumenical' reasons.

Contarini was, of course, a Catholic, but scarcely 'basically' a Catholic. 'Basically' he was an eclectic, not out of vacillation or weakness of character, but because he felt himself compelled to do justice to all his different allegiances, as a man of the Renaissance, of the Church, and of the Curia. There can be no doubt about his inner integrity when his fundamental convictions were at stake. The difficulty arose, however, when a conflict arose between his various loyalties, where his concern for Christian unity clashed with his allegiance to Catholic truth. It is in the light of this crisis, in which priorities had to be determined, that the nature of Contarini's Catholicism is best revealed. Under pressure, the liberal Contarini was forced back on the traditional authoritarianism.

A reassessment of Contarini's Catholicism will therefore have to keep the following factors in mind. First of all, Contarini found that he had to dissociate himself from the Protestants not on their 'central article' of justification, which, indeed, he believed they understood better than some Catholics, but in their doctrine of Church and sacraments.

Secondly, the refusal of the Protestants to abandon their views on Church and sacraments was regarded by him as sheer obstinacy, for it was in no way the logical outcome of the doctrine of justification but a wilful refusal to accept the authority of the Church. The important point here is not that Contarini's attitude to the Church's authority was the traditional Catholic one, but that he was able to hold it at the same time as he adhered to a doctrine of justification acceptable to the Protestants, for this shows that his understanding of justification must also have been radically different from the Protestant one far more clearly than any detailed examination of his theological terminology. The acid test of one's appreciation of the doctrine of justification by faith alone is, after all, one's interpretation of the nature of the Church and the sacraments.

This has relevance for the whole debate about Italian 'evangelism', of which Contarini is one of the most notable exemplars.[18] How is its Protestant-sounding terminology to be evaluated? Contarini's case would appear to throw some light on this. For while accepting a doctrine of imputed righteousness he is able, as it were, to insulate it off from the other doctrines. The doctrine of justification by faith is not, as for Luther, *the* article of belief around which all the others must be grouped, in terms of which they must be interpreted or reinterpreted. Its relevance tends rather to be restricted to the realm of private piety, to the spiritual life of the individual. It is not far removed from being a gnostic teaching for the spiritual élite, and one suspects that Italian evangelism as a whole was not altogether free of this tendency.

This leads, thirdly, to the question of the authority of the Church. Luther had radically 'reduced' the Church to the eschatological community in which and into which the Gospel was bodied out in Word and sacrament. For Contarini, on the other hand, the *eschaton* has receded to the limits of time, the imminent Kingdom has been replaced by the mystical fellowship of the Church with its transcendental doctrines. The task of the Church is primarily didactic not proclamatory.

Hence personal faith is not enough. Side by side with an emphasis on the sole sufficiency of grace and faith for the salvation of the believer stands an insistence on the necessity for an objective, supra-personal authority, whose function it is to provide the framework within which this individual faith can be nourished. To put it pointedly, the presupposition to faith in Christ is faith in the

[18] Cf. McNair, pp. 1–50.

infallibility of the Church within which this Christ is preached and believed.

The controversy over transubstantiation at Regensburg made this quite clear. The unconditional faith which the Lutherans reserved for the incomprehensible Word of forgiveness and release, for the Gospel, must also be given, according to Contarini, to the teaching authority of the Church. His refusal even to entertain the thought that a properly constituted Council could err in its definitions of the faith sprang logically from his conviction that the Word is not limited to the preaching of Scripture, but can find and has found incarnation in the dogmatic tradition of the Church. In the hierarchy of the Church he sees the divinely ordained guardian of this dogmatic tradition, to whom the appropriate response is that of humble submission.

Unlike Luther Contarini had not remoulded his whole doctrine of the Church in terms of his understanding of justification. The various elements in his thought seem, at least to one in the Protestant tradition, to lie unresolved beside one another. Certainly there is nothing comparable to Luther's teaching on the Word of God, with its implications for the nature and the structure of the Church and for the relation of theology and philosophy, nor is there any parallel to Luther's eschatology. This does something to explain Contarini's astonishment at Regensburg when he discovered what the Protestants' views on the Church actually were, and his inability to explain their adherence to them except as pure obduracy.

Perhaps, however, there was a still greater obstacle than the strictly theological one to an understanding between Contarini and the German Protestants. His heritage was that of the Mediterranean. He was a Latin through and through. His ideals were the Classical ones. He still believed in the triumph of reason and order and harmony. His world remained fundamentally intact.

In Germany, on the other hand, the medieval synthesis of rationality and superstition had been replaced by a new dialectic of despair and defiant faith, a dialectic to which, of course, Marx and Freud stand closer than modern Protestantism. On the basis of this a cultural upheaval of unparalleled dimensions had taken place.

Thus Contarini found himself regarded at Regensburg as the representative of an outdated cultural imperialism. His reaction was

one of pain and puzzlement, and it will take uncommon patience
if we are to begin to understand this confrontation. For to all of us
Regensburg is an irritant. It irks the 'tolerant' by its failure, the
Catholic by its divergence from Trent, the Protestant by its deviation from Lutheranism. Yet Contarini and Regensburg explain
one another, and it is quite illegitimate to laud the one and damn
the other. The Catholicism of Contarini can as little be understood
apart from Regensburg as it can be reconciled with that of Trent.

We shall have to move towards a rather more differentiated
conception of pre-Tridentine Catholicism if justice is to be done
to Contarini, and cease regarding it as a rather inadequate stepping-
stone for pilgrims towards Trent. For the historian at least there is
nothing inevitable about the progression of events which eventually
led to Trent. It is time that per-Tridentine Catholicism was studied
in its own terms and for its own sake.

Contarini's activity at Regensburg mirrors the richness and
elusiveness of this Catholicism. The very fact of his presence at the
Diet cannot be wondered at enough. It is at least as significant as
the eventual failure of his mission. For if it was the inner contradictions of pre-Tridentine Catholicism, as exemplified in Contarini,
which were to be so cruelly exposed by the Diet, it was these same
contradictions which had enabled an exercise in reconciliation to
take place at all.

Contarini may have understood something of Lutheran theology.
Of Protestantism he had not the slightest comprehension. His
ecumenical concern and his understanding of justification prepared
him only to deal with the former. Hence his retreat when faced by
the full implications of a Protestant Church and a Protestant culture, first to a confessional Catholicism, and then to an intolerant
Curialism.

The dialogue between Protestantism and Catholicism at the Diet
of Regensburg in 1541 did not fail. It never took place.

BIBLIOGRAPHY

PRIMARY SOURCES

ALBERI, EUGENIO (ed.). *Relazioni degli ambasciatori veneti al Senato.* Series 1, vol. iv; Series 2, vol. iii. Florence: 1846, 1860.

BRETSCHNEIDER, CAROLUS GOTTLIEB (ed.). *Corpus Reformatorum.* Vols. iii, iv, xi: *Philippi Melanchthonis Opera quae supersunt omnia.* Halis Saxonum: Apud C. A. Schwetschke et filium, 1836–43.

BRIEGER THEODOR (ed.). 'Zur Correspondenz Contarini's während seiner deutschen Legation: Mitteilungen aus Beccadelli's Monumenti', *Zeitschrift für Kirchengeschichte,* iii (1879), 492–523.

—— 'Aus Italienischen Archiven und Bibliotheken: Beiträge zur Reformationsgeschichte', *Zeitschrift für Kirchengeschichte,* v (1882), 574–622.

BROWN, RAWDON (ed.). *Calendar of State Papers and Manuscripts, relating to English Affairs:* existing in the Archives and Collections of Venice and in other Libraries of Northern Italy. Vols. iii, iv. London: Stationery Office, 1869.

BUCER, MARTIN. *Alle Handlungen und Schriften zu vergleichung der Religion durch die Key. Mai. Churfürsten, Fürsten und Stände aller theylen Auch den Päbst. Legaten auf jüngst gehaltenen Reichstag zu Regensburg verhandlet und einbracht*... Strassburg: bei Wendel Kihel, 1541.

CARDAUNS, LUDWIG. *Zur Geschichte der Kirchlichen Unions- und Reformbestrebungen von 1538 bis 1542* (Bibliothek des Kgl. Preuss. Historischen Instituts in Rom, v). Rome: Verlag von Loescher, 1910.

CONTARENUS, ALOISIUS (ed.). *Gasparis Contareni Cardinalis Opera.* Parisiis: Apud Sebastianum Nivellium, sub Ciconiis in via Jacobaea, 1571.

DITTRICH, FRANZ (ed.). *Nuntiaturberichte Giovanni Morones vom Deutschen Königshofe. 1539, 1540* (Quellen und Forschungen aus dem Gebiet der Geschichte. In Verbindung mit ihrem Historischen Institut in Rom herausgegeben von der Görres-Gesellschaft. I. i). Paderborn: 1892.

—— (ed.). 'Die Nuntiaturberichte Morones vom Reichstag zu Regensburg. 1541', *Historisches Jahrbuch der Görres-Gesellschaft,* iv (1883), 395 ff., 618 ff.

—— *Regesten und Briefe des Cardinals Gasparo Contarini.* Braunsberg: Verlag von Huye's Buchhandlung (Emil Bender), 1881.

ECK, JOHANN. *Apologia pro Reverendis. et illustris. Principibus Catholicis, ac aliis ordinibus Imperii adversus mucores et calumnias Buceri, super actis Comiciorum Ratisponae: Apologia pro Reverendiss. se. ap. Legato et Cardinale, Caspare Contareno.* Cologne: M. Novesian, 1542.

—— *Replica Jo. Eckii adversus scripta secunda Buceri apostatae super actis Ratisponae* . . . Ingolstadt: A. Weissenhorn, 1543.

ERASMUS, DESIDERIUS. *De Amabile Ecclesiae Concordia.* Basel: Ionnis Oporinus, 1563.

FRIEDENSBURG, WALTER (ed.). 'Beiträge zum Briefwechsel der katholischen Gelehrten Deutschlands in Reformationszeitalter: Aus italienischen Archiven und Bibliotheken', *Zeitschrift für Kirchengeschichte*, xvi (1896), 470 ff. (Aleander) xviii (1898), 106 ff. 233 ff., 420 ff., 596 ff. (Cochlaeus); xix (1899), 211 ff., 473 ff., (Eck); Vol. xx (1900), 59 ff., 242 ff., 500 ff. (Fabri and Nausea); Vol. xxi (1901), 537 ff. (Nausea); Vol. xxiii (1902), 110 ff., 438 ff. (Pighius, Wauchop).

—— *Politische Correspondenz der Stadt Strassburg im Zeitalter der Reformation* . . . (Urkunden und Akten der Stadt Strassburg, Part 2, vol. v). 1879.

GROPPER, JOHANN. *An die Römische Keyserliche Maiestat unsern Allergnedigsten Herren Wahrhafftige Antwort und gegenberichtung h. Johan Gröpper Keyserlicher Rechten Doctor Canonichen des Dhoms und Scholastern zu sanct Gereon zu Cöllen:* Uff Martini Buceri frevenliche Clage und angeben wider im D. Gröpper in eynem jüngst aussgangen Truck beschehenn. Cologne: Iaspar Gennepaeus, 1545.

—— *Enchiridion Christianae Institutionis sive Institutio compendiaria doctrinae christianae* in *Canones Concilii Provincialis Coloniensis.* Cologne: Quentel, 1538.

HERMINJARD, A. L. (ed.). *Correspondance des réformateurs dans les pays de langue française:* Recueillie et publiée avec d'autres lettres relatives à la réforme et des notes historiques et biographiques. Vols. vi, vii: 1541–2. Geneva: H. Georg, Libraire-Editeur, 1886.

HÜNERMANN, FRIEDRICH (ed.). *Gasparo Contarini: Gegenreformatorische Schriften (1530 c.–1542)* (Corpus Catholicorum, vii). Münster in Westfalen: Verlag der Aschendorffschen Verlagsbuchhandlung, 1923.

JEDIN, HUBERT. *Contarini und Camaldoli* (Edizioni di Storia e Letteratura: Estratto dall'Archivio Italiano per la Storia della Pietà), vol. ii (1953).

LÄMMER, HUGO (ed.). *Monumenta Vaticana historiam ecclesiasticam saeculi XVI. illustrantia:* Ex tabulariis Sanctae Sedis Apostolicae secretis excerpsit prolegomenisque et indicibus instruxit H. L. Friburgi Brisgoviae: 1861.

LENZ, MAX (ed.). *Briefwechsel Landgraf Philipps des Grossmüthigen von Hessen mit Bucer.* 3 vols. (Publicationen aus den preussischen Staatsarchiven, v, xxviii, xlvii). Leipzig: 1880–91.

LE PLAT, J. *Monumentorum ad historiam Concilii Tridentini potissimum illustrandum spectantium amplissima collectio.* Vol. ii: 1518–40; vol. iii: 1541–8. Louvain: 1782–3.

LUTHER, MARTIN. *Werke:* Kritische Gesamtausgabe. Weimar: Hermann Böhlau, 1883 ff.

MELANCHTHON, PHILIPP. *Acta in Conventum Ratisbonensi continentia haec quae sequuntur:* librum propositum delectis Collocutoribus. Articulos oppositos certis locis in libro . . . Impressum Viteberge per Iosephum Klug, 1541.

MORANDI, GIAMBATTISTA (ed.). *Monumenti di Varia Letteratura:* tratti dai manoscritti di Monsignor Ludovico Beccadelli arcivescovo di Ragusa. 2 vols. in 3 parts; Bologna: Nell'Instituto delle Scienze, 1797–1804.

Nuntiaturberichte aus Deutschland. Edited by the Preussisches Historisches Institut in Rom. Part 1: 1534–59. Vols. v–vii. Gotha: 1909–12.

PASTOR, LUDWIG VON (ed.). 'Die Correspondenz des Cardinals Contarini während seiner deutschen Legation (1541)', *Historisches Jahrbuch der Görres-Gesellschaft,* i. 321 ff., 473 ff. . .

QUIRINI, A. M. (ed.). *Epistolarum Reginaldi Poli S.R.E. cardinalis et aliorum ad ipsum collectio.* Vols. i–iii. Brixiae: 1744–8.

ROTH, F. (ed.). 'Zur Geschichte des Reichstages zu Regensburg im Jahre 1541: Die Korrespondenz der Augsburger Gesandten Wolfgang Rehlinger, Simprecht Hoser und Dr Konrad Hel mit dem Rathe, den Geheimen und dem Bürgermeister Georg Herwart nebst Briefen von Dr Gereon Sailer und Wolfgang Musculus an den letzteren', *Archiv für Reformationsgeschichte,* ii (1905), 250 ff.; iii (1906), 18 ff.; iv (1907), 65 ff., 221 ff.

SCHULTZE, VICTOR (ed.). 'Actenstücke zur deutschen Reformationsgeschichte: (i) Dreizehn Depeschen Contarini's aus Regensburg an den Cardinal Farnese (1541); (ii) Fünfzehn Depeschen aus Regensburg vom 10. März bis 28. Juni 1541', *Zeitschrift für Kirchengeschichte,* iii (1879), 150 ff., 609 ff.

SOLMI, EDMONDO (ed.). 'Gasparo Contarini alla Dieta di Ratisbona secondo i documenti inediti dell'Archivio Gonzaga di Mantova'. *Nuovo Archivio Veneto,* xiii, n. s. xxv (1907), 5 ff., 68 ff.

WEISZ, LEO (ed.). 'Schweizerquellen zur Geschichte des Regensburger Reichstages von 1541', *Zeitschrift für Schweizerische Kirchengeschichte,* xxviii (1934), 51 ff., 81 ff.

SECONDARY SOURCES

AGOSTA, GIUSEPPE. *Il Card. Gaspare Contarini e il Luteranesimo.* Trapani: 1950.

AUGUSTIJN, C. 'De Gesprekken tussen Bucer en Gropper tijdens het Godsdienstgesprek te Worms', *Nederlands Archief voor Kerkgeschiedenis*, n. s. xlvii, 208–30.

BORNKAMM, HEINRICH. *Martin Bucers Bedeutung für die europäische Reformationsgeschichte* (Schriften des Vereins für Reformationsgeschichte, No. 169). Gütersloh: 1952.

BRANDI, KARL. *Kaiser Karl V:* Werden und Schicksal einer Persönlichkeit und eines Weltreiches. 6th edn. München: Verlag F. Bruckmann, 1961.

BRAUN, WILHELM. *Kardinal Gasparo Contarini oder der 'Reformkatholizismus' unserer Tage im Licht der Geschichte*. Leipzig: 1903.

BRIEGER, THEODOR. *Gasparo Contarini und das Regensburger Concordienwerk des Jahres 1541*. Gotha: Perthes' Buchdruckerei, 1870.

—— 'Die Rechtfertigungslehre des Kardinals Contarini, kritisch dargestellt und verglichen mit der des Regensburger Buches', *Theologische Studien und Kritiken*, xlv (1872), 87–150.

CANTIMORI, DELIO. *Italienische Häretiker der Spätrenaissance*. Translated from the Italian by Werner Kaegi. Basel: 1949.

CASPAR, BENEDIKT. *Das Erzbistum Trier im Zeitalter der Glaubensspaltung* (Reformationsgeschichtliche Studien und Texte, 90). Münster: Aschendorff, 1966.

CHURCH, FREDERICK C. *The Italian Reformers, 1534–1574*. New York: Columbia University Press, 1932.

CISTELLINI, ANTONIO. *Figure della Riforma Pretridentina* (Studi e documenti di storia religiosa). Brescia: 1948.

DITTRICH, FRANZ. *Gasparo Contarini, 1483–1542: eine Monographie*. Braunsberg: Druck und Verlag der Ermländischen Zeitungs– und Verlagsdruckerei (J. M. Wichert), 1885.

—— *Miscellanea Ratisbonensia a. 1541*. Braunsberg: 1892.

DÖLLINGER, J. J. I. VON. *Die Reformation: ihre innere Entwicklung und ihre Wirkungen im Umfange des Lutherischen Bekenntnisses*. 3 vols. Regensburg: G. Joseph Manz, 1846–8.

DOUGLAS, RICHARD M. *Jacopo Sadoleto, 1477–1547: Humanist and Reformer*. Cambridge, Mass.: Harvard University Press, 1959.

EELLS, HASTINGS. 'The Failure of Church Unification Efforts during the German Reformation', *Archiv für Reformationsgeschichte*, xlii (1951), 160–74.

FERRARA, ORESTES. *El Cardinal Contarini: Un gran embajador veneciano*. Madrid: 1956.

FRIEDENSBURG, WALTER. *Kaiser Karl V. und Papst Paul III., 1534–1549* (Schriften des Vereins für Reformationsgeschichte, No. 153). Leipzig: 1932.

—— 'Zur Geschichte des Wormser Konvents 1541', *Zeitschrift für Kirchengeschichte*, xxi (1901), 112–27.

GUTIERREZ, P. C. 'Un Capitulo de Teologia Pretridentina: El Problema de la Justificacion en los primeros Coloquios religiosos alemanes 1540–1541', *Miscelanea Comillas*, iv (1945), 7–32.

HACKERT, HERMANN. *Die Staatsschrift Gasparo Contarinis und die politischen Verhältnisse Venedigs im sechzehnten Jahrhundert* (Heidelberger Abhandlungen zur mittleren und neueren Geschichte, Nos. 68, 69). Heidelberg: 1940.

HARTUNG, FRITZ. *Deutsche Verfassungsgeschichte vom fünfzehnten Jahrhundert bis zur Gegenwart.* 5th edn. Stuttgart: 1950.

HEER, FRIEDRICH. *Die Dritte Kraft: Der europäische Humanismus zwischen den Fronten des konfessionellen Zeitalters.* Frankfurt-am-Main: S. Fischer Verlag, 1959.

HEIDRICH, PAUL. *Karl V und die Deutschen Protestanten am Vorabend des Schmalkaldischen Krieges* ... (Frankfurter Historische Forschungen, v, vi). Frankfurt: 1911, 1912.

HERGANG, CARL THEODOR. *Das Religions-Gespräch zu Regensburg i. Jahre 1541 und das Regensburger Buch: nach andren darauf bezüglichen Schriften jener Zeit.* Nach Quellen bearbeitet ... Cassel: Fischer, 1858.

HOLSTEN, WALTER. 'Christentum und nichtchristliche Religion nach der Auffassung Bucers', *Theologische Studien und Kritiken*, cvii, n. s. ii (1936), 105–94.

HÜNERMANN, FRIEDRICH. 'Die Rechtfertigungslehre des Kardinals Gasparo Contarini', *Tübinger Theologische Quartalschrift*, cii (1921), 1–22.

JANSSEN, JOHANN. *Geschichte des Deutschen Volkes seit dem Ausgang des Mittelalters.* Vol. iii: *Seit dem Ausgang der socialen Revolution bis ... 1555.* Edited by Ludwig Pastor. 15th edn. Freiburg im Breisgau: 1899.

JEDIN, HUBERT. 'Zur Entwicklung des Kirchenbegriffs im sechzehnten Jahrhundert', *Biblioteca Storica Sansoni*, n. s. xxv (Relazione del X Congresso internazionale di Scienze Storiche. Vol. iv, 1955), 59–73.

—— *A History of the Council of Trent.* Translated from the German by Dom Ernest Graf O.S.B. 2 vols. London: Thomas Nelson and Sons Ltd., 1957–61.

—— 'Ist das Konzil von Trient ein Hindernis der Wiedervereinigung?' *Ephemerides Theologiae Lovanienses*, xxxviii (1962), 842–55.

—— *Kardinal Contarini als Kontroverstheologe* (Katholisches Leben und Kämpfen im Zeitalter der Glaubensspaltung, No. 9: Vereinsschriften der Gesellschaft zur Herausgabe des Corpus Catholicorum). Münster in Westfalen: Aschendorffsche Verlagsbuchhandlung, 1949.

—— *Katholische Reformation oder Gegenreformation?* Ein Versuch zur Klärung der Begriffe nebst einer Jubiläumsbetrachtung über das Trienter Konzil. Luzern: Verlag Josef Stocker, 1946.

JEDIN, HUBERT, *Kirche des Glaubens—Kirche der Geschichte:* Ausge-
wählte Aufsätze und Vorträge. 2 vols. Freiburg: Herder, 1966.

——— 'Das Konzil von Trient und der Unionsgedanke', *Theologie und
Glaube*, xl (1950), 493–519.

——— *Girolamo Seripando: Sein Leben und Denken im Geisteskampf
des sechzehnten Jahrhunderts* (Cassiacum, ii, iii). 2 vols. Würzburg:
1937.

——— 'Ein Streit um den Augustinismus vor dem Tridentinum 1537–
1543', *Römische Quartalschrift*, xxxv (1927), 351–68.

——— 'Das Turmerlebnis des jungen Contarini', *Historisches Jahrbuch
der Görres-Gesellschaft*, lxx (1951), 115–30.

——— 'An welchen Gegensätzen sind die vortridentinischen Religionsgespräche zwischen Katholiken und Protestanten gescheitert?',
Theologie und Glaube, xlviii (1958), 50–5.

JUNG, EVA-MARIA. 'On the nature of Evangelism in Sixteenth-Century
Italy', *Journal of the History of Ideas*, xiv (1953), 511–27.

KORTE, AUGUST. *Die Konzilspolitik Karls V. in den Jahren 1538–1543*
(Schriften des Vereins für Reformationsgeschichte, No. 85). Halle:
1905.

LÄMMER, HUGO. *Die Vortridentisch-Katholische Theologie des Reformations-Zeitalters aus den Quellen dargestellt.* Berlin: 1858.

LECLER, JOSEPH. *Toleration and the Reformation.* Translated by T. L.
Westow. 2 vols. New York: Association Press, 1960.

LECLERCQ, DOM JEAN. 'Le Bˣ Paul Giustiniani et les ermites de son
temps', *Italia Sacra: Studi e documenti di storia ecclesiastica*, Vol. i.
Padua: 1960.

——— *Un Humaniste Ermite: Le Bienheureux Paul Giustiniani (1476–
1528).* Rome: 1951.

LIPGENS, WALTER. *Kardinal Johannes Gropper (1503–1559) und die
Anfänge der katholischen Reform in Deutschland* (Reformationsgeschichtliche Studien und Texte, No. 75). Münster in Westfalen:
1951.

LORTZ, JOSEPH. *Die Reformation in Deutschland.* 2 Vols. 4th edn.
Freiburg im Breisgau: Herder, 1962.

MACKENSON, HEINZ. 'Contarini's Theological Role at Ratisbon in 1541',
Archiv für Reformationsgeschichte, li (1960), 36-57.

——— 'The Diplomatic Role of Gasparo Contarini at the Colloquy of
Ratisbon of 1541', *Church History*, xxvii (1958), 312–37.

MCNAIR, PHILIP. *Peter Martyr in Italy: An Anatomy of Apostasy.*
Oxford: Oxford University Press, 1967.

MADER, FELIX. *Stadt Regensburg* (Die Kunstdenkmäler von Bayern:
Regierungsbezirk Oberpfalz, xxii). Vols. i–iii. Munich, 1933.

MATTINGLY, GARRETT. *Renaissance Diplomacy.* London: Jonathan Cape,
1955.

MICHAELIS, OTTO. 'Zur Frage des Missionsverständnisses der Reformatoren', *Zeitschrift für Missionskunde und Religionswissenschaft*, xli (1926), 337–43.

NESTLER, HERMANN. 'Vermittlungspolitik und Kirchenspaltung auf dem Regensburger Reichstag von 1541', *Zeitschrift für Bayerische Landesgeschichte*, vi (1933), 389–414.

OFFELE, WOLFGANG. 'Julius Pflugs Irenik im Spiegel seines Katechismus', *Theologisches Jahrbuch*, 1966, pp. 545–59.

PASTOR, LUDWIG VON. *History of the Popes from the Close of the Middle Ages*. Translated by R. F. Kerr. Vol. xi: *Paul III (1534–1549)*. London: Kegan Paul, 1923.

—— *Die Kirchlichen Reunionsbestrebungen während der Regierung Karls V*. Aus den Quellen dargestellt . . . Freiburg im Breisgau: 1879.

PIEPER, ANTON. *Zur Entstehungsgeschichte der ständigen Nuntiaturen*. Freiburg im Breisgau: 1894.

POLMAN, PONTIEN. *Die polemischen Methoden der ersten Gegner der Reformation* (Katholisches Leben und Kämpfen im Zeitalter der Glaubensspaltung, No. 4), Münster in Westfalen: 1931.

RANKE, LEOPOLD VON. *Deutsche Geschichte im Zeitalter der Reformation*. 6 vols. 5th edn. Leipzig: 1873.

Realenzyklopädie für protestantische Theologie. Edited by A. Hauck. 24 vols. Leipzig: J. C. Hinrichs'sche Buchhandlung, 1896–1913.

REPGEN, KONRAD. *Die Römische Kurie und der Westfälische Friede*. Vol. I. i: *Papst, Kaiser und Reich 1521–1644*. Tübingen: 1962.

ROSENBERG, MANFRED. *Gerhard Veltwyck: Orientalist, Theolog und Staatsmann*. Wiesbaden: Friedmann, 1935.

ROSS, J. B. 'Gasparo Contarini and his Friends', *Studies in the Renaissance*, xvii (1970), 192–232.

SCHATTENMANN, JOHANNES. 'Die Regensburger Religionsgespräche von 1541 und 1546 in der Schau von heute'. *Zeitwende*, xix (1947–8), 44–52.

SCHENK, W. *Reginald Pole: Cardinal of England*. London: Longmans, Green and Co., 1950.

SEEBERG, REINHOLD. *Lehrbuch der Dogmengeschichte*. Vol. IV. ii: *Die Fortbildung der reformatorischen Lehre und die gegenreformatorische Lehre*. 3rd edn. Erlangen: Deicherst'sche Verlagsbuchhandlung Dr. Werner Scholl, 1920.

SPAHN, MARTIN. *Johannes Cochlaeus: Ein Lebensbild*. Berlin: 1898.

STÖCKER, H. 'Luthers Stellung zum Regensburger Religionsgespräch im Jahre 1541', *Allgemeine evangelische Kirchenzeitung*, lxxiv (1941), 114 ff., 126 ff., 134 ff.

STUPPERICH, ROBERT. *Der Humanismus und die Wiedervereinigung der Konfessionen* (Schriften des Vereins für Reformationsgeschichte, No. 160). Leipzig: 1936.

STUPPERICH, ROBERT, 'Der Ursprung des "Regensburger Buches" von 1541 und seine Rechtfertigungslehre', *Archiv für Reformationsgeschichte*, xxxvi (1939), 88–116.

TAVARD, GEORGE H. 'The Catholic Reform in the Sixteenth Century', Church History, xxvi (1957), 275–88.

TRUSEN, WINFRIED. *Um die Reform und Einheit der Kirche* (Katholisches Leben und Kämpfen im Zeitalter der Glaubensspaltung, No. 14). Münster in Westfalen: Aschendorffsche Verlagsbuchhandlung, 1957.

VETTER, PAUL. *Die Religionsverhandlungen auf dem Reichstag zu Regensburg.* Jena: 1889.

WIEDMANN, THEODOR. *Dr Johann Eck: Eine Monographie.* Regensburg: 1865.

ZEEDEN, E. W. 'Die Einwirkung der Reformation auf die Verfassung des Heiligen Römischen Reiches', *Trier Theologische Zeitschrift*, lix (1950), 207–15.

ZIEHEN, E. 'Frankfurter Anstand' und deutsch-evangelischer Reichsbund von Schmalkalden 1539', *Zeitschrift für Kirchengeschichte*, lix (1940), 342–51.

INDEX

Albert, Archbishop of Mainz, Cardinal, Elector, 4, 7, 11, 18 f., 22, 55, 61, 70, 73, 79, 84 f., 87, 92, 112, 150 f., 156, 160, 167

Aleander, Girolamo, Cardinal, 11, 15, 22, 57, 153, 164

d'Aquilar, imperial ambassador in Rome, 75

Ardinghelli, Niccolò, secretary to Cardinal Farnese, 83, 151

Arras, Bishop of see Granvelle, Antoine

Augsburg, city of, 55, 68, 91

Augsburg, diet of (1530), 6 f., 70, 73, 76, 89, 91, 101, 107, 109, 123, 126, 146, 158, 165, 169

Badia, Tommaso, Master of the Sacred Palace, 102, 104, 111, 127, 154

Bavaria, Dukes of see William and Louis, Dukes of Bavaria

Beccadelli, Ludovico, secretary of Contarini, 38, 43, 49

Bembo, Pietro, Cardinal, 99

Bologna, city of, 40, 43 f.

Brandenburg, see Joachim II

Braun, Conrad, jurist, 61

Brück, Gregor, jurist from Electoral Saxony, 8, 149

Bucer, Martin, 7 f., 12, 17 ff., 23 ff., 26 ff., 43, 48, 68, 78, 87 f., 91 ff., 107, 110 ff., 117, 123, 130 f., 133, 136, 138, 141 f., 145 f., 158, 175

Burckhard, Franz, chancellor of Electoral Saxony, 110, 127, 136

Calvin, John, 23, 109, 113, 174

Campeggio, Thomas, Bishop of Feltre, nuncio at Worms (1540), 22 f., 33 f., 55 f., 65

Capito, Wolfgang, Strasbourg theologian, 23, 28 ff.

Caraffa, Gianpietro, Cardinal, 153, 164

Carlowitz, chancellor of Ducal Saxony, 7 f.

Cervini, Marcello, Cardinal, legate to Charles V, 16, 21

Charles V, Emperor, 6, 8, 11 ff., 16 ff., 21, 23 ff., 27 ff., 34 f., 36, 39, 41 ff., 46, 50, 54 ff., 60 f., 63 ff., 79 ff., 84 ff., 97 ff., 110, 124 f., 131, 133 f., 136 ff., 143 f., 147, 149 ff., 157 ff., 164 ff.

Cleves, 55, 157, 169

Cochlaeus, Johann, Catholic controversial theologian, 3, 49, 92, 111

Colonna, Ascanio, 74 f.

Contarini, Francesco, Venetian ambassador to Charles V, 64, 157

Cortese, Gregorio, Benedictine abbot of S. Giorgio Maggiore, Venice, 48, 111

Cruciger, professor at Wittenberg, 127

Dandino, Girolamo, nuncio to Francis I, 36, 54, 71

Eck, John, Catholic controversial theologian, 4, 12, 23, 33 f., 42 f., 61, 67, 92 ff., 98, 100, 102 ff., 110 f., 120, 129, 132, 152, 159, 164 f.

Erasmus, Desiderius, 5 f., 27

Farnese, Alessandro, Cardinal, Secretary of State, 11 ff., 36, 40, 54, 57, 60, 66, 72, 75, 100, 111 f., 126, 151 ff.

Ferdinand, King of the Romans, 8, 11 ff., 17, 20, 55, 81 f., 170

Feige, jurist from Hesse, 8, 28 f., 141

Flaminio, Marcantonio, Italian humanist, 37, 48

France, 59, 67, 68, 71 f., 75, 87, 125, 150, 157, 160, 169

Francis I, King of France, 11 f., 28, 71, 152, 162

Frankfurt, diet of (1539), 9 ff., 17, 19, 42, 146

Frederick, Count Palatine, brother of Elector Louis, 55, 70, 72, 76, 80, 93, 102, 118

George, Duke of Saxony, 7

Wied, Hermann von, Archbishop of Cologne, Elector, 3, 19, 22

William and Louis, Dukes of Bavaria, 18 f., 22, 55, 67, 69 ff., 79, 84 f., 87, 94 f., 104, 150 f., 156, 159 f., 164 f.

Witzel, George, Catholic theologian, 4, 8, 103

Worms, colloquy of (1540), 21 ff., 31, 33 f., 54 f., 61, 65 f., 70, 74, 110

Worms, diet of (1521), 41, 146

Württemberg, 30, 69